MILITARY CHAPLAINCY IN

D0706111

The presence of Christian chaplains on the battlefield focuses in a very sharp way the wider tension between a gospel of peace and the need for armed force in a brutal world. I welcome this book as a much needed and valuable contribution from those with first-hand experience of the role and the willingness to think theologically about that tension and the dilemmas it poses.

Professor the Rt Revd Lord Richard Harries

Chaplaincy highlights the need for faith and society to re-engage with vital moral questions. Military chaplains continue to operate within the dynamic tension between faith communities, the armed services and society, offering a distinct moral presence and contribution. Drawing the reader into the world of the military chaplain, this book explores insights into the complex moral issues that arise in combat (especially in Afghanistan), and in everyday military life, These include the increasing significance of the Law of Armed Conflict and the moral significance of drones.

Through the unique chaplain's-eye-view of the significance of their experience for understanding the ethics of war, this book offers clearer understanding of chaplaincy in the context of the changing nature of international conflict (shaped around insurgency and non-state forces) and explores the response of faith communities to the role of the armed services. It makes the case for relocating understandings of just war within a theological framework and for a clear understanding of the relationship between the mission of chaplaincy and that of the military.

Explorations in Practical, Pastoral and Empirical Theology

Series Editors

Leslie J. Francis, University of Warwick, UK
Jeff Astley, St Chad's College, Durham University, UK
Martyn Percy, Ripon College Cuddesdon and The Oxford
Ministry Course, Oxford, UK

Theological reflection on the church's practice is now recognized as a significant element in theological studies in the academy and seminary. Ashgate's series in practical, pastoral and empirical theology seeks to foster this resurgence of interest and encourage new developments in practical and applied aspects of theology worldwide. This timely series draws together a wide range of disciplinary approaches and empirical studies to embrace contemporary developments including: the expansion of research in empirical theology, psychological theology, ministry studies, public theology, Christian education and faith development; key issues of contemporary society such as health, ethics and the environment; and more traditional areas of concern such as pastoral care and counselling.

Other titles in the series include:

Military Chaplaincy in Contention
Chaplains, Churches and the Morality of Conflict

Edited by

ANDREW TODD
Cardiff Centre for Chaplaincy Studies, UK

ASHGATE

Published by
Ashgate Publishing Limited
Wey Court East
Union Road
Farnham
Surrey, GU9 7PT
England

Ashgate Publishing Company
110 Cherry Street
Suite 3-1
Burlington, VT 05401-3818
USA

www.ashgate.com

British Library Cataloguing in Publication Data
Military chaplaincy in contention : chaplains, churches and
   the morality of conflict. -- (Explorations in practical,
   pastoral and empirical theology)
   1. Military chaplains. 2. Great Britain--Armed Forces--
   Chaplains. 3. War--Moral and ethical aspects. 4. Military
   ethics.
   I. Series II. Todd, Andrew.
   355.3'47-dc23

The Library of Congress has cataloged the printed edition as follows:
Military chaplaincy in contention : chaplains, churches, and the morality of conflict / edited
by Andrew Todd.
      pages cm. -- (Explorations in practical, pastoral, and empirical theology)
   Includes bibliographical references (pages   ) and index.
   ISBN 978-1-4094-3157-2 (hardcover) -- ISBN 978-1-4094-3158-9 (pbk) --
ISBN 78-1-4094-3159-6 (ebook) -- ISBN 978-1-4094-7117-2 (epub) 1. Military chaplains.
2. Just war doctrine. 3. War--Moral and ethical aspects. I. Todd, Andrew, 1961-
   UH20.M56 2013
   355.3'47--dc23

                                                                                        2012043237

   ISBN 9781409431572 (hbk)
   ISBN 9781409431589 (pbk)
   ISBN 9781409431596 (ebk – PDF)
   ISBN 9781409471172 (ebk – ePUB)

Printed and bound in Great Britain
by MPG PRINTGROUP

Contents

Notes on Contributors

Jonathan Ball is an Anglican priest living in Salisbury. He studied history at Oxford University and theology at Leeds University whilst training for the ministry at Mirfield. After a curacy and incumbency in the Lichfield Diocese he became an army chaplain in 1996 and served on operations in Northern Ireland, Congo, Kosovo, Afghanistan and Iraq. As Staff Chaplain to the Chaplain General, he contributed to the compilation of the Tri-Service Operational Service Book 2007, and was awarded the Cardiff University MTh with distinction. On leaving the army he became Bishop's Chaplain to Dr David Stancliffe, Bishop of Salisbury, with whom he shared a passion for liturgy. Jonathan has a particular interest in current liturgical practice in the post-modern context. He is currently Operations Manager of the Royal Marines Charitable Trust at Fleet Headquarters, Portsmouth.

Colin Butler was ordained in 1984 and served in parishes until 1999 when he joined the Royal Army Chaplains' Department. He is currently Brigade Chaplain for north-west England. Since joining the army he has served in operational theatres in Cyprus, Northern Ireland, Iraq and Afghanistan. In 2006–7 he was chaplain to a battlegroup in Basra city. From 2007 until 2010 he was senior chaplain in the West Midlands and was appointed MBE. He is a graduate of the Cardiff MTh course. He is currently studying for a PhD on the relationship between the military covenant and society.

James Coleman served as a Church of Scotland chaplain with both the RAF and the army for a total of 19 years, and completed his doctoral research into 'Models of Ministry in the RAF' during this period. Now working in Yorkshire as a synod development officer with the United Reformed Church, he tutors on the MTh in chaplaincy in Cardiff looking at moral issues in the context of military chaplaincy, with particular attention being given to a reappraisal of just war thinking.

David Fisher teaches ethics and war at Kings College, London, where he was recently awarded a PhD in war studies. He was a senior official in the Ministry of Defence, Foreign Office and Cabinet Office, serving as defence adviser to the Prime Minister and UK Defence Counsellor to NATO. He is Co-Chairman of the Council on Christian Approaches to Defence and Disarmament and regularly contributes to books and journals on defence and ethics. His publications include *Morality and War: Can War be Just in the Twenty-First Century?* (2011, pbk 2012) and *Just War on Terror? A Christian and Muslim Response* (2010) which he co-edited. He won the 2012 W.J. Mackenzie book prize for *Morality and War* as the best book of the year in political science.

Mark Grant-Jones is currently serving as a Brigade Senior Chaplain in the Royal Army Chaplains' Department. Following a career as an exploration geologist Mark became a Baptist minister having completed his graduate studies at Cardiff University. Having joined the Chaplains' Department at the outset of the Iraq war in 2003, he has served as a chaplain to infantry, armoured and training regiments over the last nine years. As part of continuing professional development Mark completed the master's degree in chaplaincy studies at Cardiff University followed by the postgraduate teaching qualification. His operational experience during this time has included Iraq, Northern Ireland, Kosovo and Afghanistan. Mark is married to Sarah and they have four teenage girls. He is currently preparing to return to Afghanistan.

Peter Howson spent 25 years as an army chaplain with his final posting being as the Principal of the Armed Forces Chaplaincy Centre at Amport House. He then completed 10 years as the Superintendent of the Inverness Circuit of the Methodist Church. During this time he wrote his doctoral thesis on British army chaplaincy in the period 1960 to 2000. He joined the staff of the Centre for Chaplaincy Studies in 2005 with responsibility for teaching a module in the MTh in chaplaincy that looked at military chaplaincy in operational settings. Since 2012 he has been a part-time minister for the Methodist Church in Byfleet and Weybridge. He has recently contributed a chapter to a collection of essays on chaplaincy during the First World War, as well as writing a study of the organisation of British army chaplaincy during that conflict (published by Helion). Having started his career as a teacher in Malawi he has retained links with that country and made a number of visits in recent years. He is an elected member of the Council of the Society for Army Historical Research. His next project is an investigation of the role of the Religious Affairs Branch within the British Control Commission Germany between 1945 and 1949.

Philip McCormack is a Baptist minister, who joined the Royal Army Chaplains' Department in 1997. Currently he is the Chief Instructor/Deputy Principal of the Armed Forces' Chaplaincy Centre (AFCC), Amport House. In the Birthday Honours List, June 2011, he was awarded an MBE (Military Division), not least for his work as a senior chaplain in support of operations in Iraq and Afghanistan. He completed a PhD through Queen's University of Belfast in 2001, the Cardiff University MTh, with distinction, in military chaplaincy; and is in the final stages of a second PhD, at Cranfield University, Shrivenham, with the title, *The British Soldier: Warrior or Weapons Platform a Philosophical Framework*. A paper on his research was published in 2012 by the Defence Academy of the UK.

Peter Sedgwick is Principal of St Michael's College, Cardiff, Ministry Officer for the Church in Wales and honorary lecturer at Cardiff University. He is a Metropolitical Canon in the Church in Wales. From 1996 to 2004 he was policy officer for the Church of England on Home Affairs, leading on the anti-terrorism agenda after 9/11. He has taught at the universities of Birmingham and Hull, and is a life fellow of the Center for Theological Inquiry, Princeton. He is the author of many books and articles on social ethics, and a member of the Anglican Roman Catholic International Commission (ARCICIII) which is working on a study of the differences in theological ethics between the two churches. He teaches the ethics module on the Cardiff MTh in chaplaincy studies, where he has learnt much from serving chaplains.

Stephen Sharkey started his military involvement as a Territorial Army soldier from 1986 until 1991 and became a chaplain to West Lowland Army Cadet Force where he served for seven years. Father Stephen joined the Royal Army Chaplains' Department as a regular chaplain on 15 September 2008. He is currently chaplain to 2nd Battalion the Yorkshire Regiment in Cyprus, Episkopi Garrison chaplain and the only Roman Catholic chaplain in British Forces Cyprus. He also served in Cyprus with 2nd Battalion the Duke of Lancaster Regiment and with 4 Rifles based in Bulford, Wiltshire returning from Afghanistan on 2 October 2009 after a four-month tour on OP HERRICK 10 where he was in Nad Ali, Helmand Province, with 4 Rifles as part of the Election Surge Force. Fr Stephen was chaplain also during 4 Rifles, A Company deployment to HERRICK 11 where the Battalion lost five soldiers.

Andrew Todd is the Director of the Cardiff Centre for Chaplaincy Studies, a partnership between Cardiff University and St Michael's College, Cardiff. Andrew has more than 17 years' experience of theological education (and is a past president of the Cambridge Theological Federation). He is a practical theologian and linguistic ethnographer, with particular interests in the implications of chaplaincy for an understanding of religion and spirituality in public life. Recent publications include: 'Responding to Diversity: Chaplaincy in a Multi-Faith Context', in Miranda Threlfall-Holmes and Mark Newitt (eds), *Being a Chaplain* (SPCK, 2011) 89–102; and 'Chaplaincy Leading Church in(to) the Public Square', in *Crucible: The Christian Journal of Social Ethics*, October–December 2011. Also in 2011, he delivered the research report, 'The Role and Contribution of a Multi-Faith Prison Chaplaincy to the Contemporary Prison Service', to the National Offender Management Service, who commissioned the research.

Andrew Totten is an Assistant Chaplain General and the British Army's Anglican Director of Ordinands. He has been on operations in Bosnia with the Worcestershire and Sherwood Foresters (1996) and the Light Dragoons (1998); in Kosovo with the Royal Scots Dragoon Guards (2000) (subsequently appointed MBE); in Northern Ireland with the Royal Irish Regiment and then the Irish Guards (2001 to 2004); and in Iraq with 7th Armoured Brigade (2005). A graduate of the MTh in chaplaincy studies (with distinction), he was Director (Army) at the Armed Forces Chaplaincy Centre (2006 to 2009). Accompanying 16 Air Assault Brigade to Afghanistan (2010), he spent seven months in Helmand Province as the British Task Force Chaplain.

Foreword

The Right Reverend Lord Eames OM, Archbishop of Armagh 1986–2006

I had known him through the difficult years as a growing sense of vocation to ministry confronted him with increasing urgency; through the times when he pondered if there were reasons rather than excuses to close his mind to God's call; through the days when demands of family life seemed to offer a strange comfort to remain in secular employment rather than the unknown paths of ordination. Then I had known him in the days leading up to the moment when I would lay my hands on him with the words: 'Receive the Holy Ghost for the office and work of a Priest in the Church of God ...'.

Now, he sat again in my study. Through the years of parochial ministry he had developed and grown in the ups and downs of pastoral experience. Yet again, he had a question. The call was to offer himself to the ministry of a chaplain in the armed services. His question returned to me time and time again as I have read the words of this book: 'What am I called to be in particular?'

What, in particular, are the gifts, the strengths and the insights of a chaplain in today's forces? What is the precise nature of the challenges to the spiritual life and service of a chaplain in the changing circumstances of service where the Christian tradition must witness alongside other faith practices to an increasing degree? What is the chaplain called to be when moral issues about the nature of armed combat multiply in a world far removed from the apparent simplicity of those early theories of 'the just war'? Where should the voice of the Christian chaplain be expected to be heard in the world where the drone can inflict suffering and death at the decision of strategists thousands of miles from the scene of conflict? What is the chaplain called to do when confronted by questions about justice, human rights and suffering; when war itself is a subject of contention between nations represented in international organisations such as the UN, or between superpowers, or regional groupings of states?

It has been my privilege to witness at first hand the worth of chaplains through the long years if military involvement in the Troubles of Northern Ireland, in Iraq and, more recently, to be with them in Afghanistan. I have talked and listened to them about their work just as I have listened to the reactions of servicemen and women to the role they play in their everyday lives.

So, when I attempt to pen this short foreword, it is real people I think of; it is real situations where no textbooks could prepare chaplains for life and death realities; it is courage, fear, uncertainty and hope within pastoral caring and ministry; and it is about human need searching for reassurance and hope.

'What am I called to be in particular?'

Faced with some of the complex issues analysed in this book, my colleague could well reflect the frustration felt by many clergy in the Troubles of Northern Ireland. Then, instantaneous theology demanded by critical human situations often provided no time for reflection. Of course, it was impossible to prepare for every situation. But being there as it happened, being with people in their devastation and need, sharing all the burden of death and suffering rather than theorising meant only one thing – when they forgot what you said, they remembered you were there.

In the pages which follow, the reader will find the personal testimonies of chaplains which have the ring of truth that experience alone can provide. For me, this book provides more questions than answers – but therein lies its strength. My admiration for the work of chaplains I have seen and experienced over the years convinces me that 'being there' far outweighs any sense of failure an individual feels when confronted with a situation in which words seem totally inadequate.

I believe this book is published at a most critical time in the history of chaplains. Not only is the international scene making new and profound demands on armed services, but on the ways they become involved in disputes. The web of moral issues about the use of force and particularly 'collateral damage' in conflict raise new aspects of the eternal debate on justice and injustice, right and wrong. As humankind designs new ways of killing, questions about 'the faith once delivered' and armed conflict multiply.

In the centre of this cauldron, the Church sends chaplains to be called to serve. Too often, the 'sending church' sees this as a point of departure for responsibility and identity for chaplains. There are serious questions here for the mainstream churches of the UK and for their leadership.

It is a real privilege to be invited to write this foreword. I would express the wish that this book provokes much discussion at this critical time of change for the world of chaplains. Perhaps my abiding impression and indeed my prayer is best summed up thus – 'when they forget what you said, they'll remember you were there …'.

Robin Eames

Preface

This book is offered as a contribution to the debate about the morality of armed conflict and military service. A central question of the book is how churches engage with the morality of war and the moral ethos of the military community, as it seeks to serve the state under the authority of government, in the interests of peace and justice. Chaplains offer a unique insight into these questions, as the following pages reveal. And their moral role is dependent on the answers. The book would not have been possible without their participation as contributors, but also in the research workshops which gave rise to this volume. As editor I wish to thank all those who participated in those workshops, chaplains, former chaplains and colleagues; those who have written, or contributed to, the chapters which make up the book; and the British Academy for supporting the research through a small grant. I would also like to thank those whose permission has made the book possible: The Ministry of Defence, for permission for serving chaplains to contribute; the Senior Chaplain at the Royal Military Academy Sandhurst, for permission to reproduce the Commissioning Order of Service on page 119; and the Revd Brian Elliott and Canterbury Press, for permission to reproduce the hymn on pages 126–7. The book is offered out of respect for those who serve in the armed forces, and in particular their chaplains; and so that the voice of military chaplaincy may be heard more clearly.

Andrew Todd
January 2013

PART I
Chaplaincy in Contention

Chapter 1
Chaplaincy in Contention

Andrew Todd

Introduction

This book is about the moral role of military chaplains. It offers interlocking perspectives on the nature of that role, on the challenges which it presents for chaplains, and on chaplains' creative engagement with those challenges. In one sense, it grew out of a series of research workshops, supported by a small grant from the British Academy, and convened by the Cardiff Centre for Chaplaincy Studies, which drew together chaplains from the British Army and the RAF and academics, who were together interested in investigating the connections between military chaplaincy and the ethics of conflict. Many of the participants have contributed chapters to this book.

In another sense, the book grows out of military chaplains' involvement in recent operations involving the British armed forces and, in particular, those located in Afghanistan. This book represents the first full discussion so far of the changing moral role of British military chaplains, in the light of their involvement in Afghanistan. Just as involvement in Afghanistan has represented a sustained operational tempo for the armed services, not known in recent decades, so military chaplains have also experienced the effects of that tempo, with frequent and recurring deployments to the theatre of operations. With their colleagues in the services, chaplains have also been in the public eye. And sometimes chaplains have had their own public profile, through their role in repatriations of those who have been killed, for example, or through media interest, such as that represented by the television programme *Commando Chaplain*, broadcast as part of the Channel 4 'Revelations' series on 12 July 2009.

This book offers a portrayal of chaplains as very much 'in contention', in the sense of their being at the centre of an international conflict. But it also reflects something of the contentious nature of campaigns including Afghanistan, and investigates the way in which such contentions have reshaped military chaplaincy. The current situation places chaplaincy, as part of the armed forces, at the centre of a national debate about British involvement in Afghanistan (and previously in Iraq). In their moral and pastoral role chaplains often receive questions from military personnel that arise from their involvement in operations conducted in the public gaze, and where they become almost instantly aware of media portrayal and comment. But the chaplains' role and involvement can itself be a public question – to what extent is a largely Christian, religious presence appropriate in this public context? What moral message is communicated by chaplaincy involvement in an international military coalition in Afghanistan, or elsewhere?

Such contentious issues sharpen other questions. Apart from a small number of civilian world faith chaplains to the military, British military chaplains are Christian, representing a variety of sending churches. Churches are, on the whole, supportive of their chaplains in the armed forces. But they may be at the same time critical of current military operations. This book explores the way in which these churches do not necessarily connect these two areas. In particular they do not always listen to the voices of chaplains on the contentious issue of the involvement of Christians in military operations, which include the authorised use of lethal force. These chaplains' voices raise questions about the coherence of church positions, which support military chaplaincy, on the one hand; but which do not fully engage with contemporary questions of the ethics of armed conflict, on the other.

It is the contention of this book that military chaplains, with occasional exceptions, exercise a positive moral role on the international stage, including in Afghanistan. Their role is a significant public religious contribution to the debate about contemporary policy concerning the role of the military in defence and foreign policy. At the same time the book contends that the very success of that role raises sharp theological and ethical questions which need to be fully addressed by chaplains' sending churches, as well as by chaplains themselves.

This chapter locates subsequent discussion in the chaplain's experience of Afghanistan, before introducing the themes which emerge from that experience. Two chaplains have contributed short reflections, which explore the reality and implications of being at the sharp end of military chaplaincy in the twenty-first century.

Moral Courage

Stephen Sharkey's narrative takes us very much to the sharp end of chaplaincy – to a Forward Operating Base in Afghanistan in the wake of the death of a soldier. In many ways this is an uncompromising account. Stephen is very clear that the moral and physical courage of a chaplain in such circumstances does not have to do with the niceties of rational debate. Rather it is the instinctive reaction of the pastor, who can do no other than be with the soldiers he serves. Nonetheless, the story does raise key questions which do need to be addressed in other contexts, including those provided by subsequent chapters of this book.

Three things stand out. First, the moral role of the chaplain is also intimately connected with the morale of the soldiers. Because the chaplain's key role is first of all to be present, he has the capacity to respond to the human needs of the military personnel – to see their need for sleep, a listening ear or physical contact and respond accordingly. The second striking feature of the tale relates to the chaplain's ritual, or liturgical, role. The central account of the memorial service to the dead soldier speaks volubly of the power of this act to hold the unit, despite their coming under fire. This is not only about holding their attention, but also about holding them as a community and holding their grief – through an act that is both moral and theological.

Both the first two noticeable aspects of the narrative connect, however, with the third significant feature of the account, which introduces a less comfortable concept. This is the idea that, through their pastoral, ritual and moral presence, chaplains become 'force-multipliers' – they contribute, whether intentionally or not, to the military effectiveness of the unit. Without Stephen's presence and interventions, the soldiers would have been less able to cope with the continued demands of the tour of duty. This raises the vital question for chaplains, and for their sending churches, about how far both parties need to be in sympathy with the 'mission' of the armed forces. This is, of course, sharpened by the fact that most chaplains are commissioned and wear military uniform as part of their role.

A further question that is implicit in this narrative concerns how chaplains are educated, trained or formed. How can they be appropriately prepared to act with 'instinctive' moral courage in situations of crisis? What enables them to offer military personnel appropriate care, including through the medium of ritual and liturgy? And what moral formation enables them to cope with their role, whether intended, or unintended, as a 'force multiplier'?

Stephen Sharkey's Account

I was chaplain to a particular battalion on operations in Afghanistan. We had two companies based in Helmand District, in two Forward Operating Bases (FOBs). At around 11 a.m. one morning I was told by the Commanding Officer that we had lost a soldier, who had been killed by an Improvised Explosive Device (IED) less than an hour previously, and that the Platoon Sergeant had been seriously injured; his life was described as critical. Thankfully today he is still serving and has made an almost full recovery, a real sign of physical courage for all to see!

At the point I was told the news it was on a need to know basis, the question was asked of me, 'Where do you think you need to be Father?'. I had the choice between heading back to Camp Bastion for the eventual repatriation or to the FOB, from where the soldier had left just a few hours previously for the last time. For me it was what I would term a 'no brainer', it was natural for me to want to be with those who were left behind, to be with the company who were based in the FOB, most especially with those who had been with the soldier who had died, as they faced the darkness of losing one of their comrades, friends.

The FOB was approximately six kilometers from another FOB where I had been with another company. It was a dangerous road often travelled by these soldiers, just off the route where the soldier had been killed earlier that day. To make the journey by road was an easy decision, but a risky one for all involved, it involved the usual risk of IEDs, attack by insurgents; and the fact that it was more than 45 degrees made it a very tough and dangerous journey to rendezvous with the Company and travel to their FOB.

The journey took around 13 hours. It was not without excitement as we came under fire at times and because I sat in the back of a vehicle having to avoid telling the news that the soldier had died. The boys knew, but I just could not confirm it; it was not advantageous to break the news at that time and it would not have helped matters. The news would be better broken in the safety of the FOB.

Arriving at the FOB was a relief. It was still very warm and the mood of the FOB was one of sadness, one of anger from some people. It was also a place where I witnessed for the first time the humanity of a British soldier. This was a man who would in anyone's view be considered a giant; he was physically massive. But here in the FOB in the heat of the night and the realisation of the happenings of the day he was a broken man, he was sobbing, feeling guilt, angry but not violent. He had stood beside the dead soldier as he stepped around the side of the vehicle, as the pressure plate of the IED was activated, whether by the vehicle or by the soldier.

The moral and physical courage of a chaplain in many ways can be seen in these instances. I did not think how to act morally or with any courage, it was a natural reaction for me to travel to the FOB, to be with this company; to offer my prayer, consolation, and what I feel was most appreciated: my presence. Just being there was worth more than words would ever explain.

The heads were down, the morale was very low. It was a scene of a morose lot, and to be honest I could not blame them. But, this attitude was not healthy, I knew it and so did all of those involved and those based in the FOB. The first action I had to do was the most basic human action that we can ever do, it was to give that massive guy a hug. It was to get a grip of him and hold him and tell him not to worry, all was going to be OK; he was to relax. Then, which was I suppose an act of moral courage, I told this massive lump that he had to go to bed; I ordered him into his tent, telling him he was to shut his eyes and keep them shut until the daylight was shining through his eyelids. Thankfully he went, he lay down on his bed and he managed to get a few minutes or hours of sleep.

During the next day I wandered around talking to all in the FOB, preparing for a Memorial Service at 1800 hours, just as the sun was setting and the coolest part of the evening. We had come under some small arms fire during the day, it was sporadic, nothing too concerning.

The Memorial Service was as all such services were in Afghanistan. It was to be just a time of quiet, a period of prayer and remembrance, a show of solidarity. It was all these apart from the quiet. The quiet was broken because we came under attack by a group of insurgents. It was as though they knew we had lost one of our own and they were determined to spoil this important time of healing.

With the parade of around 150 from the battalion and attached personnel gathered around me on three sides, we started in quiet, the heat of the day was starting to reduce and the light was decreasing. The service started and the quiet reflectiveness was suddenly broken by the sound of a rocket propelled grenade landing next to one of our guard-posts. It was just at that point that all went mad, and we came under a steady stream of fire from one area outside the FOB. The gunfire could be heard as a pop in the distance but overhead the whizz of the bullets could be heard uncomfortably close. It felt as though we could almost jump up and catch the bullets.

I stared out of the side of my eye towards the Officer in Charge of the Company, and the Sergeant Major. They made no move, they did not give any signal to me and I felt happy at that point to continue on, to complete the Memorial Service. A few soldiers peeled off to assist with the Sanger under fire, firing back and suppressing the insurgent; but practically all stayed on parade. The Service continued and the most memorable point was to be during the minute's silence, the Bugler sounded Last Post and all our soldiers stopped firing, the incoming rounds continued but we never retaliated, that is until after the minute's silence and Reveille sounded and our Mortar Line went into action.

With the Memorial Service ended at the Blessing, everyone fled to their appropriate places to guard the FOB all round. The Memorial Service was a fitting memorial to the soldier who had died, but, from the very start of the sad events that resulted in the Memorial Service, I had to deal as a chaplain with various difficult decisions that could have had life and death implications not just for me. I don't say this knowing that I had to ponder these decisions, but in the knowledge that they were just natural decisions that did not need to be cerebrally thought out and risk assessed, they were natural reactions and decisions that I would go as far as to say were instinctive.

Going to the FOB, I would say, did not involve any form of moral decision; it was not an act of courage, a big decision; rather it was a natural reaction and desire to be there for those who needed to be supported. It was not a response to an invitation but simply a duty to be there where and when needed. I did however think of those transferring me between the FOBs and would never have put them at risk just for me. I knew that they were needed to protect the route along which the vehicle involved in the soldier's death would be recovered for inspection.

Within the FOB I was in some sense a free spirit. I was welcomed into the homes of the soldiers, simple tents, but they were for many months the place they would eat, sleep and drink. They were essentially home from home. Although daunting at times, with the usual 'What can I say', I was dropping in to speak to the soldiers, drinking coffee and just 'being', spending some time talking and most importantly listening. As a chaplain I would call this 'wasting time fruitfully', but in the light of the soldier's death it was tinted with the fear and grief associated with the death of a mate, a fellow soldier. As most priests would recognise, sometimes silence speaks louder than words. We don't need to have all the answers, we just need to be there; they need our presence just as much as our moral guidance.

The Memorial Service proved to be one of the most incredibly moving, and I would say at times somewhat frightening, experiences I have had ever. It was a test of nerve, in many ways, of courage. Perhaps this would even be considered moral courage, given that we were definitely determined not to allow the threat of attack to mar the memory of this soldier. It was difficult trying to assess the risk, that is the risk that at any time we could have been attacked even more ferociously, or even have experienced an attempt to overrun the FOB. There was also the risk that a stray round could hit any one of us on parade. The service has been talked about in various accounts by various people, some present and some second-hand. It was for me an example of what we are, what we do, how we show our love. The decision to go to the FOB was as I said an almost unconscious decision, by that I mean a reaction to need rather than a formulated or calculated assessment. The decision to continue the Memorial Service was slightly different. I did take into account the severity of the incident as it unfolded, and the reaction of the Company Commander and the Company Sergeant Major was pivotal to resultant completion of the service, but the ultimate decision to continue was mine. It was however not a difficult decision, but one that did prove to be a 'force multiplier' for that Company, as they went on to complete a successful tour of Afghanistan. If the service had stopped prematurely, even if it was completed later that night, it is said that we as a fighting force would not have been as charged and focused and so not as 'Operationally Effective'.

The Padre and the Legal Officer

If the first chaplain's account reveals the full potential for the chaplain's role to have an impact on soldiers serving in Afghanistan, the second illustrates the way in which a continuing historic role is exercised in a changing context. Mark Grant-Jones' narrative is short and to the point, and has one main focus. His account makes very clear that an increasing emphasis on legal requirements and the Law of Armed Conflict in particular may circumscribe both moral consideration of operations (at least at the tactical level) and the historic role of the chaplain. This raises a question of wide significance, for commanders and governments, as well as for the padre, of the dynamic between moral argument (including the application of just war traditions to current operations) and legal frameworks. It further asks chaplains and churches, and those concerned with the public role of religion, about whether theology may provide a third corner of the triangle, with ethics and law.

Mark Grant-Jones' Account

Throughout the preceding century we have seen the increasing secularisation of just war theory and a movement away from a moral and theological foundation towards a strictly legal and diplomatic base. Concurrent with this, the chaplain's contribution that is not currently well utilised is that of ethics. In current military ethics where theology has been replaced with law so has the chaplain by the lawyer at the commander's table. Today it is clear that there is currently a strong dependence on law to guide the moral process in modern warfare and it is also clear that the complex interplay between political, humanitarian and military goals means legal parameters are complex.

On 20 August 2009 in a Forward Operating Base in the Helmand town of Sangin, the chaplain was present in the operations room when a situation began to develop on the outskirts of the town. A group of around 10 men had gathered and formed a vehicle checkpoint stopping and questioning people as they arrived from the rural regions. Given that this day was Election Day across Afghanistan it was presumed that these men were Taliban and seeking to intimidate or coerce local people against voting. This activity was observed for a while until a decision was made by the Commanding Officer to deal with these men. Having taken advice from the regional Brigade headquarters and being satisfied that these men, armed, were not part of any official grouping and therefore were Taliban insurgents, an Apache attack helicopter was called on site. When this helicopter arrived, it was given permission to kill the insurgents which it promptly and efficiently did. The sound of its chain gun was heard as the visual image was beamed into the control room via on-board cameras. It was hard to see much detail in the dust but the immediate aftermath was clear. At no point in this exercise was there a discussion with or even reference to the chaplain. Once the legal criteria were met then the fate of those 10 men was sealed. They had not obviously killed anyone, nor were they an immediate and present danger to ISAF forces.

It was coincidence that the chaplain was present at the time these events played out. During the course of events the chaplain was able to ask the Commander what the process of decision-making was and the basis of the action was made clear. The operation was a tactical move made on the basis of current legal parameters in operation. The event illustrated the difficulty of locating ethics in a theological framework in a secular organisation.

To give some colour to the challenges facing UK military personnel in Sangin on Election Day, two of their number died in an explosion that evening whilst on patrol in the town.

The Padre's Mission

The preceding sections paint a vivid picture of the reality of contemporary military chaplaincy. They indicate that the chaplain's moral role is built on the foundations of their pastoral and liturgical roles – morality is integral to their being people of faith who lead others in acts of faith. This requires the chaplain to have developed a coherent faith response capable of integrating these dimensions, which, given the moral courage required on occasion, also needs to be rooted in a strong sense of calling. Moral courage exercised instinctively, or as the result of an in-built sense of duty (as in Stephen Sharkey's account), needs to be interwoven with a faith which the chaplain inhabits at some depth; as thoroughly as he or she inhabits their own skin.

The chapter thus far also illustrates something of the challenge of living out that vocation and integrated theology and spirituality in the military context. That may mean addressing the issue of being a 'force multiplier'; it may mean recognising the way in which the chaplain's role can on occasion be circumscribed by tactical reality and the complex demands and requirements that military personnel and those in command must fulfil in the theatre of operation. Such challenges add to the need for the chaplain to be clear about his or her mission in this setting, so that theology can be lived and articulated, with respect for the military world and ethos; but also with the courage that theology is a distinctive voice, that offers wise questions and insight.

This mission needs to be inclusive, because the chaplain is there for all, irrespective of whether they espouse a particular faith or not. Chaplains exercise an 'all souls ministry' that respects and embraces the diversity of the military community. Mission is often expressed, therefore, as being present (as in Stephen Sharkey's account). For the Christian chaplain this may well be accompanied by a theology of incarnation; that the Christian faith is about the presence of God in the midst of creation and humanity in the person of Jesus Christ. So for the chaplain faith is communicated by being as much as by doing; and by example, rather than by seeking to convert. Space is made for the faith of those with whom the chaplain engages; and when members of the British military community wish to explore questions of faith, that is welcomed. But the chaplain's own faith, although it may be shared, is never imposed. The Christian gospel is communicated by the way in which the chaplain participates in military life, by the quality of their pastoral care, and by their moral example and engagement.

Such an inclusive approach allows the chaplain to lead a corporate act of remembering in a FOB that makes space for all present to remember, according to their own faith, or belief, the colleague who has been killed. But it also allows the act to be a corporate one, a single shared rite of remembering that centres on a moment's silence which braves incoming fire.

The chaplain's mission must also be inclusive and responsive (rather than dogmatic) because of the particular sensitivities of the chaplain's role as part of an occupying force in a country with its own strong religious traditions. This is also in keeping with an emerging role for the chaplain in a setting like Afghanistan, as the subject-matter expert on religion (although this is more likely to be articulated this way amongst American forces than British ones). If the chaplain has a quasi-official role with respect to the religion, and religious officials, in Afghanistan, it is of enabling greater understanding of the religious dimensions of Afghan life, and perhaps of engaging in a dialogue with local leaders, from a position of mutual respect for each other's traditions.

The above raises wider questions of appropriate models of mission in a twenty-first century multi-cultural and secular setting. This is a question for chaplains, for sending churches in their support for chaplaincy, and for churches in their wider mission. Alongside that question is the specific one about how the chaplain's theology of mission includes a theology of war, given that his or her mission is aligned with the military mission and the authorised use of lethal force.

Recent approaches to the Christian understanding of mission have emphasised its breadth. This is expressed, for example, in the 'Five Marks of Mission' first developed by the Anglican Consultative Council, and set out in their 1984 document, 'Bonds of Affection'.[1] According to this view, mission is characterised by the following aims, or goals:

> To proclaim the Good News of the Kingdom
> To teach, baptise and nurture new believers
> To respond to human need by loving service
> To seek to transform unjust structures of society
> To strive to safeguard the integrity of creation and
> sustain and renew the life of the earth.

This provides a frame for understanding the balance within mission espoused by military chaplaincy. If chaplains feel a primary call to offer loving service in the face of human need, and if they rightly understand evangelism and nurturing faith as about quiet presence and making space, their involvement with the military requires them to balance these principles with an approach to unjust social structures, if not also their role in renewing the life of the earth.

Indeed their pastoral care and faithful presence in the midst of military operations might suggest the need for quite a bold approach to the transformation of unjust structures. This might involve believing that the role of the military, in keeping with the just war tradition, is the re-establishment of peace and justice; that this may involve armed conflict as a necessary step on this road; and that chaplains actively support the armed forces in this mission. It might also include support for those who see their service within the forces as a way of living out their faith, and as a contribution to restoring, or developing, just social structures at a global, as well as local, level.

Depth of faith; an understanding of the chaplain's mission as inclusive; a bold approach to an integrated understanding of the relationship between the chaplain's mission and that of the military; these are the facets of chaplaincy identity and practice that underpin the chaplain's moral role. They provide for the possibility that the chaplain can be a moral presence; can exercise moral courage; can play their part in training, in character formation and the development of core values; and, when the occasion demands it, can offer the kind of critical friendship to the military community that would justify the role characterisation of 'moral compass'. How this interplay of faith, understanding of mission or calling, and moral role is played out, including in theatres of operation, is the subject of this book, together with the moral and theological questions arising.

---

[1]   ACC-6, p. 49. See http://www.anglicancommunion.org/ministry/mission/fivemarks. cfm.

Following the Threads

Many, although not all, of the threads with which this book is concerned have therefore already been raised in the preceding chaplains' accounts of their role and experience in Afghanistan, and in the initial discussion of their role as faith practitioners in the military context.

Totten deepens and extends the picture of the chaplain's role in Afghanistan. He focuses particularly on the question of the chaplain's role in relation to soldiers' morale. The theme of morale orientates his exploration of two issues pertinent to military chaplaincy, namely its integrity and its influence. The first issue has attracted much pacifist criticism, typically hinging on the role of chaplains in the maintenance of morale. Totten's chapter, written largely in Afghanistan, seeks to rehabilitate that role through a historical and philosophical reconnection of morale to its moral roots.

Working from this historical and philosophical survey, Totten argues that chaplains need to work with morale, by restoring the moral dimension to the military understanding of morale, rather than colluding with the perspective that sees it in purely psychological terms; and by resisting the temptation to take a corresponding, purely pastoral, approach, of supporting military personnel in the midst of the horrors of war. Thus chaplains need to work with the military in shaping the moral character of those who serve, as part of their preparation for conducting war well (alongside the development of corporate discipline and understanding of the legal framework of military operations). Totten proposes that this is key to sustaining morale which is rooted in the understanding that military personnel can act justly in the midst of conflict; and can have a quietness of mind about the morality of their role. He further argues that for chaplaincy to contribute effectively to the moral basis for morale, it needs to keep alive, and indeed promote the contribution of their Christian perspective, as an important 'second language' alongside a more prominent secular discourse. The extent to which this renewed stress on the just war context of chaplaincy translates into influence in the modern battlespace is discussed with particular reference to the chaplaincy team that accompanied 16 Air Assault Brigade on Operation HERRICK 13.

In a way that complements Totten's work, McCormack offers a critical evaluation of some of the difficulties chaplains face, in acting as an effective 'moral compass' in the midst of complex contemporary military operations. He casts a particular light on the place of international law in contemporary military operations. Rooted in a careful analysis of the Western philosophy of war, he evaluates the place of international law within the 'new wars' of which the conflict in Afghanistan is a prime example. He concludes that international law evolved within an understanding of war being waged by states on each other, and in which war is always political. However, in new wars in which non-state actors play a prominent part, the framework of international law is required to do a job for which it was not designed. This is a consequence of non-state actors, insurgents (perhaps motivated by cultural and religious considerations, rather than just by those which are straightforwardly about inter-state politics), both ignoring international law and using it as part of their campaign. In the latter case, insurgent action may be designed to manoeuvre state forces into actions against civilians which are outside the boundaries of international law. This creates a propaganda victory for insurgent forces, which may sufficiently shift public opinion so as to undermine state intervention, by eroding public support for engagement. This shift in public opinion in turn influences state governments, whose calculations about operations are expressed in a new narrative of 'exceptional circumstances' and 'military necessity'.

McCormack concludes that such changed circumstances, in which the application of international law is not straightforward, require ethical resources which ought to be offered by chaplains and churches, amongst others. His contention, however, is that the churches have failed to recognise the changing reality of military operations in the twenty-first century. In consequence, they have continued to work with ethical approaches appropriate to previous conflicts, often resulting in an evaluation that operations cannot be justified. Rather than developing a renewed ethic for 'new wars', which might resource chaplains and those they serve, McCormack suggests that churches have tended to contribute to public calls for withdrawal, which in turn offered the propaganda victory sought by non-state actors. The chapter concludes that this amounts to a silence from the churches, which renders the chaplain silent in the face of complex ethical questions inherent in situations such as Afghanistan.

Sedgwick and Fisher, offering a perspective from outside the world of military chaplaincy, both broaden the picture of the challenges presented to military chaplaincy by the wider context. Sedgwick's chapter explores the development of two parameters within which military chaplaincy must operate. One parameter has to do with the complex interaction of insurgency, terrorism and religion in British military operations since 1945. The other parameter is concerned with the conduct of counter-insurgency operations, and the use of enhanced interrogation techniques in particular. The historical development of these two parameters is explored by Sedgwick with reference to Northern Ireland from 1969 to the end of the twentieth century, before he turns to more recent operations in Iraq and Afghanistan.

Working within these parameters sets military chaplains a range of challenges, which include the moral, the theological and the pastoral. Thus the chaplain, someone who is increasingly regarded as the subject-matter expert, is called on to account for the religious motivation of the insurgents, especially post-9/11. They are also challenged to offer an alternative religious perspective, alongside their role in ensuring the moral accountability of the armed forces. Sedgwick suggests that the greatest challenge is in the chaplain responding to the use of enhanced interrogation techniques. He argues from a position of considerable respect for chaplaincy, but suggests that in being involved in military counter-insurgency operations, 'it walks a cliff edge high up in the mountains, where the path is not clear, the danger of a fall is fatal, and the weather is often murky'. Set alongside

McCormack's contribution, this chapter reinforces the case for chaplaincy being both supported and well-resourced, both from within the military community, but also from the sending churches.

Fisher takes us into the world of technological warfare, with his focus on the use of drones. He offers a picture of the drone operator detached from the theatre of operations, but nonetheless directing lethal force (in the shape of missiles) into the locus of the conflict, such as Afghanistan. Fisher asks whether this way of waging war has rendered traditional approaches to the ethics of war (including the just war tradition) obsolete. He argues that this is not the case, demonstrating clearly that the actions of the drone operator can be, and need to be, directed by just war principles, especially those of proportionate use of force and discrimination between combatants and non-combatants.

Fisher's contention is further that therefore those involved in war conducted at a distance must be trained and formed morally, as well as technically. The virtue of drone operators is as important as their technical skill. This enables him to revisit the question raised at the beginning of his chapter, about whether the 'robotisation' of war reduces the need for courage in the conduct of military operations. He suggests that if the requirement for physical courage is less, the need for moral courage has increased. In support of this he cites recent examples where moral courage has been lacking in military operations. His conclusion is that the technology of war makes it necessary that those who conduct such operations need to be formed in virtues such as a sense of justice, self-control and respect for others, so that they may act with appropriate moral courage. This chapter stands alongside Totten's call for chaplaincy to be engaged in shaping the moral character of military personnel.

If the two chapters of the book by Totten and McCormack deepen understanding of the chaplain's moral role, and of the challenges chaplains face in realising that role; and if chapters 4 and 5 (by Sedgwick and Fisher) explore dimensions of the wider context in which chaplaincy is set; then the chapters that follow (by Howson, Ball, Coleman and Todd with Butler) offer different perspectives on the ecclesial context of chaplaincy. In particular, they offer insight into the relationship between chaplains and their churches, and offer suggestions about how questions arising may be addressed; not least by the churches, if they wish to engage fully with military chaplaincy and the moral issues which it raises.

Howson offers a carefully researched, historical account of a number of facets of the relationship between churches and their chaplains in the last 60 years. He offers a particular evaluation of the way this relationship has been realised, or not, in the structures responsible for the governance of army chaplaincy. The chapter acts as a sequel to McCormack's case-study of the relationship between the Church of Scotland and its military chaplains, by highlighting a number of examples where there have been tensions between chaplains and their sending churches. In a number of cases, church criticism of particular military operations has been offered with little reference to chaplains, and has undermined their sense of being supported by their denomination. Howson argues that, not least in the

Cold War period, churches developed a 'functional pacifism' which has stood at odds with their sponsorship of chaplains.

He subsequently charts both the decline in the churches' involvement in the governance of army chaplaincy, and the increase in the control of chaplains by the army. In the first case, Howson shows how the Inter-denominational Advisory Committee on Army Chaplaincy Services, brought into being during the First World War, had ceased to function by 1968 (the year of its last meeting). This body was constituted of representatives of the sending churches, and was chaired by the Permanent Under-Secretary at the War Office. The Chaplain General was not a member and came to meetings only by invitation.

In the second case, Howson demonstrates the increasing role of the Royal Army Chaplains' Department (RAChD), under the leadership of the Chaplain General, in managing chaplains, especially in the wake of the 1999 McGill report on the 'Spiritual Needs' of the British Army. He points both to the process of 'convergence', whereby Roman Catholic chaplains were brought within a single RAChD structure, with chaplains from other churches; and to the development of 'all souls ministry' which emphasises the chaplain's role of being available to all members of a particular unit. Howson suggests that this significantly alters the chaplain's sense of whom he or she represents, especially in relation to their sending church. His chapter concludes with a plea for a renewed structure to support chaplaincy that recognises that they operate under dual authority – that of the church, or faith group, as well that of the army.

Ball's chapter also explores chaplains' dual membership of the military and of their faith communities, but from a rather different angle. He considers the ritual and liturgical role of the military chaplain, which sits alongside and is inextricably linked with the moral role. He identifies a series of dilemmas that go with the ritual role: to what extent should the military chaplain assume the consent of personnel to be objects of prayer in a way which a civilian counterpart in a peacetime context could not possibly take for granted? To what extent can or should military ceremonial and ecclesiastical ritual be permitted to have blurred boundaries, and at what point does ecclesiastical ritual cease to be what it is meant to be and become military ceremony (and can chaplains collude with this)? And to what extent can requirements by a church only to use authorised services and forms of words be ignored should it appear expedient on pastoral grounds? He explores these dilemmas against the background of the Christian liturgy being used on Operations today; and of liturgical reform both within and outside the military and its effect on liturgies used, and on the ownership of liturgy by the non-committed.

Ball sets the wider context for the above by offering an overview of church decline; of the changing relationship of young people (especially generations X and Y, typical of the military community) and the church; and of the development of liturgy in the military context, in the light of the Afghan campaign and of the return of chaplains to a front-line role. He draws on a variety of perspectives on ritual in order to wrestle with the way in which a chaplain may offer to lead a liturgy for military personnel, understanding it to mean one thing, while those for whom it is provided may interpret it very differently. He acknowledges the risk of the chaplain being perceived as saying, through an act of prayer or worship, that 'God is on our side', rather than asking the question, 'Are we on the side of God?'.

Nonetheless, Ball offers a positive picture of the ritual role of the chaplain, especially in relation to operations in Afghanistan, which has been well received by those deployed there, and which has enabled them to wrestle with questions of meaning and identity raised by their involvement in conflict. As Ball indicates, the positive response, even if it does not occasion attachment to the institution of the church, still asks questions of the churches about their wider response to generations X and Y; and once again about churches support for chaplains in this demanding and complex, yet prophetic, role.

Coleman's chapter leads us back to the starting point of the research which gave rise to this book: the question of the contemporary relevance of traditional ethical approaches to conflict and of just war thinking in particular. He argues in particular that, in relation to recent conflicts, an over-reliance on international law by politicians, and a corresponding use of just war criteria as little more that a convenient checklist of legitimacy, has removed the just war theory from its theological context. Further, the way in which the theory is now constructed, so that it appears to be a self-sufficient set of principles, exacerbates this tendency. Coleman argues, therefore, for a radical reappraisal of the theology of just war.

For this he turns to the work of Bonhoeffer. Drawing on the work of Green (2005), Coleman turns our attention to Bonhoeffer's thinking about his participation in the plot to kill Hitler, in tyrannicide, in the context of his well-known commitment to pacifism. More than the points of contact between the ethics of tyrannicide and of just war (including questions of last resort and legitimate authority) Coleman is drawn to Bonhoeffer's theological rationale for participation in the plot. This constitutes an understanding of the Christological imperative of resisting tyranny, and the corresponding decision to act freely in pursuit of peace, accepting responsibility for that action. That decision to act carries with it an acknowledgment of the guilt incurred, which requires a dependency on the grace of God that transcends any human justification of the act.

Coleman proposes that Bonhoeffer's approach, which is much more than just a set of ethical principles, and which places involvement in conflict in the wider context of sin, guilt and grace, offers a theological frame for reconsidering just war theory. He pursues that reconsideration of just war thinking as an ethic of peace-making, especially by investigating recent work on *jus post bellum*. He then pursues the implications of this for the role of the military chaplain. Arguing the necessity in contemporary warfare for all military personnel being regarded as moral beings, who take responsibility for their actions, Coleman points to the chaplain as a living example of a moral life in the midst of conflict. More than this, he proposes that a key role of the chaplain is to be concerned with, and to promote, reconciliation and forgiveness. This can, in turn, enable military personnel and others to conceive of military operations as disciplined service in the pursuit of justice.

Chapter 9 (by Todd, with Butler) returns, therefore, to the question of the different ways in which the chaplain can and does live and act as a moral example, within a moral military community. As with previous chapters, it focuses on the dual accountability of chaplains to the military and to their faith communities, taking this as a starting point for a discussion of their present moral role. That role is unpacked in relation to an understanding of the British military moral ethos that has developed over the last two decades, and a specific investigation of chaplains' own perspectives on the dimensions of the way in which they act as a 'moral compass' to the military community.

The investigation, carried out as part of the research workshops sponsored by the British Academy out of which this book has grown, looks at: questions asked of chaplains; questions asked about chaplains; and chaplains' responses to the various questions. The investigation concludes that chaplains' moral reasoning is significantly situational, but that they are not afraid to work with and deploy particular moral norms, drawn from the military context, wider society and their own faith community. The chapter further suggests that the 'genius' of military chaplaincy lies in their ability to connect different moral norms and foster dialogue between them, enabling military personnel to work, for example, with the tension between moral questions arising out of the working week, and being off-duty; or between moral issues relevant to the UK setting and those that arise on operations. Chaplains' ability to connect domains is facilitated specifically by their ambiguous social location; by the way in which they simultaneously belong to the military and symbolise a wider world.

The chapter characterises this moral role as one of being an 'interpreter' of plural traditions. The chapter suggests, drawing on Gadamer (1979), that this requires the chaplain to inhabit those different traditions; and that chaplains' critical role depends, not on their detachment from the military ethos, but precisely on their involvement in it, alongside their involvement in other traditions, especially their faith tradition. This gives rise to the proposal of a model of mission for chaplaincy (derived from Bosch 1991) which is contextual, concerned to discern where God is active in the military setting (as well as where God's presence is frustrated). However, one aspect of the chaplain's contextualisation, and inhabiting of the military tradition, is that he or she has to be aligned with the military purpose of exercising lethal force, when authorised and required to do so. This alignment need not be exercised uncritically, but once again is actually fundamental to the chaplain acting as a critical friend within the military community. The chapter concludes that, if the sending churches are to be supportive of their military chaplains, then they too must be in critical alignment with the military purpose, and believe that serving in the military can be a Christian vocation.

Chapter 2

Moral Soldiering and Soldiers' Morale

Andrew Totten

Introduction

In May 2010 the Chaplain General brought a 'pastoral key issue' to the attention of the British Army's Directorate of Personal Services:

> There has been a noticeable number of commanders, soldiers and families discussing with their chaplains what can only be described as "fearfulness", particularly prior to deployment to Afghanistan. This is not altogether surprising, and it is certainly understandable that they may wish to share this with the chaplain rather than colleagues or even family. In the case of those in command positions these fears are not so much about personal safety but their responsibility for their soldiers and how they will cope if their soldiers are killed, especially in instances of multiple casualties. (Robbins 2010)

Although offering no solutions beyond vigilance, the Chaplain General clearly touched a nerve: his text, suggestive of a risk to morale, was copied to senior officers across the army. It would not have come as a surprise to those in command of experienced troops preparing for another deployment: the hunger among newer recruits for operational experience has largely abated by the time they are on their second or third Afghan tour. A few days after circulation of the Chaplain General's remarks, a Company Commander at 3 PARA, a battalion training for a third deployment to Afghanistan with 16 Air Assault Brigade, told the *Daily Telegraph*: 'there are only a certain number of times that you can dance with the devil and get away with it. There is a sense of nervous anticipation among the men' (Major Nick French, quoted in Harding 2010a).

That reference to the devil is less an attempt to demonise the enemy than a tendency, seen also in journalistic wordplay on 'hell' and 'Helmand', to draw on religious imagery to communicate the intensity of combat in Afghanistan. Soldiers' own accounts of that combat, avidly read by the general public and each successive wave of new troops, make mention of religious practices to ward off personal harm. A Royal Irish officer who has seen several tours with 16 Air Assault Brigade echoes the sense of playing against the odds:

> It wasn't as if I had many of my nine lives left. During my time in Garmsir, in southern Helmand, in 2006, I had survived by the skin of my teeth. Almost

every day I was in a situation where I could have been killed, yet for whatever reason fate conspired to keep me alive whilst others around me were being shot, burned, and blown up, left maimed, scarred and disfigured, both physically and mentally. Some would lose limbs. More than a few would lose their lives. I was lucky to have made it out of there. Almost every step of the way I had been terrified. I'd prayed to God, made pacts with the devil, done anything that might keep me safe and allow me to return to a loving family, and a future. And guess what? It had worked. Despite everything, I had made it out of that Helmand hell. Lady Luck had been on my side. (Beattie 2009: 8)

This heightened sense among soldiers of the possibility of their injury or death does not necessarily manifest itself in a call on the chaplain; but as the Chaplain General observed, it has markedly increased the likelihood of such pastoral engagement, particularly before tours begin. This business of caring for those caught up in war is a much-repeated self-description of modern British chaplaincy. Usually accompanying that description, however, is an attempt to maximise the distance between chaplaincy and the fighting itself: 'my job as a padre is not to oil the wheels of war but to help the humanity caught up in it' (the Revd Clinton Langston, quoted in Mallinson 2011).

Despite considerable involvement by chaplains in the British Army's formal programme of moral education over the past decade, they remain reticent about offering specific endorsements of soldiers' fighting role, perhaps heedful of the prevailing pacifist mood of their sending churches. Facing tricky navigation between muscular Christianity and Christian misgiving – with holy war and pacifist perfectionism on their outer flanks – chaplains switch tack from moral issues to soldiers' pastoral needs. This chimes with the current sentimentality that views soldiers primarily as victims. However, it fails to recognise that pastoral care – even a simple ministry of presence – has its own moral implications. The critic is certainly suspicious:

the military chaplain has in fact contributed to the strengthening and maintenance of the morale of the fighting forces. Even if we grant that this has not been the intention nor that it would be accepted by him as a definite role obligation, it remains an almost inseparable and inescapable *effect* of his activities. By his very presence, the pastor in uniform represents a symbol of legitimacy in the eyes of most observers and participants; for, as the argument would go, if it were not permissible for the believer to take part in the war, would the priest be there? (Zahn 1969: 112)

Zahn is correct in his assessment of the historical influence of the military chaplain on morale. He is correct too to see the moral strand as inextricably woven into the fabric of military chaplaincy. (When interviewing chaplains, for example, journalists almost inevitably raise moral questions about conflict.) But the contention here, contrary to Zahn, is that the maintenance of morale can indeed be embraced as an obligation of chaplaincy. If the cause or simply the conduct of the fighting soldier are justified, why would the maintenance of his morale not be a proper object of concern? Equally, would drawing the attention of the soldier and others to his just conduct not assist in this maintenance? Also, what form of morale needs to be maintained in order to keep his conduct justifiable? Such interlinked questions – along with the challenge of translating the answers into influential practice – help define the agenda for a chaplaincy that is properly engaged with just war theory.

But a lack of clear definitions plagues the debate. This is not to say that tidier semantics would resolve the problem: those of a pacifist persuasion will still find the following effort to reconstitute morale in moral terms unacceptable, if by default they have ruled out a moral framework for the use of force. But a clearer etymological understanding of how 'morale' has shifted away from its roots is a necessary step towards reconfiguring and re-contesting the place of chaplaincy within just war thinking (for those who accept such thinking as a valid framework), while also ensuring that this reinforces the integrity of chaplaincy, rather than calling it further into question.

An etymology of chaplaincy itself seems in order too, for a moral and political context shaped the understanding of the chaplain's duties from the outset. This appeal to etymology is not made because original meanings are somehow more authentic or definitive: it is accepted that 'language and culture evolve throughout history and terms take on a variety of semantic registers in accordance with the changing social, cultural and political contexts in which they operate' (Carrette and King 2005: 33). Instead:

> Examination of the genealogy of terms … remains an important task in identifying how such concepts have been used and what connotations they bring forward as 'traces' from earlier epochs. Such attention to genealogy allows us to see the effects of power operating in the construction of ideas. (Carrette and King 2005: 33)

Both the institution of military chaplaincy and also the perception of its role in soldiers' morale have evolved and expressed themselves in a multitude of cultures over the centuries, but to go back to their roots should throw their current expression into sharper relief and illuminate domains that remain open for chaplains to contest and influence.

Integrity of Chaplaincy

Chaplaincy owes its name to pre-battle liturgical practices of the eighth-century armies that culminated in the military machine with which Charlemagne revived the Roman Empire in the West. Walahfrid Strabo, writing at the Frankish court in the ninth century, explains:

> *Cappellani* [chaplains] originally came from the *cappa* [cloak] of blessed
> Martin; the Frankish kings commonly took it with them in battle because it
> helped them to victory; because they carried it and cared for it with other saints'
> relics, clerics began to be called chaplains. (Harting-Correa 1996: 193)

There was nothing new about priests ministering to soldiers on campaign.
Relics were paraded and masses said as far back as the days of the Roman legions.
After 742, however, those chaplains gained a significantly enhanced role. In that
year, Boniface, the English missionary, and Carloman, uncle of Charlemagne,
presided over the *Concilium Germanicum*. It was Carloman who undertook the
unprecedented step of reissuing the decrees of the *Concilium Germanicum* as
a capitulary, underscoring a deep interest in military-religious reform. Troop
morale was the issue at stake. Quite simply, 'the Church role in developing the
soldiers' morale owed much to government policies' (Bachrach 2001: 147).
At the heart of it all was a provision for the making of private confession by
soldiers, for which the council's decrees are the earliest surviving evidence.
Pre-Constantinian prohibitions on soldiering had long since disappeared, but
killing in war was still widely viewed as sinful. 'Forever in the background ...
lurked the Christian doubt of how Christ's blessing of the peacemakers might
be reconciled with the impulse of the man on horseback, even if he rode under a
papal banner' (Keegan 2004: 290).

During the fourth and fifth centuries a soldier who confessed his sins and
received penance was expected to leave the army: Pope Leo I (d.461) made that
point explicit. With inevitable consequences for morale, this obliged soldiers to
choose between ending their careers and risking death in battle in a state of sin. The
introduction of repeatable, private penance offered a way out of this predicament.
Historians are agreed that wherever and however private penance emerged, the
Irish Church in the monastic period made it general practice. MacCulloch observes:

> When missionaries from Ireland and Scotland started spreading their faith in
> northern and central Europe in the seventh century, they brought tariff books
> with them; these were the first "penitentials" or manuals of penance for clergy
> to use with their flocks. The idea was hugely popular ... It became the basis of
> the medieval Western Church's centuries-long system of penance. (2009: 333)

It also underpinned the second canon of the *Concilium Germanicum*. In addition
to the overall commander's bishop and attending chaplains, who were responsible
for relics and masses, now the commander of every unit in the Carolingian army
had to have on his staff a priest capable of hearing confessions and assigning
penances in the period before battle. The Irish had thus radically changed the older
Christian concept of confession as a single public event in a person's life – like a
second baptism – into a repeatable private encounter with a priest, with penalties
laid out in tariff books. Of course the system flew in the face of Augustine's
theology of grace, and the issue eventually helped split the Western church at the

Reformation; but in its original Irish context the primary impulse, paradoxically, was to show that no sin was so terrible as to be beyond the saving grace of God.

Applied within the context of the Frankish military, as Bachrach points out, 'the development of repeatable confession and the control this gave to individual soldiers over their own personal salvation opened an entirely new area of military-religious practice' (2003: 43). It was no less than the legally mandated expansion of the duties of the chaplain to provide individual pastoral care to all serving soldiers. Indeed, it may be proper 'to identify the *Concilium Germanicum* as the legal origin of the chaplain's office in the Latin West' (Bachrach 2004: 76). From now on:

> As combat loomed, early medieval chaplains sought to maintain the morale of their fighters and seized the moment to accomplish their broader mission of pastoral care … The belief that war arose out of sin, and that the outcome of battle was a form of divine judgment reinforced the menace of death to encourage penitential rites of purification and supplication. (McCormick 2004: 54)

The dark side of this – realised in crusading, itself construed as a penitential act – was the trend towards holy war, with the Franks regarding themselves as God's chosen people and the true successors of the Israelites. It is this 'Constantinian settlement' of faith with nationalism that so exercises modern critics of military chaplaincy, even though no modern alignment of church, state and military exists to exert such a strong gravitational pull on British chaplaincy. Quite the opposite: concern is more often centred on the increasingly tenuous links between church and state and church and military. One way or another, however, it seems that military chaplaincy has had to reckon with political considerations from the outset. Probably within all state institutions, the pastoral is political. At the same time, the morale which those medieval chaplains sought to maintain was also rooted in the moral soil of a just war ecology (however mixed up with nationalism that may have been). Morale amounted to much more than a feel-good factor. Indeed, if a war was just, as Augustine taught (2003: 862), that was a cause for lamentation rather than celebration, for if it was unjust one would not have had to engage in it (which finds an echo in the remark attributed to the Duke of Wellington after Waterloo: 'there is only one thing sadder than winning a battle and that is losing it'). The combination of attitudes which this entails – pride in one's profession of arms and remorse that its application is necessary (mixed in with emotions ranging from grief at the loss of comrades to professional satisfaction to the thrill of the chase) – has probably never been a stable one. But the point remains that those early chaplains were not simply 'caring for those caught up in war': they were also committed to the righting of wrongdoing and the proclaiming of justice in the theatre of war.

Turning to the etymology of 'morale', it should be noted first of all that the mental and emotional attitudes to which the word now refers – confidence, hope, zeal, willingness – are at least as old as the military, but this English usage dates only from the mid-nineteenth century. The word emerged a century earlier simply as a variant of 'moral', with the spelling indicating a particular stress, much in the same way as 'locale' relates to 'local' or 'rationale' relates to 'rational'. Ultimately 'moral' derives from Cicero, who invented 'moralis' to translate its Greek predecessor 'ethikos'. Both terms referred to 'disposition' or 'custom', though 'the Latin term from which "moral" comes emphasizes rather more the sense of social expectation, while the Greek favours that of individual character' (Williams 1985: 6).

Much of the early use of 'moral' in English simply suggested 'practical': it was not seen as a domain separate from the religious or the legal. That separation began to happen from the mid-seventeenth century onwards, in the aftermath of the Wars of Religion, as the search began for a non-divisive alternative to religion as the ground for common life. 'Morality' came to denote:

> that particular sphere in which rules of conduct which are neither theological nor legal nor aesthetic are allowed a cultural space of their own. It is only in the later seventeenth century and the eighteenth century, when this distinguishing of the moral from the theological, the legal and the aesthetic has become a received doctrine that the project of an independent rational justification of morality becomes not merely the concern of individual thinkers, but central to Northern European culture. (MacIntyre 1985: 39)

It was in the mid-eighteenth century that 'morale' emerged as a stress-variant of 'moral'. From the mid-nineteenth century its meaning would gradually be transposed to the psychological register, and most military thinking of the past century has dealt with it in such terms, examining the role of small groups in maintaining morale, for instance, or the importance of prior training to offset the horrors of the battlefield (Strachan 2006).

Britain's citizen army of the Great War brought issues of emotional endurance particularly to the fore. It is instructive to note how often cheerfulness, either as a personal attribute or as an emotion generated in others, features in medal citations for chaplains during that war (Madigan 2011: 115–18). Philosophically, what hastened the shedding of the older sense of 'morale' in favour of psychological freight may well have been the early twentieth-century relegation of moral utterance to the arena of the emotions. Be that as it may, it is fascinating that the heated and seemingly intractable debate over chaplains and morale, whereby morale-building by chaplains has come to be seen as morally disconnected if not morally dubious, seems to be one more symptom of the disordered state of moral language of which MacIntyre has warned (1985: *passim*). Thus, taking a psychological context for morale for granted, Challans can write of the confusion that arises in US military doctrine when it:

> conflates "moral" with "morale", the first referring to the ethical, and the second to the psychological. Since the two referents are then used interchangeably, we

have the unfortunate consequence of thinking that moral superiority flows from psychological dominance. (2007: 14)

British military doctrine occasionally demonstrates the same Nietzschean tendency, whereby morality is seen as 'no more than a camouflaged way of imposing our will on others' (Sacks 2005: 42). However, as will be shown, echoes do persist in British military thinking of morale's older moral context, even in such self-cancelling dismissals as that of General Rupert Smith, for whom its basis need not 'be "ethical" in any sense, other than the ethos of the particular group in question at the time' (2001: 43).

The central accusation of the debate over chaplains and morale – namely that chaplains are too easily stripped of their religious role and reduced to functionaries who exist solely to help maintain morale – waned as a contention during the Second World War (having been a particular focus for pacifists during the 1930s), but re-emerged in the shadow of the Cold War, Vietnam, and various post-colonial conflicts. In his study of RAF chaplaincy as a 'role in tension', Zahn (1969: 109) considered it worth bringing the 'critical mass' of his analysis to bear on the 'distinction between morale-building and moral guidance as elements of the essentially pastoral role claimed by the chaplains'. Again, Zahn is correct to note the tendency of modern chaplaincy to retreat to the pastoral domain as supposedly non-contentious territory. However, his own tendency to treat morale-building and moral guidance as mutually exclusive is just as dubious.

It has to be acknowledged that some chaplains have put the cart before the horse. Field Marshal Montgomery's chaplain, for example, believed that 'the padre's way to an army's heart is through conviction that religion assists its fighting' (the Reverend Frederick Llewelyn Hughes, quoted in Louden 1996: 76). Also, as with the 'holy grocers' of the Great War, chaplains' contributions to morale may at times have had more to do with material matters than moral. 'Woodbine Willie' at least had a Christian message to accompany the cigarettes: de-Christianisation could leave his successors with just the latter.

For now, though, chaplains have retained a clear sense that morale bereft of a moral base (a deficiency pacifists seem to consider inherent), would indeed be simply a matter of managing or manipulating the necessary fighting spirit, a process with which Christian chaplaincy could have no involvement without loss of integrity. For the British Army too, 'being an effective killing machine is not enough; it is not an end in itself' (Bowyer 2009: 155). The army's own doctrine, while observing that 'some of the most barbarous armies in history have had tremendous morale and will to fight' (ADP 2010: 0220), and while observing that they have been successful, draws an immediate distinction:

> This may suggest that victory is what counts, regardless of the methods used to achieve it. But the British armed forces are, in their modern origins, rooted in the spirit of democracy. This has created a clear necessity to act within the bounds of popular understanding of what is thought to be right. Soldiers should use

force from a position of moral strength, reflecting the contemporary customs and
conventions of the Nation, adjusted to be realistic within the unusual exigencies
of conflict and war. (ADP 2010: 0220)

The 'spirit of democracy' is a moot point given that democracies too can lose
their grasp on justice: 'the military community, disciplined and characterised by
firmly held values of its own ... may even find itself morally in conflict with a
more bloodthirsty public' (Torrance 2000: 205). A democracy can also become so
averse to the use of force as to render its military impotent. Nevertheless, British
military doctrine retains traces of its lineage. It may have been bowdlerised of
Christian references in favour of something called 'national morality' (ADP 2010:
0220), but still 'the most obvious source of ethics ... of the British Army is the
Christian religion and the Bible' (Deakin 2008: 17). Archbishop William Temple
rightly observed that 'the worst of all things is to fight and to do it ineffectively'
(quoted in Burleigh 2010a: 503), but in general, Christian teaching on 'the restraint
of force to the minimum necessary ... has had some profound effects in Western
civilisation, where the elimination of anything that looked like extravagance in
sanctions or penalties has been a consistent theme' (O'Donovan 1999: 260). Thus,
the use of just the minimum necessary force has been an aspiration of the British
Army since at least the days of the Raj, stemming not only from the need to avoid
provoking the subcontinent but also to live up to Victorian evangelical images
of a civilising empire (Thornton 2004).That Christian approach has its own
roots in Judaism, where despite an impression of bloodthirstiness, the purpose
of Deuteronomic liturgy and ritual was actually 'to construct a wall around the
encounter of battle, to make an unbridgeable difference between the ordinary
relations which bind peoples to neighbouring peoples and the exceptional moment
of antagonistic confrontation' (O'Donovan 2003: 4). The modern suspicion is
that the combination of religious practice with soldiering will tend to promote
not restraint but fervour; but the evidence, certainly from the Second World War,
indicates otherwise:

> If chaplains and other representatives of organised religion played a key role
> in supporting soldiers' morale on and off the battlefield, it seems equally clear
> that, despite the exhortations of their commanders and others, religious ideals
> seldom served to *motivate* soldiers to fight. Nevertheless, evidence from across
> the United States, British and Canadian armies suggests that religion very often
> proved to be a critical source of personal *support*, especially in times of crisis.
> (Snape 2010: 151–2, Snape's italics)

That dominance of the pastoral over the motivational might suggest a
diminishment of the moral too; but as we have seen, the pastoral probably cannot
be divorced from the moral or the political where state-funded chaplaincy is
involved. Another moral dimension persists too, highlighted paradoxically by the

very lack of force of religion (and specifically, crusading imagery) as a motivator in the Second World War:

> the evidence suggests that a crusading identity was far more commonly ascribed than actually felt … Besides plain ignorance and basic indifference, an obvious reason why Allied soldiers found such rhetoric and ascriptions unconvincing was because their experience of war and of military service was so often antithetical to those moral standards in civilian society that were usually identified with the good Christian life. Naturally, the elemental savagery of war was all too apparent to front-line soldiers … However, much more widely felt were the moral pitfalls of army life and of an existence beyond the confines and restraints of home. (Snape 2010: 146)

The nature of the fighting in which soldiers found themselves engaged, as well as the moral climate of their day-to-day routine, thus corroded their acceptance of attempts to state the justice of their cause. This is of abiding importance for just war theory, a clear indication that *jus in bello* reaches back to touch *jus ad bellum*. Essentially, it was soldiers' own moral sense that militated against moralists' attempts to justify war. In a reversal of the obvious sequence, *how* they fought and conducted themselves abroad seems to have had an effect on *why* they fought. The implications of not maintaining the moral high ground within the organisation as well as in combat are clear. As for chaplains, their effectiveness or otherwise in combating the 'moral pitfalls of army life' is probably easier to assess than the extent to which religious instruction (or belief itself) placed moral restraints on how soldiers actually fought. In the Second World War, the *how* seems to have been much more influenced by the *where* – from the vast spaces of north Africa to the jungles of south-east Asia to the tall hedgerows of Normandy. As always, standards were also subject to erosion in the fear and heat and horror of battle. The desire, particularly among infantrymen, to kill for the first time, to be blooded, must be reckoned with too. 'Place', 'situation', and 'person' could (and can) combine to horrific effect (Zimbardo 2007). Crucially, however, 'most soldiers in Western armies remained civilians in spirit and came from societies that had not encouraged them to hate' (Burleigh 2010a: 362). In the absence of deterrents such as the death penalty, British soldiers as citizens of a Western democracy 'needed to be coaxed, reassured, supported and reasoned with to an unprecedented extent' (Snape 2010: 138); and as products of a culturally Christian society, 'it was inevitable that religion and religious agencies should play a significant role in this complex and ongoing process of negotiation' (Snape 2010: 138).

This raises the issue – to be addressed in the next section – of how modern chaplaincy can continue to exercise moral influence within an army whose soldiers decreasingly hail from a culturally Christian society; but it is sufficient for now to have registered the multifaceted historical reality and integrity of chaplains' contribution to morale, and (given Snape's comments above) their contribution to soldiers' reasoning.

Such reasoning is not abstract: for soldiers, just war theory is not just theoretical. It is much better understood as a 'proposal of *practical* reason … about how we may enact just judgment even in the theatre of war' (O'Donovan 2003: 6–7, his italics). This approach to just war theory offers not just the possibility of engaged moral reasoning, but also the rigour of spiritual exercise such as pacifists might commend. Indeed, O'Donovan talks of its 'spirituality', by which he means 'its capacity to make the reflecting subject conscious of his or her own responsible position before God in relation to other members of society who have their own differently responsible positions' (2003: ix). Essentially, the question the soldier must resolve in the course of his reasoning (if not exactly in O'Donovan's vocabulary) is: 'what does the praxis of judgment require of *me*, a soldier, in *this* armed conflict *now*?' (2003: 17, O'Donovan's italics).

The quiet mind of the soldier who has resolved that question, and can live with his consequent actions, best expresses morale as it is conceived here. (Conversely, a soldier's morale eventually suffers if he is not at ease with his conscience.) 'Never go mindlessly into situations where angels and sensible people fear to tread,' writes Zimbardo, in commending 'mindfulness' as one strategy for resisting malign social influences (2007: 453). British military doctrine, in stressing that 'no doctrine, plan or formula for conducting warfare or other military activity is likely to succeed without the maintenance of morale', notes that this 'depends upon affording personnel … a sense of justifiable purpose' (ADP 2010: 02A3). Morale thus retains a moral axis, albeit one on which it once turned more clearly. Strengthening that axis is now the crucial task, for there seems even more reason to endorse Mileham's words, written though they were before the conflicts in Iraq and Afghanistan, that 'in the expeditionary era, moral conduct on operations is at once a vital constituent and a consequence of morale' (Mileham and Willett 2001: 68).

Influence of Chaplaincy

Chaplaincy, it seems, has been quite capable of promoting morale with integrity, guilty of neither warmongering, nor of stifling moral reflection. It is all far removed from the sort of morality-free morale that Monsignor Stephen Louden, formerly the British Army's Principal Roman Catholic Chaplain, seems to envisage in his charge that army chaplains 'attempt to be no more than morale sustainers' (1996: 7). For Louden, chaplains should confine themselves 'to their core role of ministry of word and sacrament' and 'present war as a consequence of human sin and aberration' (1996: ii). Of course the latter is theologically true, and is rightly reflected in word and sacrament; but if that is all that is being communicated, then (as with the ruling of Pope Leo I) it does not take the serving soldier very far.

Augustine's message to Boniface, deeming military action an obligation of love to the neighbour, has much more mileage in it. Admittedly, as long ago as Augustine it was recognised that those who are trained for war are often trained not to love peace; and for a soldier who has been sickened by war, what Louden commends may have merit. (Even a soldier whose actions have been entirely in accordance with the rules of engagement can come to feel the need for forgiveness and atonement. Recent counter-insurgency training seems to have left a number of veterans of earlier tours of Afghanistan regretful of more forceful and less discriminating approaches that once seemed appropriate, and determined to make amends.)

But quite how a message that simply labours the sinfulness of the enterprise to which the soldier's training is constantly geared would ever encourage that soldier to reflect on his present, specific and practical responsibilities within the battlespace, is never spelt out. It is an approach that leaves chaplaincy shorn of the possibility of meaningful contribution to practical reasoning, of what O'Donovan calls a 'discipline of deliberation, a way of focussing and posing questions of political responsibility to oneself and to others at that frontier of human experience where action is in danger of breaking down into mere reaction' (2003: 16). This discipline redirects attention away from opinions over the justice of a cause, which initially at any rate tend to wax and wane in line with media coverage, to the judgements and actions required of the soldier in the present moment:

> If the ordinary soldier had first to reach a clear and informed view of the right and wrong of the prince's decision ... he could never get to the point of considering his own rôle and responsibility. It was, of course, acknowledged that the point could be reached where a private soldier understood the cause he supported as insupportable; and at that point he must extricate himself from it as best he could. But the point of the proposal was not to try to resolve that point first, working theoretically and deductively downwards from a premise, 'this war is just,' to a permissive conclusion, 'I may take part in it'. It was to mount a deliberative exploration outwards from a given point of practical engagement. (2003: 16)

Thus, a good deal of the preparation for Afghanistan is geared precisely to 'judgemental training'. Soldiers are exposed to realistic scenarios that demand judgement calls, most crucially concerning whether or not to open or call in fire. It was a desire to reduce casualties in real-life situations that finally led General Stanley McChrystal, US commander of the international force in Afghanistan, to introduce new guidance in August 2009, recognising that to destroy a life or a home or a property jeopardises families and creates more insurgents. The catchphrase until the summer of 2010 was 'courageous restraint'. However, given that soldiers were feeling restrained from returning fire even in self-defence (with mounting anger and frustration as casualties were taken), and given that a more robust approach was required to make local communities feel protected from intimidation, the phrase was replaced by concepts of patience and precision, the latter greatly assisted by the introduction to Helmand of advanced surveillance techniques. The effort in Helmand, backed up by such technology and extra troops on the ground, became centred on understanding what the military calls the 'human terrain'. A veteran of all three of 3 PARA's Afghan tours puts it like this:

> In 2006, it was "man the ramparts", the next time it was strike ops and we didn't have much interaction with the locals. This time it seems a hell of a lot more geared to winning over the population – we have to deal with the people and are sensitive to their feelings. The locals are more helpful now because we are out there a couple of times a day. We know their faces, they know our names. (Lance Corporal Andrew Wiltshire, quoted in Harding 2010b)

A basic principle remained that of avoiding civilian casualties. Indeed, General David Petraeus, McChrystal's successor, in line with the counter-insurgency aim of protecting the people in order to build their confidence in the forces of law and order, deemed such protection to be a 'moral imperative'. The worth of this from a humanitarian perspective is clear, as indeed it is from a utilitarian perspective: in this media age of the 'strategic corporal', the actions of an individual soldier can have campaign-level consequences. That is not to suggest that the soldier has to start applying deep intellectual and moral reasoning when faced with the decision of whether or not to use force: on the street corner speed may be of the essence. Moreover:

> One does not normally expect to educate soldiers in psycho-philosophy. They are trained chiefly to interpret their rules of engagement, which are carried around on a small card – supposedly condensed from thick law books – giving guidance on the practical application of the law ... The point is that in military activities, the serviceman or woman needs to be predisposed towards acting swiftly and correctly, when correctly may have wide-ranging physical, intellectual and moral ramifications. We have to assume the "strategic corporal" will get it right. (Mileham and Willett 2001: 62)

That corporal's officers (and chaplain) have an enduring responsibility to keep him on the right path, much of which boils down to good leadership and supervision. The roving chaplain, resistant to the 'evil of inaction' (Zimbardo 2007: 317), has a particular role to play in reminding him of his home and humanity. One young corporal in a difficult outstation in Helmand told the author, who had addressed him by his Christian name, that he had almost forgotten how that felt. Much further up the chain there are the judgements of politicians and generals concerning the strategy and resources and troop numbers that affect operating conditions, not least the force density upon which largely depends the soldier's ability to act in a restrained or patient manner (and not simply react to being outgunned). But it is at the soldier's level that the sudden life or death judgement calls are so often made. It is here that the issue arises of the soldier's instincts, and also his readiness to expose his colleagues or himself to the additional risk that was implied by '*courageous* restraint', and is still potentially involved in being patient and precise, particularly after friends have already been killed or injured.

What this boils down to is how best the soldier can be helped to use force judiciously, can be predisposed towards correct action. It is about remaining vigilant for darker institutional currents, but it is also about forming and sustaining the character of the soldier so that his judgement can withstand corrupting situational forces. The challenge, ethically, is to generate morale that is grounded in civilised behaviour.

The linkage between character and morale was made explicit during the First World War, partly under the influence of French texts on the subject. 'What exactly constituted "morale" was complex, but it was generally recognised that the stronger the character of the individual soldier, the stronger and more combat-ready the group he was attached to would be' (Madigan 2011: 109). Vulnerable though such morale was to simple equation with the emotion of combat-willingness, moral references persisted in this concept of 'character':

> discipline, courage, selflessness, and devotion to duty were viewed as the outward expression of "strong" character. Character, moreover, was understood as something that could be developed. It could be strengthened and civilians could be turned into combat troops by cultivating the soldierly spirit through "character-training". (Madigan 2011: 109)

Chaplains were seen as having a religious role to play in such character training. Even their less evidently spiritual work – hosting concert parties, organising sporting events, distributing cigarettes – could be interpreted in terms of building relationships between chaplains and soldiers and thus making the latter more amenable to the Church's influence. In the Second World War, too, chaplains made significant contributions to educating and influencing soldiers. A case in point is one highly successful endeavour fittingly initiated within the 1st Airborne Division, an antecedent to 16 Air Assault Brigade:

> Intended to provide an element of religious instruction (and thereby enhance motivation, discipline and morale) padre's hour took the form of a weekly meeting for informal discussion between chaplains and ordinary soldiers, discussions which took as their subject any one of a host of religious and moral questions … [It] seems to have become a genuinely popular institution … the largest exercise in adult religious education ever undertaken in British or Canadian history. (Snape 2010: 139)

The challenges facing chaplaincy in seeking to retain such roles for the Church in character formation have proved formidable, however, particularly since the 1960s. Secular agencies have gradually assumed responsibility for soldiers' welfare; pacifists in the wider Church have scorned the caricature of the morale-raising padre; faith-free codes of conduct have been devised; the connections between religious allegiance and character have been increasingly repudiated. Padre's Hour eventually became a parody of itself. In common with other Christian representatives in the public square, military chaplains are discovering that a specifically Christian perspective is no longer the common currency.

As MacIntyre observes above, the moral, the theological and the legal have developed into separate domains since the late seventeenth century, and the theological is no longer the master narrative. Quite the reverse. And any tradition that is marginalised by the dominant social, cultural, moral and political order will struggle to convince others of the answers that stem from its justice and its rationality:

> Theories of justice and practical rationality confront us as aspects of traditions, allegiance to which requires the living out of some more or less systematically embodied form of human life, each with its own specific modes of social relationship, each with its own canons of interpretation and explanation in respect of the behaviour of others, each with its own evaluative practices. (MacIntyre 1988: 391)

Thus far the British Army has probably retained more of its Christian tradition than other British public institutions, but what is urgently required of all chaplains is translation of ideas across the emerging cultural boundaries, undergirded by dialogue, aiming at mutual understanding if not acceptance, thereby ensuring that a Christian perspective persists, if only as a second language:

> There is a first and public language of citizenship which we have to learn if we are to live together. And there is a variety of second languages which connect us to our local framework of relationships: to family and group and the traditions that underly them. (Sacks 2005: 64–6)

Problematically, the 'first and public language' must retain sufficient resonance with each secondary language for it to be spoken with conviction and integrity, yet those secondary languages may be increasingly incompatible with each other. Each person may also have more than one 'second' language. (For a soldier, this can set up dissonance between life on leave and life in barracks, or – if he has a Christian faith – between life in barracks and life in church.)

However, this difficulty of conflicting languages is not a new one, for all that modern lifestyle choices, the disintegration of Christendom, and the rise of new media may have exacerbated the situation. Indeed, one of the oldest and lasting clashes of languages and their associated value systems is that between the warrior and the priest. Nietzsche identified Christianity as the force that suppressed the warrior's healthy, aggressive instincts by creating a sickly morality of kindness, humility, obedience, forgiveness, love of the enemy, and justice. It undermined the warrior tradition: 'Christianity aims at mastering *beasts of prey*; its modus operandi is to make them *ill – to* make feeble is the Christian recipe for taming, for "civilizing"' (Nietzsche 2000: 27, Nietzsche's italics).

The occasional task for the military chaplain, on that Conradian 'pilgrimage amongst hints for nightmares' where Nietzsche's disciples are encountered, may not be to find accommodating language to reconcile opposites, but to contend against those darker dynamics to which the world of the soldier, and particularly the combat infantryman, is susceptible. The renewed if tentative engagement with Christianity among soldiers in Helmand is certainly a wholesome corrective to disturbing spiritual tendencies that could otherwise emerge, given the quasi-religious sense of belonging among men at war. 'Accept that since wars are going to be around for a long time, we need to be prepared to wage them, while seeking to do so in a just and proportionate fashion, with officers in firm control of men who might be tempted to stray on to the dark side', argues Burleigh, adding that 'the job I'd like least is probably that of an armed forces chaplain' (2010b: 75). It is a matter of the chaplain knowing when to converse and when to confront.

Complicating that judgement is the role model of the awkward prophet, prompting the view that the Church cannot engage in dialogue with the world but simply has to be a witness to the world – 'our task is not to make these nations the church, but rather to remind them that they are but nations' (Hauerwas 1981: 110). Weber notes two factors behind such a religious perspective: the belief that 'the political apparatus of force could not possibly provide a place for purely religious virtues' (1978: 593); and the belief that martyrdom – the suffering of force rather than the exercising of it – is the true demonstration of religious commitment:

> it is very striking that under the glorious regime of the Maccabees, after the first intoxication of the war of liberation had been dissipated, there arose among most pious Jews a party which preferred alien hegemony to rule by the national kingdom. This may be compared to the preference found among some Puritan denominations for the subjection of the churches to the dominion of unbelievers, because genuineness of religion can be regarded as proven only in such churches. (Weber 1978: 593)

This certainly strikes at the root of most forms of chaplaincy, particularly its military expression. However, not only does it disregard the need to remain a contender within the public arena, it also abandons an enduring task of pastoral theology: to determine 'what it means to have responsibility to the city' (Sedgwick 2000: 171). This wider moral context requires a response beyond that of ministry to the individual or the chosen group.

Neither should the city walls be a limit. Perceiving a bleak modern situation, MacIntyre urges 'the construction of local forms of community within which civility ... can be sustained' (1985: 263); but such a retreat to the ghetto risks neglecting both the city and the society beyond it. MacIntyre himself later observes that whenever 'in the ancient world justice was extended beyond the boundaries of the *polis*, it was always as a requirement of theology' (1988: 146):

> Christian theology cannot renounce the secular world on two counts. First …
> its teachings on creation and incarnation stand opposed to such Manicheanism.
> Secondly … Christians are part of the secular world, they work in it, with it,
> and buy the goods … The retreats to fundamentalism and neo-conservatism do
> not redeem the secular. They do not therefore bring healing, salvation, and the
> conviction of what is sinful and what is good. They just leave the secular to rot.
> (Ward 2000: 69)

Given that soldiers' own responsibility extends to killing or dying for the
city – and in humanitarian or counter-insurgency campaigns, for those beyond
its walls – the task of pastoral theology is never more acute than when addressing
their situation. And in modern British history their situation has rarely been as
acute as it has been in Helmand, where the moral terrain has been at least as
challenging as the physical (if not actually compounded by the latter). The author
repeatedly observed soldiers in high temperatures and burdened with kit, patiently
encouraging local nationals to support the people and processes of civil society,
safeguarding civilians who would otherwise be caught up in any return of fire, and
keeping that return of fire precise and proportionate. It may be useful, in closing, to
outline some measures that were intended to keep chaplaincy engaged with such
soldiers' needs and experiences.

In April 2010, as part of the preparation for 16 Air Assault Brigade's
deployment to Afghanistan, Brigadier James Chiswell MC convened a conference
of all commanding officers and chaplains at Amport House (the Armed Forces
Chaplaincy Centre), which helped shape a set of 'Standard Operating Instructions'
for chaplaincy during Operation HERRICK 13 (Totten 2010). The specific aim of
the conference was to examine what sustains and guides commanders and those
in their care (with particular reference to religious observance on operations),
incidentally exploring the relationship between commanding officer and chaplain.
Speakers addressed the history of military morality and the implications of values-
based leadership. The Chaplain General took questions on whether religious
observance on operations amounted to compulsory worship or necessary ritual.
Two decorated commanding officers from recent HERRICK tours spoke of their
expectations and experiences of chaplaincy. The former Archbishop of Armagh,
Lord Eames OM, was due to talk on Christian leadership until air travel was
disrupted by a volcanic eruption, but he subsequently visited the Brigade in
Helmand itself and preached at its homecoming service.

While recognising that contemporary conflicts – wars among the people – do
not necessarily have a space or time of 'pure' battle that can be clearly demarcated
as in Deuteronomy, the importance of services to mark each individual regiment's
deployment and homecoming was widely accepted at the conference. Borrowing
the collect of the twenty-first Sunday after Trinity from the Book of Common
Prayer for the soldiers to say in unison at the outset, those liturgies would fuse
penitence with the concept of morale outlined earlier:

Grant, we beseech thee, merciful Lord, to thy faithful people pardon and peace,
that they may be cleansed from all their sins, and *serve thee with a quiet mind*,
through Jesus Christ our Lord. Amen.

A collect written specifically for 16 Air Assault Brigade was also approved at
Amport, and subsequently issued to all soldiers on a small plastic card that many
carried throughout their time in Helmand. Its crafting, both in terms of theology
and also its use of pentameter as a martial and memorable rhythm, attracted interest
from chaplains and commanding officers alike. The collect, while recalling the
four cardinal virtues of wisdom, justice, temperance and courage, was also worded
to evoke the theological virtues of faith, hope and love underpinning St Paul's
'most excellent way' of 1 Corinthians 13:

O Lord, the author and lover of peace,
from whom all wisdom and justice proceed:
we humbly beseech thee to remember
members of 16 Air Assault Brigade.
Keep us bold in deed and true in spirit;
lift us with courage on wings like eagles;
and show us now the most excellent way;
through him who loved us, Jesus Christ our Lord.
Amen.

Separately, the chaplain to 2 PARA conducted a commanders' pre-deployment
study week on moral issues, and the chaplain to 3 PARA contributed to the moral
section of the unit's operational aide-memoire. In Afghanistan itself, the chaplain
to the Army Air Corps sat in with attack helicopter pilots as they viewed and
discussed recordings of their missions; the chaplain to the Irish Guards perpetuated
the battalion's tradition (whether in barracks or on operations) of holding a
church service for all ranks every Tuesday morning; the chaplain to the Counter
Improvised Explosive Device Task Force, at the request of his soldiers, gave them
a collect of their own to recite at repatriation ceremonies; and all chaplains kept
to a pattern of Sunday services at the larger bases and occasional field services in
the outstations.

Of great assistance in this effort to maintain a public (or at least a military)
culture with a religious dimension – one, moreover, that can influence the
character of soldiers – is that people (and soldiers more than most) 'have not
stopped identifying themselves as religious individuals, and have not yet stopped
thinking in religious ways ... The biblical tradition survives in our culture —
marginal, endangered, a survival to be sure, but still there' (Sacks 2005: 34). This
is particularly evident among the many Commonwealth soldiers who currently
serve in the British Army. It also underlies the Irish ethos of two battalions that
served on HERRICK 13. Encouragingly, too, junior ranks across the board seem
to remain open to moral and religious debate:

They can take round-table discussions on matters of military morality with enthusiasm ... even if they continue to look for leadership and example from their seniors. They can grasp right and wrong and all the shades in between. They can understand moral imperative, duties and obligations as well as moral restraint and scrutiny. Their moral imagination, judgement and integrity can be developed fully, so that the morale of their unit can be promoted and maintained to a high level, while they remain alert to moral as well as physical danger. (Mileham and Willett 2001: 69)

The difficulties of maintaining the Church's voice in the military are considerable and likely to increase, but something in the very nature of military service may be helping to keep the channel open:

wherever the light of religion has not died out from armies, men seem to hunger for its consolations on the eve of action ... it does seem that something – a pause, a moment of reflection, a summoning of force, a dedicatory act, a prayer of intercession – must be added to the purely material and administrative dispositions made by an army if its men are to commit themselves to battle with the stoutest hearts they can find. (Keegan 1991: 327)

If the contention of this chapter is broadly correct, then it is not just a matter of stout hearts, but quiet minds too; and by taking soldiers' present and future quietness of mind as the touchstone of morale, chaplains have a special role in preventing men straying. They have a responsibility too to publicly commend conduct that is commensurate with the Christian just war tradition. Thus, although debate will continue to rage over whether the original political commitment of troops to Afghanistan had a reasonable chance of success or the right intent, and while acknowledging soldiers' own acute sense of moral ambiguity, it seems fitting to finish with a commendation of the actual conduct of 16 Air Assault Brigade on Operation HERRICK 13, not only in terms of protection of the innocent and use of proportional force as a last resort, but also determination to restore a just and peaceful society.

Conclusion

Christian pacifist criticism will probably always deny theological integrity to military chaplaincy on the basis of its own readings of scripture and Christian tradition. The unpacking of the concept of morale, however, suggests that at least within a just war context – itself the outcome of Christian reflection on scripture and tradition – chaplaincy does have an historical and philosophical integrity. Chaplains need not fight shy of morale, though they face a battle reclaiming it from psychological territory. Equally, they must resist the tendency to retreat to the 'purely' pastoral: in the field of military chaplaincy in particular, the pastoral is never independent of the moral or the political, and the moral is at least as much about organisations and systems as it is about individuals. Remaining alive to those contexts is essential for chaplains as they seek to exercise influence and nurture morale with integrity.

As for the extent of that influence: since the Wars of Religion, religious positions have had to reckon with the rise of legal theory and secular forms of justice, and there will always be the need to confront the darker aspects of human nature and institutions that have withstood the Enlightenment; but the defining tone does not have to be antagonistic. The challenge for the Church is to contest each domain when necessary, but where possible to promote 'its particular vision of the common good through influence, conversation, shared resources and the making of common cause' and on the basis of 'a differentiated model for the church's social contribution which leads to neither domination, nor cultural captivity, nor isolation' (Fergusson 2004: 164). The challenge for today's chaplains, in turn, is to ensure that Christian chaplaincy remains a contender; to ensure that a Christian 'second language' and presence stay sufficiently influential to impact on the form of human life that is British soldiering.

Chapter 3
'You've Been Silent, Padre'

Philip McCormack

Background

The background to the central premise of this chapter is located in the impression left upon the writer following a targeting planning meeting prior to 19 Light Brigade's deployment on Operation HERRICK 10 (March–October 2009). As part of the Brigade's pre-deployment training, this planning meeting was designed to practise the structural aspects of the procedures that would be used when developing 'targeting packs' once in theatre. The British Army has an extremely detailed set of procedures and guidelines which have been developed in accordance with the UK's adherence to, and enactment of, the Law of Armed Conflict. The MoD's (Army) explanation of the Law of Armed Conflict, along with the rules of engagement specific to a particular campaign, is intended to 'actually prescribe and take account of most of the possible moral breaches during operations'.[1]

The planning meetings were detailed and lengthy. Those required to attend were all directly involved in the deliberate artillery and air strikes planning and decision-making process once in Helmand. The Brigade's Chief of Staff (COS),[2] SO1 Joint Fires[3] (along with his immediate staff) and the Brigade's Chief Legal Officer[4] formed the central core of this grouping. The Brigade chaplain's request to attend one of the meetings was welcomed but he did not, nor was he expected to, form part of this planning or decision-making process. At the end of this particular exercise the COS commented, 'You've been silent, Padre. Do you have any comments or observations?'

---

[1] Mileham (2008: 53). Whether this is still a valid conclusion in an asymmetric setting will be discussed later in this chapter.

[2] The Brigade Chief of Staff, among his many roles, is intimately involved in the planning process of every brigade level mission, and many battle-group level processes.

[3] SO1 (Staff Officer or Lt Col, or OF4 rank) was the Commanding Officer of the Artillery Regiment attached to the brigade. His/her designation as 'Joint Fires' reflects that HERRICK is a joint operation comprising of Naval, Army and Air Force elements. His/her role is to co-ordinate planned air and artillery strikes against targets that have been developed in the planning process.

[4] The brigade's legal officer is an experienced lawyer, specialising in the application of the UK's Law of Armed Conflict.

The Brigade chaplain responded that he did but that the group might not appreciate them. Nevertheless, the COS invited the chaplain to share them with the group. The chaplain noted that NATO's mission in Afghanistan, and in particular the UK's involvement in this NATO/American operation, is frequently defended using moral or ethical language. In essence, the public are repeatedly told that the mission has a strong moral or ethical foundation justifying it.[5] Consequently, the actions of NATO/American forces, especially its air and artillery strikes, are undertaken in support of this political imperative that has a strong moral/ethical foundation.

The Joint Fires planning process, though meticulous, is necessarily mechanistic and has the Law of Armed Conflict as its guiding principle. This process can appear akin to a mathematical equation in which if all the parts are applied in the correct sequence and are legally coherent any action taken will not only meet the requirements of the Law of Armed Conflict but will therefore be ethical/moral because the overall mission has an ethical/moral foundation. The chaplain suggested that there were several potential problems with this reasoning.

Firstly, although something may be legal, it does not necessarily make it ethical or moral. For example, a person walking down a street who sees a child being attacked by an adult, in the UK, is under no legal requirement to become involved. Depending on the cultural expectation of such a society, the adult might well be expected, morally, to contact the police as a bare minimum. Secondly, the essential use of law, in terms of what the law is, is essential to this discussion. Those who maintain a 'positivist' use of the law see no ethical value in the law. In other words the law is not interested in whether something is ethical or not but rather whether or not an action is lawful. The chaplain suggested that what often resonates with the general public is the moral impact of an attack or incident and not the finely balanced niceties of legal judgements.

The Brigade chaplain suggested that there was a profound disconnect between the structural or methodological approach employed and the desired outcome, which was frequently defined as ethical, equally as much as legal. The chaplain noted that, although the legal framework had been established, an ethical one had not. This had the consequence of sidelining the ethical component of the campaign structurally from the formal decision-making process. The chaplain reminded the group that although something may be legal, it does not necessarily make it ethical or moral. The silence of the chaplain throughout the planning meeting, at least to some extent, reflected the structural absence of a moral/ethical framework for use in seeking to achieve an outcome frequently defended using moral/ethical language. To his credit the COS agreed with the argument but simply commented that they were obligated to use the solely legal mechanism.

It is important to state that the Brigade chaplain witnessed the meticulous care and detailed planning and discussions that took place throughout what was

---

[5]　This position is debated in the countries of those nations supplying troops to this mission.

a difficult and costly tour. This writer knows of no instances when the Chain of Command did not seek to apply the structural mechanism required of it. This chapter implies no criticism of UK forces. The greatest possible care is taken over the use of lethal force. Rather this chapter seeks to state the claim of military ethics independent of military law and to ask the national churches of the United Kingdom why they have been silent in this matter? The silence of the Brigade chaplain, this chapter will maintain, reflects the complete, formal disengagement of the national churches of the United Kingdom from this vital area of the United Kingdom's international interests and obligations, with the consequence that a purely and largely 'secular' mechanism is the only option available to the United Kingdom's Armed Forces. That this has been allowed to happen whenever the moral rectitude of the United Kingdom is questioned through its involvement in the conflicts in Iraq and Afghanistan is nothing less than astonishing. This chapter will seek to highlight not only some of the issues involved but also suggest a potential way forward.

The first section will briefly consider the Western philosophy of war as a means of offering a basic historical context for the Western approach to war. This is essential as this particular cultural context, I will argue, also provides the foundation for the current international system of states and international law. The entire international system is founded upon a Clausewitzian and Cartesian worldview. The phenomenon of what are known as 'new wars' has created a paradigm shift in the nature of war. This shift is not only diametrically opposed to the established international system and the norms that exist between states, the morality of these new wars may well also operate outside the Churches' traditional moral understanding of war. This new reality is one that may present a formidable challenge to the traditional concept of the status of non-combatants. The phenomenon of these new wars, and of asymmetric warfare, has created the conditions in which the language of exceptionalism and of military necessity have become all too familiar phrases. Faced by non-state players who either reject or ignore international law and international norms, state players have sought to justify their actions on the grounds that a particular response was an exception to the norm or a military necessity forced upon them by the actions of X. The final section will look at how the Church of Scotland responded to the ongoing war in Afghanistan.

A Western Philosophy of War

The origin of the Western way of warfare,[6] according to the military historian John Keegan, is to be found in classical Greece (1993: 388). Keegan maintains that:

---

[6]   The intention is only to give a brief introduction to this concept rather than a detailed treatment of it.

It was they who in the fifth century BC, cut loose from the constraints of the primitive style, with its respect above all for ritual in war, and adopted the practice of the face-to-face battle to the death. This departure, confined initially to warfare among the Greeks themselves, was deeply shocking to those outside the Greek world who were first exposed to it. (1993: 389)

The Persians in contrast, according to Keegan, were unprepared for enemies that could not be bought or talked off but rather sought direct engagement.

What made the Greek expression of face-to-face battle so unique in the ancient world was the close-knit and tightly drilled phalanx of hoplite warfare, comprised largely of citizens of the city-state. The Homeric depiction of Achilles, the archetypal warrior, had inspired generations of Greeks.[7] However, as the centuries passed and Greek warfare evolved, what was required by the 'state'[8] also evolved. Achilles was a one-man killing machine; effective, brutal and obsessed with personal glory.[9] Whereas in hoplite warfare, what was required was conformity and unity of purpose; as evidenced in the tightly knit formations of the Greek phalanx where individual identity was subsumed into the identity of the whole.[10]

Coker maintains that the Greek way of warfare was important because it was absorbed and developed by the Romans (2002: 38). What, he argues, 'made the Roman experience decisive was that they introduced system into Greek warfare – they systematized it' (2002: 38). 'Nothing', he contends, 'matched the bureaucratic ethos of the Roman legion' (2002: 39). The supremely well-drilled legionnaire, professional officer corps, systematic and ruthless application of force made the Roman war machine without match in the ancient world.[11] Like any military force in history, it suffered defeats in battle, for example, the series of losses against Hannibal, the famous Carthaginian general. However, unlike Hannibal's force which was largely drawn from groups of mercenaries, the Roman legions of the Republic were mainly drawn from its citizenry.

Rome therefore had the capacity to field armies continually, even after it had lost a battle. Even the hugely talented and imaginative general Hannibal was ultimately defeated by the systematic nature of the Roman machine. The Greek historian Polybius was convinced that the defining difference between the two

---

[7]   The myth of Archilles is still very much alive even in this modern age; as evidenced in the Hollywood blockbuster *Troy*, with Brad Pitt in the role of the ancient warrior.

[8]   In this case 'city-state'.

[9]   See the *Iliad*, 18.121 where Achilles says, 'But now, may I win heroic glory!'.

[10]   See Hanson (2005a), which gives an excellent and detailed account of hoplite warfare during the Peloponnesian War.

[11]   The Romans did more than copy Grecian warfare; they developed it, incorporating cavalry and ballistic weaponry into their tactics. What distinguishes Roman warfare most from Greek warfare was the Roman ability to adapt in battle to the fluidity of actual combat. The Greek phalanx was large and difficult to defeat in confined spaces. However, it suffered from inflexibility to adapt in battle and had little defence against cavalry in open terrain.

great ancient empires was that Rome could rely upon the bravery of its own citizens whereas the Carthaginians relied upon the courage of professional mercenaries. Hanson makes this telling observation:

> in the near constant fighting of the first-century BC, whether Roman soldiers battled against trained gladiators, rebel legionaries, seaborne mercenaries, eastern phalangites, or Northern tribal irregulars, the result was almost always the same: eventual battlefield victory, slaughter of enemy combatants, absolute elimination of gifted adversaries. (2005b: 53)

The rediscovery of classical learning in Renaissance Europe ushered in what Coker refers to as a dialogue with the past (2002: 58). Niccoló Machiavelli wrote a seven-volume work called *Art of War* (1519–20) in which he forcefully contended for the need for a well-trained citizen army. He was critical of what he considered the over-dependency of many European city-states that relied upon hired professional mercenaries. During this period of medieval history this dependence upon and use of mercenaries had been a central feature of much of European warfare. The great Prussian military theorist Carl von Clausewitz 'found Machiavelli to be a very sound judge of military matters, with some new insights'.[12] One of the great works of this period that indicates a dynamic dialogue with the past was Thomas Hobbes' translation of the classic work of Thucydides, *History of the Peloponnesian War*. It was and continues to remain influential.[13] Likewise, the compendium of Flavius Renatus Vegetius, *Concerning Military Matters*, produced around AD 390, was also translated widely and even used by George Washington (Parker 2005: 4). However, the fascination with classical antiquity in the later Enlightenment period did not end with interest in military theory; it permeated British art and culture during the nineteenth century.

Throughout the mid-to-late Victorian period classical and medieval myths were re-created and adapted for new generations, of all ages; chivalric myths and Arthurian legends were common themes in paintings, poetry, music, literature and even architecture (MacKenzie 1992: 111). Underneath this intense interest lurked fears of physical degeneracy in the British male, heightened after humiliating defeats during the Boer War at Stormberg, Magersfontein and Colenso.[14] Throughout the 1880s there had been growing speculation concerning the physical degeneracy of the British urban male (Pugh 1999: 114). Underneath many of these fears was the closely related idea that physical deterioration was inextricably linked with decadence and decadence to moral decline (Paris 2000: 85).

Victorian Britain had delved deeply into the classics to find examples that inspired a culture obsessed with what were considered manly noble virtues. In

---

[12]   'Letter to Fichte (1809)' in Paret and Moran (1992: 281).

[13]   Howard (1983: 16), referring to the reasons for the war between Athens and Sparta, maintains that, 'you can vary the names of the actors, but the model remains the same'.

[14]   This became known as the 'Black Week' of 10–15 December 1899.

a similar fashion, many Victorians looked to antiquity for parallels with their present situation. Yes, England had been like Athens in her glory, but now she was in danger of resembling Athens in its days of decay (Jenkyns 1980: 293). Although Britain emerged victorious from the Boer War, nevertheless, the war in Africa was readily identified with Athenian defeat at Syracuse (Jenkyns 1980: 336). Similarities were also made between the decay of the Roman Empire and the danger of decadence and decay within Britain and her empire. Jenkyns contends that, 'The Romans of the first century had differed from the British in being wholly unaware that their empire would ever come to an end' (1980: 335). The glory of ancient Athens, Sparta, Macedon and Rome had faded into history. The story of the West during the Renaissance and Enlightenment is, quite simply, a living dialogue with classical antiquity, one that Britain had enthusiastically engaged in.

Clausewitz: The Philosophical Premise of Modern Western War

The philosophical premise underpinning the modern Western way of war is located mainly in Carl von Clausewitz's *magnum opus*, *Vom Kriege*, or *On War* (1993). Although originally published in 1832 this work continues to be considered the equivalent of 'a Copernican shift' in military thinking. It is simply not possible to understand the modern Western philosophy of war without a basic grasp of Clausewitzian theory.

It is possible to detect something of Clausewitz's mature philosophical reflection on his understanding of the nature of war in this confident assertion:

> I shall not begin by expounding a pedantic, literary definition of war, but go straight to the heart of the matter, to the duel. War is nothing but a duel on a larger scale. Countless duels go to make up war, but a picture of it as a whole can be formed by imagining a pair of wrestlers. Each tried through physical force to compel the other to do his will; his *immediate* aim is to *throw* his opponent in order to make him incapable of further resistance. *War is thus an act of force to compel our enemy to do our will.*[15]

Clausewitz's philosophical world was very much Kantian, in that he believed or accepted that an archetypal form of war existed (Leonard 1967: 6–7). In other words, he would have sought to identify what it was about war that conformed to the basic Kantian notion of the 'thing-in-itself' (*Ding-an-sich*). Throughout *On War* Clausewitz maintained the proposition that not only did war have an objective

---

[15] (1993: 85, emphasis original). This quote comes from chapter 1 of *On War*, the only chapter Clausewitz satisfactorily completed of his final revision before his death. In that regard it represents his later, and arguably, more refined thoughts on a philosophy that he had been honing for a number of years.

nature (stated above), it also had a subjective nature.[16] The notion that things had an objective and subjective nature was an accepted part of German philosophical thought at this time. Modern Clausewitzians continue to argue that the objective nature of war is, and will always remain, unchanging (Gray 2005: 31). Whether this is true for those who hold to a post-modern world construct is highly doubtful.

For Clausewitz, politics gave war its purpose, shaped its goals and set its desired outcomes. He explained that:

> We deliberately use the phrase 'with the addition of other means' because we also want to make clear that war in itself does not suspend political intercourse or change it into something entirely different … The main lines along which military events progress, and to which they are restricted, are political lines that continue throughout the war into subsequent peace … War cannot be divorced from political life; and whenever this occurs in our thinking about war, the many links that connect the two elements are destroyed and we are left with something pointless and devoid of sense. (1993: 605)

Clausewitz uses the political component of war to give the expression of real/limited war its sense of purpose and meaning:[17] 'war is only a branch of political activity; that it is in no sense autonomous' (see 1993: 731–7).

One of Clausewitz's most effective military metaphors is his notion of the 'remarkable trinity' which serves as an indispensable, integral part of his philosophy of war.[18] It succinctly encapsulates his understanding of the necessary political interaction between a government, the people and the army:

> War is more than a true chameleon that slightly adapts its characteristics to the given case. As a total phenomenon its dominant tendencies always make war a paradoxical trinity – composed of primordial violence, hatred, and enmity, which are to be regarded as a blind natural force; of the play of chance and probability within which the creative spirit is free to roam; and of its element of subordination, as an instrument of policy, which makes it subject to reason alone.
>
> The first of these three aspects mainly concerns the people; the second the commander and his army; the third the government. The passions that are to be kindled in war must already be inherent in the people; the scope which the play of courage and talent will enjoy in the realm of probability and chance depends on the particular character of the commander and the army; but the political aims are the business of the government alone.

---

[16]   See (1993) Book 1, chapter 1.20 and 21 for Clausewitz's use of these terms.

[17]   Howard (2002: 52) observes that 'policy was the guiding intelligence, war only the instrument'.

[18]   Howard (Clausewitz 1993) translates this as 'paradoxical trinity'.

> Our task therefore is to develop a theory that maintains a balance between these
> three tendencies, like an object suspended between three magnets. (1993: 101)

The simple and yet striking analogy of war being 'like an object suspended between three magnets' goes some way to encapsulate the essence of his philosophy. The Clausewitzian trinity of war (the people, the army and the government) continues to lie at the very foundation of an essentially Enlightenment and Western understanding of what war is.

International Law and War

Clausewitz briefly, and rather dismissively, mentions what he refers to as, 'certain self-imposed, imperceptible limitations hardly worth mentioning, known as international law and custom, but they scarcely weaken it' (1993: 83). The irony is that the international system is underpinned by the essential philosophical creation articulated by Clausewitz (Brown 1997: 113). According to Brown, 'war is a normal feature of international relations, a normal part of the functioning of the international system' (Brown 1997: 113). Gray describes this as the realist paradigm, which he contends shows no convincing evidence that it is undergoing some transformation (2002: 227). Brown is not convinced. For him, there is a growing suspicion about what he calls 'state-centricity'. The political conception of war is an example 'of international relations not behaving quite in the way it is supposed to. In reality, the malaise here goes much deeper. A Clausewitzian view of war is an essential requirement for the balance of power to operate; the two institutions stand together, and if, as suggested here, they fall together the whole state-centric edifice is in ruins' (Brown 1997: 122). Clausewitz never envisaged the evolution of a body of law that would describe and regularise relations between states. For him, war was a violent clash of wills, bloody and terrible. The single reference to international law in *On War* is in itself testimony to his disregard for this emerging idea.[19] However, what is self-evident is a clear and undeniable link between a Clausewitzian construct of the state, war, international relations and international law.

Clausewitz's dictum that war is the continuation of state politics contains within it the logical consequence that war was essentially a 'phenomenon' that occurs only between states.[20] This logically expresses two related and important

---

[19]   See M. van Creveld (1991: 66) for a consideration of the rules of war regarding prisoners as the applied to him personally and how these changed radically within a generation.

[20]   In *On War* Clausewitz is very aware of the role of irregular troops and Revolutionary War. However, one should be cautious in reading back into earlier nineteenth-century warfare, an early twentieth-century meaning of these concepts. Clausewitz emphasised that war was essentially about the decisive clash and the annihilation of the enemy's military

derivatives: firstly, that in order for this to occur, the state must have a monopoly, or sole ownership, of violence and, secondly, that the establishment of a condition of peace can be formally guaranteed on the basis of that monopoly of violence.

Stumpf argues that the emergence of the territorial state in Europe, in conjunction with a secularisation within the legal tradition, saw a growing public debate on the role of international law and how relations between states could be subjected to more formal structures (Stumpf 2006: 2–6). Previously, maintains Stumpf, there had been an understanding of law as 'a metaphysical system, supplemented by a Christological concept of legislation' (2006: 2). Best adopts a similar explanation, contending that international law 'comes to us soaked in several sorts of reason: the reason of the classical-cum-Christian natural law which originally gave life to the *jus gentium*, the reason of the Enlightenment which made international law a necessary element of civilised international relations' (Best 1994: 275).

There are several critical observations that may be deduced from this historical construct: firstly, a state-centric understanding of international relations is essentially a Western (Cartesian) paradigm; secondly, that peace is the antithetical state to war; thirdly, the international legal system is both Western in origin and grew out of the theological and philosophical foundations of the Judaic-Christian traditions. The relevance of these points requires some elaboration.

The Manual of the Law of Armed Conflict, UK Ministry of Defence is an example of how the statutes of international law may be distilled into practical directives and guidance for the UK Armed Forces. It shares a common trait with other books, like *Law on the Battlefield*, in that the historical, theological and or moral foundations that underpin international law are simply ignored (Rogers 2004). In the preface to the second edition, and in response to a particular critique of his first edition, Rogers makes no apology for his English legal background, or the impact of Western ideology. In his consideration of 'General Principles' he notes that, 'the writers of the Enlightenment, notably Grotius and Vattel, were especially influential. It has been suggested that more humane rules were able to flourish in the period of limited wars from 1648 to 1792 but that they then came under pressure in the drift towards continental warfare, the concept of the increasing destructiveness of weapons from 1792 to 1914' (2004: 1). Divorcing the motives of Grotius from his foundational moral and theological principles is striking. This approach to law is known as a form of 'legal positivism'.[21]

Legal positivism maintains that the conditions of legal validity are purely a matter of social facts. In other words, from a legal positivist perspective, the law isn't interested in right or wrong (or how that might be judged) but on whether an

---

force: 'The destruction of the enemy's military force, is the leading principle of war, and for the whole chapter of positive action the direct way to the aim. 2. This destruction of the enemy's force, must be principally effected by means of battle' (*On War*, chapter XI, 'The Use of the Battle'). Modern insurgents usually avoid major clashes against a superior force unless the clash serves an additional purpose (as propaganda, etc.).

21   See Kramer (2004: 143–71) for a defence of this approach.

act/action was legal. It is only interested in the law and its application. Morality, right or wrong is irrelevant in this particular instance. This is, arguably, the dominant position within international law. In contrast Natural Law claims that legal validity is not exhausted by social facts; theologians and ethicists would contend that Augustine's *lex iniusta non est lex*, 'unjust law is not law', raises the question of whether or not law should ever seek to divorce itself from moral considerations or foundations.

This creates an interesting dynamic especially in regard to how international law is considered. International law, as a concept, generally only exists between states. The individual citizen has no role in its classical expression; Stumpf describes this as its blindness to individuals (2006: 3). Yet despite this it has been used with a distinct moral element. Referring to the trials at Nuremburg and Tokyo as 'victor's justice', Falk notes that 'dramatizing the criminal accountability of individuals who were acting on behalf of the state did permanently escalate the claims of law in relation to armed conflict' (Falk 2005: 242). If war is only (ontologically[22]) the extension of politics, and it is a clash of political interest and will, charging individuals with the 'crimes' of a state's policy required a selective understanding of what the law is. This sense of arbitrariness concerning how states use or abuse, apply or ignore international law has been a consistent feature of modern life; a situation complicated by what some scholars have identified as 'new wars'.

New Wars

Kaldor (1999) and Münkler (2005) have argued cogently that 'new wars' have changed the parameters of war; a new reality that offers a direct challenge to the hitherto and accepted norms of international law. In these 'new wars' some of the incredibly brutal, organised violence does not appear to have any easily identifiable government structure responsible either for the violence or opposition to it. In this it is questionable whether or not these 'new wars' meet the Clausewitzian criteria of the nature of war. Both Kaldor and Münkler cite the statistic that in the early part of the twentieth century, roughly 90 per cent of those killed or wounded have been described as combatants under international law, whereas in these 'new wars' there has been a radical turnaround in the statistics. Some 80 per cent of the killed and wounded in these new wars are now civilians and only 20 per cent were, or could be considered, 'combatants' (Münkler 2005: 14; Kaldor 1999: 8, 100).

This new type of warfare, according to Kaldor, has to be understood in terms of 'global dislocation' (1999: 70). When she uses the term globalisation, she means, global interconnectedness (political, economic, military and cultural); a concept that is central to her argument (1999: 3).[23] These new, globalised wars are

---

22　　In other words, in its essence or nature.

23　　Within this process she contends that there are many who see themselves as part of a global community of like-minded people and are as yet not politicised (1999: 76).

set against the backdrop of failed or failing states, hence the dislocation. Kaldor states that 'the main implication of globalisation is that territorial sovereignty is no longer available' (1999: 86). This context is perfect for what she calls 'identity politics' (1999: 76–86).[24] In this instance, identity tends to be associated with the politics of ideas, such as religion, or a label that someone is born with and cannot change, such as an ethnic identifier (Kaldor 1999: 77). In these 'new wars', she argues, 'battles are rare, most violence is directed against civilians, and cooperation between warring factions is common' (1999: 90). The failure of the 'state' in these cases is usually accompanied by a growing privatisation of violence (1999: 92).[25] Local warlords take the place of recognised state structures, although their goal is largely financial and for the establishment of prestige.[26] 'The point', she observes in relation to these wars, is that 'the modern distinctions between the political and the economic, the public and the private, the military and the civil are breaking down' (1999: 106). Her prognosis is gloomy, 'the new type of warfare is a predatory social condition' (1999: 107).

Münkler has demonstrated, however, that the 'new wars' are not only relatively inexpensive to maintain, due to the abundant supply of lightweight automatic weapons readily available in a global market, but these wars are themselves downright cheap to prepare and wage (2005: 75). Like Kaldor he contends that these 'wars are not waged against a similarly armed enemy but mainly employ long-term violence against large parts of the civilian population' (2005: 75).[27] For Münkler the most important reason why these new wars are so cheap, and therefore easy to start, 'is that they are funded through asymmetrical relations of exchange imposed upon society' (2005: 77). What he means by this is that force becomes the dominant element in exchange, manifested in the threat of violence or in extortion. This attracts young men to a local warlord, or militia leader, 'in return for a kind of livelihood and the prospect of an otherwise unattainable reputation' (2005: 77).[28]

---

[24]   See also Gilbert (2003: 10), who also claims that new wars are manifestations of the politics of identity.

[25]   Kaldor identifies five types of groups found in these wars.

[26]   See (1999: ch. 3) for her case study of Bosnia-Herzegovina for examples.

[27]   Münkler specifically identifies the importance of sexual violence in both the strategy and economics of these new wars. Rape has been part of war in every age. However, the emergence of customs and then much later laws that provided protection for non-combatants (codified in the Geneva Convention relative to the Protection of Civilian Persons in Time of War) reduced this heinous practice in conflict. In these new wars, Münkler argues that rape is seen by some belligerents as a form for ethnic cleansing. Women, 'are no longer just booty, trophies or sex objects; the have become the conqueror's main target of attack' (2005: 82). See also Zimbardo (2007), particularly his 'Crimes Against Humanity: Genocide, Rape and Terror' pp. 12ff. The illustrations are too graphic for this writer to reproduce.

[28]   See also Ignatieff (1998: 57).

The issue at stake here, between whether Clausewitz established the eternal truth about war and those who maintain that the modern manifestation of 'new wars' is a new phenomenon, is not some kind of philosophical game constructed for an abstract proposition that has little practical worth in the 'real world'.[29] The current 'war on terror' or the insurgencies in Afghanistan or Iraq specifically revolve around competing worldviews that are diametrically opposed to one another. The idea that Clausewitz identified 179 years ago that the universal realities of war are universally applicable in any cultural setting or period of history is intellectually impossible to maintain in a post-modern world where there are no absolutes. Even Kant's categorical imperative is no longer considered universally true in every setting.[30]

The premise that the nature of war is political is not logically self-evident. It is like the preposition that states, 'I have only seen white swans, and therefore all swans are white'. This is a false preposition, in that it is not necessarily so (as the existence of black swans revealed). The relevance of this is far-reaching. Why can't the nature of war be primarily economic or religious? What is it about the 'thingness' of war which makes it political with no possibility of it being anything other? Keegan makes a similar criticism of Clausewitzian doctrine by emphasising the cultural situatedness of this particular philosophy:

> His [Clausewitz's] decision to ignore Ottoman military institutions flawed the integrity of his theory at its roots. To look beyond military slavery into the even stranger military cultures of the Polynesians, the Zulus and the Samurai, whose forms of warfare defied altogether the rationality of politics as it is understood by Westerners, is to perceive how incomplete, parochial and ultimately misleading is the idea that war is the continuation of politics. (1993: 24)

Keegan states that the belief in the primacy of politics rather than culture was not specifically personal to Clausewitz but was rather the position of Western philosophers (1993: 46); he maintains that the very belief that universal truth could be discovered was itself essentially a product of Western culture at that time. Keegan's main point is simple: the identification of politics as the essence of war is a cultural phenomenon, sited within the specific philosophical milieu of Enlightenment thinking. I would go further and contend that it is a predominately Western cultural phenomenon. While some non-Western cultures (China, India and Brazil, etc.) may have embraced it, at least to some extent, this particular cultural phenomenon continues to dominate world politics still and is embedded at the heart of international law. The problem lies, however, in the phenomenon of

---

[29]   It goes almost without saying, 'whose real world', etc. By using the term real world I am referring to the world that the average individual encounters in their daily encounter within the space outside their home.

[30]   However useful some may still find its application today.

the 'new wars', asymmetric warfare and the direct challenge that this brings to this inherited Western cultural construct.

Exceptionalism, Military Necessity and Asymmetric War

In his book detailing the genocide in Rwanda, Lebor describes in great detail how the major world powers did little to stop the fighting. Despite the moral questions raised by this failure to act, few if any international laws were broken by the major world powers (2006: 165ff.). The perception of indifference or selective adherence to international law is perhaps more graphically illustrated in regard to terrorism. Western states, according to Booth and Dunne, have consistently 'sought to deny that states can commit terrorism. The basis of terror has always been "against people and in favour of governments"' (2002: 8). States wage war: terrorists are criminals who break the law. Acts of terror perpetrated against civilians eventually prompt calls for military intervention (Gross 2010: 233). This raises the question: how will those states act? Gross is blunt:

> The baffling question is why the United States and some of its allies blatantly employ unlawful means of warfare as they wage asymmetric war against national insurgencies, international terror, rogue countries and state-sponsored guerrilla organisations. Sixty years after World War II and the great humanitarian tide of concern for basic human rights, many nations find themselves resorting to low-tech, primitive, and generally prohibited forms of warfare. Why have liberal democracies now abandoned some of the core principles of humanitarian law as they fight asymmetric wars? (2010: 2)

Gross contends that the answer lies in what he terms 'Exceptionalism' (2010: 234): 'Emergencies do not overturn or repudiate the laws of war, they simply allow for exceptions' (2010: 234).

Falk describes it in this manner, 'it is ... this context that ... leads government lawyers to grant politicians and military commanders "freedom" from the constraints of the Geneva Conventions, derided as "quaint" embodying restraints that pertain to a different age' (2005: 243). Gross contends that there is evidence that the exceptions are evolving into rules. Chomsky goes even further and accuses the United States and the United Kingdom of international terrorism in the technical sense (Chomsky 2002: 133). The sense of injustice at what might be thought of as Western double standards pervades his work. An-Na'im holds that the failure of the international community to 'in any way check or regulate the massive and indefinite unilateral response by the United States is a fundamental challenge to international legality' (2002: 162).[31] He accuses both jihadist groups and the

---

[31]   Since this was written the United States has faced greater criticism over its actions, particularly in regard its response to the insurgency following the Second Gulf

United States of exceptionalism (2002: 163). Byers also supports the position that the unilateralism of the United States leads to the making of international law by exception (2002: 124).

The reaction of many people to the guerrilla tactics of asymmetric warfare 'will doubtless be one of moral revulsion and horror' (Rodin 2006: 156). Those scholars who have been critical of the United States' attitude towards international law are conscious of the heinous and barbaric actions of those non-state actors engaged in asymmetric warfare. There is no sense of sympathy with what Booth and Dunne call the fantasies of the terrorists (2002: 4). This, however, is not the issue. Rodin maintains that 'Western forces will be judged by a higher standard to those of other states' (2006: 165). Military necessity has consistently been used by states to defend their prosecution of war (Raymond 2005); except of course where they have been defeated. Raymond observes that typical expressions used in defence of military necessity have the form 'circumstances required that I do X'. For example Tony Blair in his statement to the Iraq Inquiry said:

> It was clear following 1441 that if Saddam did not comply fully and unconditionally, military action was likely ... But for me the issue was straightforward: we had got the US to go down the UN route and give Saddam a final chance; he had not taken it; such co-operation as there was, was under the duress of military action; if we backed away now, it would have disastrous consequences for a tough stance on WMD and its proliferation; and for our strategic relationship with the US, our key ally.[32]

The rhetorical strategy behind this form of argument is 'to frame situations of circumscribed options as situations where no alternatives exist' (Raymond 2005: 4). A major difficulty with this argument is that it is one that is generally used by those engaged in an insurgency or 'new war'.

Exceptionalism and necessity are themes frequently used by jihadists. Although some of their rhetoric finds a sympathetic hearing in parts of the Muslim world (Freedman 2002: 42), it is only among some of the 1.2 billion Muslims that live around the world. The emptiness therefore, of some popularist stereotypes becomes very evident (Booth and Dunne 2002: 4). Nevertheless, the various groups that are engaged in a jihad against the West have a very specific view of international law, and its state-centric basis:

> International law and governance are likewise rejected by jihadis who view the UN as both a wholly owned subsidiary of the United States and Europe, and as

War and the situation surrounding the handling and treatment of detainees at Guantanamo Bay. However, apart from the rhetoric of condemnation, there has been little of the action implied in An-Na'im's article.

[32] See http://www.iraqinquiry.org.uk/media/50743/Blair-statement.pdf [accessed: October 2011].

proponent of a legal system at odds with Islam. The idea of international law is detested for exactly the same reason as democracy: it ignores shari'a and is based upon the non-Islamic notion that nations can "make up" any laws they please. In any case, jihadis believe that Westerners created the current international legal system to protect their own rights and not uphold true (Islamic) justice. One jihadist group traces the origins of international law to the "exclusively Christian" treaty of Westphalia, arguing that from its very inception, "International norms were established by Christian powers seeking to further their hegemony and protect their interests". Meanwhile, jihadis argue that the basic purpose of the UN is either to allow the West to maintain control over the world's wealth and resources, or to grant legitimacy to their intervention in the affairs of weak countries – most especially in the Islamic world. (Habeck 2004: 74)

If one extracts the conspiracy element from these views of the West, there is a great deal about their understanding of the origins of the state-centric system, the legal system and the origins of democracy in the West, which emerged from the Treaty of Westphalia[33] that is fundamentally correct. That the majority of those who live in the West are unaware of the foundational role Christian theology and philosophy played in constructing the framework that evolved into what is today a largely secularised system is irrelevant. Grotius' desire to see international law develop was based upon his Christian theological convictions (Stumpf 2006). Whether they are delusional or simply see the world through a fundamentally different lens, jihadists understand the religious foundations of the Western model of state-centric view and its imposition of politics as the key to conflict resolution as a new expression of imperialism. 'The truth of the matter is that the latter-day imperialism is but a mask for the crusading spirit, since it is not possible for it to appear in its true form, as it was in the Middle Ages' (Qutb, quoted in Habeck 2004: 92).

A New Reality?

A paradigm shift has taken place with regard to conflict and the use of international law as a means of regulating armed hostilities. States no longer have the sole monopoly of violence[34] and consequently in many settings cannot arbitrarily establish a state of peace within the borders of their country. One practical

---

[33]   This is to over-simplify the process that both led to the Peace of Westphalia and its consequences. It is a hugely complex subject and beyond the scope of this chapter. For a full copy of the text of the Treaty of Westphalia see http://avalon.law.yale.edu/17th_century/westphal.asp [accessed: October 2011].

[34]   Whether this has ever been completely true in practice is doubtful. What is not, however, is the historic desire of the nation state to have sole possession of violence, which it could then employ in pursuit of its goals or agendas.

example of this is the recurring theme of a 'peace process', in which continued violence can, and frequently does, smoulder on for many years as non-state players/warlords participate in direct relation to their perception of success from the 'peace process'. New wars, and I include asymmetric warfare in this category, either ignore international law or deliberately use it as a weapon against major state players who become involved in the conflict. For example, the sight of dead American soldiers being dragged naked through the streets of Mogadishu, an act contrary to the Geneva Convention and normal international norms and conventions, was deliberately designed to send a specific and powerful message to the American public. The sense of outrage and revulsion felt by Americans who saw those images led to the rapid withdrawal of American forces from Somalia. This event and the US response to it directly influenced Osama Bin Laden, who in an interview with his followers cited the Mogadishu incident as evidence of the United States being 'a paper tiger'.[35] Non-state actors/warlords were given a macabre example of one method of changing the policy of a state player. All they needed to do was change the equation used that committed the state player to become involved in the conflict.

Martin van Creveld was the first to highlight this issue in his landmark book, *The Transformation of War*. In the section entitled 'non-trinitarian war' (1991: 49f.), van Creveld considers the implications that may be derived from a government using the phrase, 'it is our national interest'. This implies, according to van Creveld, some form of calculation. The non-state actor in this scenario no longer needs to defeat the state player militarily; it only needs to alter how the calculation is weighed. When Western states use ethical language to justify how a calculation for armed intervention is made (e.g. doing the 'right thing' by Britain and the people of Afghanistan[36]) morality and ethics become major factors in that conflict. This is not to suggest that morality and ethics have not been major factors in war up to this point; that would be absurd.

A paradigm shift has occurred. Ethics and morality have become weapons used by non-state players against states (who are signatories to international humanitarian law) but who may well, because of ideological reasons, have repudiated or ignored accepted international conventions. Falk observes that:

> When the society under occupation resists by suicide bombers attacking every target from the Red Cross to the UN, shamelessly beheading journalists and civilians, it is obvious that the restraints of international humanitarian law and elemental humanitarian ethics, have been repudiated. (2005: 244)

---

[35]   See http://www.pbs.org/wgbh/pages/frontline/shows/binladen/who/interview.html [accessed: June 2011].

[36]   See G. Brown's speech, http://news.bbc.co.uk/1/hi/8237207.stm [accessed: August 2011].

A recent incident in Afghanistan highlights this horrifically. An eight-year-old girl was killed after the package she had been given by insurgents (possibly disguised as sweets), which she was told to take to a police vehicle, was detonated by remote control.[37] Those who are prepared to plan and use young children as unwitting living bombs in aid of their cause are unlikely to take any notice of international law. Indeed the wave of revulsion felt in regard to this heinous act may well have been a desired and expected outcome by the insurgents, i.e. it was a local act designed to have an international strategic effect. This lies at the heart of the paradigm shift; those who reject International Humanitarian Law, conventions and norms, may well use these very laws, conventions and norms as weapons against their enemies because of the moral effect such actions have among the citizens of those countries.

Two recent illustrations from the conflict in Afghanistan illustrate this asymmetric strategy. In the first, a British soldier on patrol identified an insurgent armed with a rifle preparing to open fire on him. As the soldier observed the gunman through his own rifle sights he also saw a 10-year-old Afghan girl, standing directly in front of the insurgent. The soldier realised that if he fired to defend himself he risked hitting the girl but if he did not engage the gunman he would be shot. The bullet fired at Lance Corporal Craig Murfitt struck him on the left side of his helmet; thankfully, it was deflected and he was not seriously hurt.[38] Stories of women and children being used as human shields by insurgents are common in many conflicts, especially where military personnel from Western states are required to adhere to the norms of international law. This tactic serves at least two purposes for the insurgent: firstly, it provides a significant defence against military personnel who are required to adhere to international law. Secondly, it provides the opportunity to create a 'win, win situation' for the insurgent. In the case of Corporal Murfitt, if he refused to fire the gunman had a non-contested engagement; if the soldier did choose to defend himself against the real threat, the insurgent had a propaganda win, 'British soldier deliberately opens fire on innocent 10 year old girl'. The use of this type of moral story by insurgents is ubiquitous.

The second illustration regards a NATO air strike on two petrol tankers that resulted in a number of insurgents being killed as well as a large number of civilians.[39] Insurgents had hijacked two fuel tankers and then proceeded to behead both drivers.[40] However one of the fuel trucks became stuck as the insurgents tried

---

[37]   See http://www.guardian.co.uk/world/2011/jun/26/afghanistan-taliban-girl-bomb-police [accessed: October 2011].

[38]   See http://www.bbc.co.uk/news/uk-england-devon-12033002 [accessed: October 2011].

[39]   See http://www.telegraph.co.uk/news/worldnews/asia/afghanistan/6137938/Nato-air-strike-in-Afghanistan-kills-scores-of-Taliban-militants-and-civilians.html [accessed: August 2011].

[40]   See http://news.bbc.co.uk/1/hi/world/south_asia/8237287.stm [accessed: August 2011].

to cross a river. An airstrike was authorised by NATO commanders in the belief that those around the tankers were insurgents. In the meantime, the insurgents had offered the fuel from the tankers to local civilians after the tanker became stuck. The resultant airstrike killed approximately 90 people. In its report on this incident the *Daily Telegraph* said, 'Taliban militants have been accused of using civilians as human shields, or deliberately provoking battles in populated areas to incur civilian casualties for propaganda'.[41] The political fallout from this incident was significant. The German Chancellor, Angela Merkel, and her former Foreign Minister, Frank-Walter Steinmeier, faced questions in a German parliamentary inquiry into the airstrike at Kunduz,[42] as well severe criticism from opposition parties. A criminal investigation of the German commander, Colonel Klein, who authorised the attack was subsequently dropped.

Anyone who has served in a NATO Headquarters will be familiar with the meticulous protocols employed before any potentially lethal strike is used. Although I was not present in the HQ that authorised the strike at Kunduz, I am absolutely confident, because of my experience working in the HQ of Task Force Helmand, that the German commander would have sought legal advice before authorising the attack; this is the standard NATO protocol. This, I would suggest, is both a strength but more importantly the fundamental weakness of a solely law-based approach to modern conflict: demonstrating that the legality of an action does not make it moral or ethical. An action may have legal sanction and yet lack any form of moral validity in the eyes of international public opinion, which is essential if any involvement in a conflict is justified using moral or ethical language. In the case of Western involvement in the 'new wars' or asymmetric conflicts, this is one of the main battlegrounds.

While the tactics of great commanders are often studied in great depth by military students, the abiding image that remains long after the precise details of a conflict have faded is the moral and ethical one. In my ministry as a chaplain, I have often asked soldiers to conjure up in their minds an image that encapsulates the Vietnam War. For 99 per cent it is of the naked girl, Kim Phuc, running away after a napalm airstrike had stripped her of both her clothes and much of her skin. While few non-military students could name the key generals involved in this war, this particular image remains as one of the most instantly recognisable and haunting images of the Vietnam conflict. Similarly, the image of 'the highway of death' or the devastation of Iraqi military vehicles on Basra road out of Kuwait City, is a lingering reminder that what is often remembered after a conflict is not the legal protocols that authorised an attack, but the moral and ethical impact of the imagery resulting from the attack. The importance of this is magnified whenever those involved in a conflict deliberately use morality and ethics as calculated weapons.

41   See http://www.telegraph.co.uk/news/worldnews/asia/afghanistan/6137938/Nato-air-strike-in-Afghanistan-kills-scores-of-Taliban-militants-and-civilians.html [accessed: August 2011].

42   See http://www.dw-world.de/dw/article/0,,14833422,00.html [accessed: August 2011].

The tactics used by non-state players in modern conflict can frequently create operational scenarios in which terms such as exceptionalism, military necessity and collateral damage become the *lingua franca*. Some non-state actors specialise in what scholars refer to as the 'Propaganda of the Deed' or POTD.[43] POTD 'does not equate to a single act of terror – it is not an event, it is part of a process of narrative construction, reinforcement and confirmation through deeds'. POTD is more than mere propaganda. It is a process of creating a living evolving narrative, one designed to function on different levels for diverse audiences. The response of a major Western state player to a terrorist atrocity becomes in itself an organic part of the living narrative created by the non-state actor. States have been forced to respond to numerous 'exceptional' circumstances as a result of public pressure to act or the fear that inaction will only encourage continued or more virulent forms of attacks. States have increasingly found themselves in situations where 'military necessity' has dictated a particular course of action, which in itself immediately raises questions as to the moral or ethical validity of the state's involvement in that conflict. This is the deliberate objective of a non-state player/actor wishing to alter how the calculation is weighed regarding a particular state's involvement in a particular conflict.

The Church Response?

What then has been the response of the national churches in the United Kingdom to the above situation? Charles Reed asked searching questions of the way in which the British churches sought to offer counsel to governments and wider society on issues of war and peace following the end of the Cold War (2004: 110). His contention was that a pacifist tradition from the Cold War continued to dominate the Church's thinking in what had become a fundamentally different political world (2004: 73). Indeed, Reed is rather blunt when he states, 'in all instances the British churches appear[ed] to place in the public domain arguments and recommendations that politicians can rarely, if ever, implement' (2004: 73).

Perhaps one recent example of this, under the heading 'Kirk says Afghan War cannot be justified' was the vote taken on 2 June 2011 by the General Assembly of the Church of Scotland.

> The General Assembly will be asked today to call for an end to the war in Afghanistan and for the troops to be called home as soon as possible. Convenor of the Church and Society Council Mr Ian Galloway said "in 2002 the Church said the war in Afghanistan could only be justified if it met the criteria of legitimacy, liable to succeed, proportional in its implementation and limited in its effect on non combatants. Our view is that this war fails on all four counts and should be ended now. These are political not military failures however, and

---

[43] For an excellent treatment of this issue see Bolt et al. (2008).

so we recognise that there is a real need for those soldiers in Afghanistan to be supported and cared for including by the valuable work of chaplains".[44]

On its website CWM, a partnership of Churches in Mission, under the banner of Action of Churches Together Scotland (ACTS), states that:

"Just war" theory seeks to limit conflict and violence. Other Christians argue that the message of the Gospel points towards active nonviolence rather than an accommodation to war.[45]

The report,[46] *Just War Criteria and the War in Afghanistan*, produced under ACTS[47] briefly outlines the history of the just war tradition and the generally accepted criteria used in coming to a determination on the justness of a conflict or a proposed conflict. It then gives a brief outline of the current situation in Afghanistan, in which it raises the question of the legality of armed intervention, specifically mentioning the lack of a UN mandate on several occasions. The main body of the report is its systematic consideration of four of the criteria for a just war: is the war legitimate? Is there a good prospect of success? Is the harm prevented outweighed by the harm caused? Are the rights of non-combatants being respected? The conclusion is unambiguous:

The concerns explored above (paragraphs 11 to 24) lead unequivocally to the conclusion that the war in Afghanistan, given the course of events and the scale of suffering involved, can no longer (if it ever could) be justified by the traditional (or any reduced list of) "just war" criteria and that continuing military engagement in Afghanistan is questionable even if the transfer of power to a democratically elected government (and the containment or defeat accordingly of the Taliban) is regarded as the benchmark that the war has been successful. There is still no UN mandate to support the legitimacy of the OEF offensive action against the Taliban; the ISAF force is having very limited success in stabilising Afghanistan; and unacceptable levels of civilian casualties are

---

[44]   See http://www.churchofscotland.org.uk/news_and_events/news/articles/kirk_say s_afghan_war_cannot_be_justified [accessed: August 2011].

[45]   See http://www.cwmission.org/news/church-of-scotland-calls-for-end-to-afghan-war [accessed: August 2011].

[46]   The report may be downloaded from http://www.acts-scotland.org/images/stories/ pdf/afghanistanfinal.pdf. [accessed: August 2011].

[47]   The ecumenical working group that produced the report *Just War Criteria and the War in Afghanistan* for ACTS comprised representatives of the Roman Catholic Church, Scottish Episcopal Church, Methodist Church, Church of Scotland and the Religious Society of Friends.

continuing. Overall, as long as foreign troops remain, it seems that the situation is being inflamed.[48]

Whether or not this report is a fair and balanced consideration of the just war tradition, as it pertains to the present engagement in Afghanistan, is questionable. The repeated use of legality as juxtaposition to the notion of justness is fascinating. It is, at least to this author, a curious position to take particularly in reference to the UN. The UN's failure to take decisive action to prevent the genocide in Rwanda is, for some, a case of how nations can remain within UN law while simultaneously accepting the systemic slaughter of 20 per cent of an entire population. The juxtaposition of keeping within international law and morality is an interesting position to adopt: this is particularly relevant whenever one considers that a 'positive' view of international law is the dominant one (i.e. that the law is not interested in morality or ethics only what is lawful).

When the authors of the ACTS report considered the third principle of the just war tradition, proportionality of 'the harm caused by a particular action with the harm prevented', there is no indication that they had any awareness of the context of how civilian causalities may have been caused; they simply cite figures from the UN that say that 55 per cent of civilian deaths were caused by insurgents and some 39 per cent by coalition forces. There is absolutely no hint that the authors of this report, on behalf of a number of major churches in Scotland, were familiar with the realities of facing an enemy that frequently and deliberately engineers situations in which civilian causalities can be used as a propaganda weapon against coalition forces. In the report authors' view, 'non-combatant immunity is fundamental to the just war theory. The huge loss of civilian lives, regardless of whether they were directly or indirectly intended, undermines any justification of the war'.[49] Albeit unwittingly, the authors of this report may well have validated the Taliban's callous and strategic disregard for the lives of the innocent. As non-state players, insurgents do not have to defeat a state player militarily; they only need to significantly alter the moral calculation by which the state participates in that conflict. If the public, essential to Clausewitz's trinitarian formula, withdraws its belief in the morality of state intervention on the basis of civilian deaths regardless of the circumstances in which those deaths occurred, the insurgents may claim a moral victory.

The call for British troops to come home as soon as possible may be viewed as an entirely understandable position to take; it is a natural humanitarian response. It does, however, leave itself open to Reed's criticism that 'British churches appear to place in the public domain arguments and recommendations that politicians can rarely, if ever, implement' (2004: 73). The ACTS report offers little practical help to the British Armed Forces currently engaged against a callous insurgency; one that rejects the authority of the UN, International Humanitarian Law, international

---

[48]   *Just War Criteria and the War in Afghanistan*, para. 26.
[49]   *Just War Criteria and the War in Afghanistan*, para. 24.

norms and the Geneva Conventions. In this specific, it is silent. Richard Falk in contrast has called for a new 'normative consensus that combines legal, ethical and religious ideas about right conduct', which:

> Cannot be produced on the basis of reason alone, but must be built through the participation of scholars and specialists that represent the various regions and civilisations that comprise the world, and take due account of the rise of non-state actors as political players in relation to armed conflict. (2005: 246)

One example the Church could take inspiration from is Hugo Grotius.[50] Grotius was an instrumental figure in laying the foundations of international law.[51] Although fleeing a sentence of life imprisonment, as a result of his involvement in a major religious dispute between reformers and Calvinists, he remained an active participant in seeking to achieve Christian unity. Grotius is a compelling model of how Christian theological principles can act as a foundation for an active engagement and dialogue with the international law. It is perhaps a sad reflection that Grotius is a largely forgotten name in modern Christian circles while remaining a prominent figure for the legal profession: e.g. The American Society of International Law holds an annual Grotius Lecture.[52]

Conclusion

The identification of politics as the essence of war is a cultural phenomenon, sited within the specific philosophical milieu of Enlightenment thinking. It is a predominantly Western cultural phenomenon which continues to dominate world politics and is embedded at the heart of international law. The emergence of the phenomenon of 'new wars' and asymmetric warfare has created a paradigm shift in the nature of modern warfare that international law was not designed to deal with. International law was created by nation states for the regulation of a specific international world order. The 'new wars' described in this chapter along with asymmetric warfare have exposed its inherent structural weakness, in that it only works whenever all parties agree to its principles or accept its Clausewitzian worldview. Twenty-first century non-state *actors*, for religious or other reasons, frequently reject international protocols for their own strategic purposes. This is the new reality that confronts modern soldiers on the battlefield; a reality where a non-state actor deliberately uses children as suicide bombers. Where is the voice of the national British churches in this new reality? Do they have anything to contribute to an ever evolving challenge and deliberate immoral manipulation?

---

[50] For a good introductory essay see http://plato.stanford.edu/entries/grotius/ [accessed: October 2011].

[51] See http://plato.stanford.edu/entries/grotius/, 1.1 'Life' [accessed: October 2011].

[52] See http://www.asil.org/events/am07/agendafull.html [accessed: October 2011].

The silence of the chaplain at a targeting planning meeting is symbolic of the relative silence of national churches with regard to their participation in the moral and ethical dynamics that are germane to the actual conduct of operations in the twenty-first century. It is time for the spectators who stand some distance from a modern conflict like Afghanistan, producing reports on the justness or otherwise of that conflict, to become active participants in a dialogue on how to create a moral/ethical resource or framework for those who find themselves in the most morally challenging situations of our time. International law is facing a threat it was not designed or intended to meet or deal with. When the use of armed intervention is justified using moral language, the operational framework used in prosecuting that campaign should have built within it a structural, moral/ethical framework capable of working in conjunction with the application of international law. The use of NATO airstrike at Kunduz was intended to deny insurgents access to the captured fuel tankers. It almost certainly met the required legal demands for the authorised use of lethal force. However, a correct application of law was unable to mitigate the resultant moral and propaganda impact of the loss of life.

Each of the national churches has a strong pacifist tradition. This reflects a long and noble tradition within Christianity. However, the report presented by ACTS is a classic example of British churches placing in the public domain an argument that politicians can rarely, if ever, implement. Is it possible that this particular report was intended to speak to an internal constituency, in which a strong pacifist tradition could be satisfied with a reinstatement of a long held position? This raises a question: 'To whom are British/Scottish churches speaking?' Was this a carefully weighted message to influence British foreign policy or one constructed mainly for an internal Christian audience? What seems clear, at least to this writer, is that the silence of the Brigade chaplain at the targeting meeting is analogous to the silence of the major national churches in the UK on the critical situation and threat facing the use of international law in modern asymmetric warfare. How can British churches make moral and ethical comments on the conduct of modern war, if they are not actively engaged in Falk's call to create a 'normative consensus that combines legal, ethical and religious ideas about right conduct'? (2005: 246).

PART II
The Wider Context of Chaplaincy in Contention

Chapter 4

Terrorism and Interrogation, as an Issue for Chaplains on Operations

Peter Sedgwick

Introduction

In this chapter, I wish to place the role of military chaplains on current operations within two parameters. The first parameter is the fact that both the Afghan and Iraq wars involved a link between insurgency, terrorism and religion. There are two issues within this first parameter which are disputed at the present time. Firstly, how far is the Afghan war at its heart a national, or tribal, insurgency in which issues of religion and terrorism are secondary? Secondly, what is the link between contemporary terrorism and religion? (Fisher and Wicker 2010) A second parameter depends on the first. If the Afghan and Iraq wars were and are undoubtedly a counter-insurgency operation, then the response by the security forces, including the military, has involved 'enhanced interrogation' at best and outright torture at worst. What is the response by chaplains to this use of interrogation?

Chaplains have to play at least three roles in operations against insurgency, which are not easy. Firstly, they have a moral role in setting the limits of response to insurgency and terrorism. This will involve the appropriate treatment of non-combatants (itself a term difficult to define). Secondly, they have a religious role in being the witness of the Christian community to the military, but also a person about whom the military personnel may ask questions about the possible religious motivation for the insurgency. 'Padre, why do these insurgents act this way? Is it because of their religion?' Thirdly, chaplains have a pastoral role in caring for the military personnel involved. There are many others who carry out some of these roles, but not all three roles together, and not in such a complex and intensive way.

This chapter approaches these two parameters by way of a case study, which is that of Northern Ireland from 1970 to 2005. The case study is chosen because it illuminates the two parameters. After the examination of Northern Ireland, the chapter passes to a discussion of the ethical issues around terrorism, interrogation and torture in contemporary operations (Afghanistan 2001 onwards and Iraq 2003–10) (Phillips 2006; Lewis 2003; Elshtain 2003). This is not only an issue for chaplains. It also raises issues for the churches, which sponsor Christian military chaplaincy.

Chaplaincy and Counter-insurgency Forces

There was a major contribution to the debate about the moral role of chaplains accompanying counter-insurgency operations with the publication in 2011 of *War and Moral Dissonance* (French 2011). Professor Peter French is a distinguished philosopher in an American university who taught a professional development course in ethics for US Marines chaplains from 2004 to 2005. Professor French's daughter, Dr Shannon French, is also an ethicist and a professor in the Naval Academy, and father and daughter taught the course together, along with other ethicists. The opening chapter of the book tells the story of how the chaplains became increasingly overwhelmed by the conflict in Iraq, and it is a harrowing account of the psychological pressures which the chaplains felt burdened with, especially after the publication of the torture at Abu Ghraib in May 2004. The rest of the book is a philosophical reflection on the issues raised by the chaplains, including torture and enhanced interrogation, corporate responsibility and honour.

French writes about his training days between March and April 2004, at the Amphibious Base at Little Creek, Virginia. The news was worrying. American mercenaries from a corporation called Blackwater had been overpowered in Fallujah and murdered publicly. 'Some of the chaplains expressed their frustration with the Iraqi people who didn't seem to appreciate what we were doing for them.' Furthermore, a few chaplains opposed the teaching of just war theory. The argument that it would help them interact with officers on operations for discussions about what was ethical was mocked, if only by a few (French 2011: 19–20). On the other hand, other chaplains took a different view. None of what French mentions at this point is any different from chaplains on duty anywhere, except that the operation is counter-insurgency, and not a conventional war.

However in May 2004 French led another session at Pearl Harbor, Hawaii, where the treatment of prisoners under interrogation became central. The atrocities at Abu Ghraib had been reported. French raised the issue of what a chaplain might do if they were at the detention centre (the chaplains assumed none was there, but in fact there was one army chaplain present at Abu Ghraib). 'The general view was that soldiers serving as prison guards at Abu Ghraib were acting under orders. A chaplain might be seen as trying to contravene orders' (2011: 25). French argued that chaplains should be like Nathan the prophet to King David. 'Then Nathan said to David, "You *are* the man!"' (2 Samuel 12:7). Chaplains were caught off-guard by that reference, and French explained that 'you are the moral advisors to command. You are supposed to stand before authority and unflinchingly speak the unvarnished truth' (French 2011: 25).[1] The chaplains were also reluctant to commend the whistle-blower, Specialist Joseph Darby, who revealed the details of what was happening at Abu Ghraib, but who was ostracised in his home town for betraying his fellow soldiers. Chaplains argued that many of the army recruits in detention centres were from urban gangs.

---

[1]   See also his detailed discussion of Abu Ghraib (French 2011: 161–2).

However, in all the ethics training after May 2004, the issue of how detained combatants should be treated did not go away. Instead it surfaced repeatedly, interrupting the formal ethics training. Personal and professional identity was now very much at risk among the chaplains. 'At the end of each day of a PDTC (professional development training course), I would return to my room feeling that I had been entrapped in the immorality of the war in which truth had become the first victim' (French 2011: 27). French spends the rest of this first chapter discussing the stories which chaplains told about counter-insurgency operations in Iraq. Chaplains were in deep personal turmoil about the lack of moral restraint shown by US Marines in Iraq, especially since they identified closely with their troops. Chaplains became convinced that the mission in Iraq was pointless, especially since there were so many stories of the loss of innocent life on counter-insurgency operations. Issues of moral courage and moral conflict now predominated in the sessions, interspersed with questions of stress and psychological difficulties.

Much of the work of defining what is moral is of course dealt with by asking instead what is legally permissible (MoD 2005; Roberts and Guelff 2000; White 2009). The Army Legal Service (ALS) has had an enhanced role for many decades. There are legal advisory offices in every major British Army HQ in the UK and overseas. Advisory officers assist the chain of command with all legal aspects of their work. All units and individuals are trained regarding operational law (both at home and on operations abroad) prior to all operational deployments. ALS officers are often asked to advise on the most sensitive issues, as well as on international law and often on the local law of the country concerned. The Operational Law Branch (OLB) of the ALS undertakes duties in intelligence related posts, and OLB officers are present in Iraq and Afghanistan on operations. There is a close link between the OLB and intelligence work. Nevertheless there are many examples, in this book and elsewhere, of chaplains having a close relationship with their commanding officer ('Padre, what do you think?'), even when the OLB officer has delivered his opinion, and chaplains will also have very frank exchanges with soldiers on the ground ('Padre, what do you think of that?'). Defining what is legally permissible does not either end the discussion of what should be done, or settle a post mortem on what was actually carried out. I confine this chapter to Christian chaplaincy, partly for reasons of brevity, but mainly because non-Christian military chaplaincy is outside my area of expertise. It is however important to note that any discussion of terrorism should involve responses from Christians and Muslims as the excellent new book, *Just War on Terror? A Christian and Muslim Response* (Fisher and Wicker 2010), demonstrates.

The British Army has long been aware that the struggle for colonial independence in the nineteenth and twentieth centuries involved both insurgency and terrorism. Insurgency is the action of taking up arms against the occupying power. Terrorism is the use or threat of violence to influence the government or intimidate the public in an ideological cause. This definition follows the wording in the Terrorism Act 2000, which defines it as 'the use or threat of action involving serious violence, damage or danger to life and health … in order to influence government or intimidate the public in a political, religious or ideological cause'. Terrorism and insurgency are not the same, and the one can exist without the other. However there are times when the two co-exist

Until the operations in Northern Ireland it was virtually unheard of for any terrorism accompanying a nationalist insurgency to take place both in the country where the insurgency was occurring and in the United Kingdom. The classic Victorian, and indeed twentieth century view until 1970, was that there was peace 'at home', but there were also foreign wars, with military chaplains serving on the frontiers. That was true of the long Victorian peace (with a small footnote for Fenian terrorism in England in the mid-nineteenth century). It was also very much the case for the First and Second World Wars, where although there was severe bombing in the Second World War within the United Kingdom, there were no land operations in the United Kingdom whatsoever. British armies fought overseas in both world wars. Terrorism was also not an issue in the First and Second World Wars, either at home or abroad.

The only exceptions were Ireland from 1920 to 1921, and Palestine in the 1930s. Anti-colonial movements after 1945 never touched British shores. The period from 1945 continued the tradition of the armed forces fighting abroad, but with peace at home. What was different was that the insurgencies (which had always been there before 1939, as in Iraq) became far more widespread, persistent and ultimately successful. So the British government (and armed forces) began the long retreat from empire. The nature of insurgency however changed in 1970 with the struggle against the IRA, when bombs and shootings took place in England, as well as in Northern Ireland itself, and the Taliban insurgency in Afghanistan is also accompanied by Al Qaeda terrorism in the United Kingdom.[2] Those convicted terrorists who trained abroad, in Afghanistan and Pakistan, include: Richard Reid, who tried to blow up a transatlantic aircraft; Dhiren Barot,[3] who planned 'dirty bomb' attacks in England; Omar Khyam; and Mohammed Siddique Khan, one of the London suicide bombers.

In the case of the armed conflict in Ireland the Christian church in general and military chaplaincy in particular, was put in a very difficult position. It was a nationalist insurgency against colonial rule, but there was also a religious dimension to the struggle. However the relationship between the two was complex, with religion being (as I will argue) the 'tone' or colouring of a long-term nationalist movement. In Afghanistan, the counter-insurgency operation, and the struggle against terrorism, is a campaign against the Taliban and Al Qaeda who are motivated by deeply held religious beliefs. There is a global ideology based on Islam and the rejection of Christianity. That was never the case in Ireland. This was a local insurgency with a religious dimension.

---

[2]   MI5's website makes this claim, see https://www.mi5.gov.uk/output/terrorist-train ing.html.

[3]   See http://news.bbc.co.uk/1/hi/uk/6121084.stm.

The rise of international terrorism inspired by extreme Islamist ideology and directed against the United States and its allies is one of the major developments of the last 20 years, especially since the watershed events of 9/11. Novel features of the current phase of terrorism include the extent of its international networks and its reliance on attacks without warning by suicide bombers. These create new difficulties for the intelligence and security services in seeking to anticipate and prevent terrorist attacks.[4] The analogy between war and terrorism inevitably involves dissimilarity as well as similarity. Like war, terrorism can not only cause widespread loss of life and damage to the physical and social fabric, but can induce terror, or fear, in civilian populations (hence the word). Unlike war, which tends to be continuous but of limited duration, the impact of terrorism is episodic. The dilemma, with which our and other societies are currently grappling with since 9/11, is whether the challenges posed by terrorism mean that we are in a perpetual state of total war, with all that this implies in terms of continued resort to military action, executive detention and martial law.

All this leads to the often made assertion that religion is a major player on the world's political stage, in a way that would scarcely have been recognised 30 or 40 years ago. Whereas the main conflicts of the twentieth century were ideological, the main conflicts of our own time are to do with identity. Religion has come into increasing prominence as a marker of identity. Religion can and does exacerbate conflict (the English criminal law now includes the category of 'religiously aggravated offences') but it is also worth noting that many people whose motivation was principally religious (of all faiths) have taken some of the most courageous peace initiatives in alleviating conflict.

Terrorism in Ireland 1970–2005: Religious or Not?

The particular case study which I wish to contrast with contemporary operations in Iraq and Afghanistan is that of military chaplaincy in Northern Ireland. In 1970, and the decades which followed, the Provisional IRA was the main terrorist organisation in the United Kingdom, and this movement was itself deeply intertwined with religion and national identity. The official IRA was the older nationalist insurgency force, which went back to the 1920s war of independence, but it was virtually defunct by the mid-1970s. The Provisional IRA saw the position of Northern Ireland, and the Unionist leadership, as a dependency culture on the British state through a lens which was partially Marxist, partially nationalist. The news in 2010 that a Roman Catholic priest in the 1970s had perhaps been an IRA

---

⁴   The book by Philip Bobbitt, *Terror and Consent* (2008) is central to this discussion. http://www.archbishopofcanterbury.org/articles.php/616/archbishop-reviews-philip-bobbitts-new-book is the review by Rowan Williams. It is also discussed in *Just War on Terror?* by Michael Howard (Fisher and Wicker 2010: 55–62), with a reply by Bobbitt (Fisher and Wicker 2010: 199–204). See also the MI5 website.

bomber in Northern Ireland, and that this had been covered up by the Roman Catholic Church and the British government, was both very shocking and disputed information.[5] Throughout the 1970s and 1980s the 1974 Prevention of Terrorism Act was aimed at controlling Irish terrorism (Hornsby Smith 1991: 41).

The biggest selling newspaper for the Irish in Britain, which was and is the *Irish Post*, confirmed the stability of Irish Catholic identity in England, in which religious beliefs did not lead to a feeling that you should act in a particular manner politically. This is not to say that the Roman Catholic Church did not become involved in the campaign to get released those who had been imprisoned for terrorism. That was a different issue: injustice had been done in the courts, and the innocent had been wrongly imprisoned by a corrupt police force. The protest by the Catholic Church in England and Ireland was driven by a sense of unfairness. The film *In the Name of the Father*[6] expresses this sense of hurt very well. In Northern Ireland, the criminal justice system became overwhelmed by the struggle against the IRA, in ways that varied from the special courts in Ulster to outright police corruption in fabricated evidence. It raises the issue, which cannot be pursued here, as to how far a counter-insurgency strategy should be led by the military, or whether it is predominantly an issue of policing.

However the support of the Roman Catholic Church for those wrongly imprisoned (in its view) for terrorism was always accompanied by a condemnation of terrorism. Indeed Tony Blair noted in 2005 that it was completely inconceivable that the IRA would have ever sought to restore the medieval Papacy and the Inquisition. This marked it as totally different from Al Qaeda. The IRA was a nationalist struggle in which religion was not central.[7] Indeed Ian Paisley was far more likely to invoke religious justification for attacking the IRA because it embodied Roman Catholic beliefs than it would itself. The IRA would argue a defence of its bombing campaign from just war theories and consequentialist reasoning, invoking a metaphysic of blood sacrifice, destiny, history and the holy grail of 'one united nation, Gaelic and free'.

There certainly was sympathy among Roman Catholics in England for the nationalist minority in Northern Ireland in the 1980s. Seventy-one per cent felt that Northern Ireland should be part of the Irish republic, which is a far higher percentage than in the rest of the English population. But here again there was a strong rejection of political violence, both because of a belief that Christianity was about peace and harmony, and because it was felt that the Catholic Church should not be involved in politics, even if this was seen as the way to promote social justice. There was even a clear belief by ordinary mass-going Catholics in

---

5   *Guardian*, 24 August 2010.

6   Sheridan (1993), A film by Jim Sheridan. The website which describes the content is http://www.imdb.com/title/tt0107207/.

7   Shanahan (2008). Blair's comments were recorded in the *Houston Chronicle*, 30 July 2005.

England in the 1980s that housing, poverty and racial justice should be pursued non-politically (Hornsby Smith 1987: 166).

However, the Roman Catholic Church consistently condemned this nationalist appeal when it became inclined to violence, especially terrorism. There was an explicit condemnation by Pope John Paul II in Drogheda, County Louth, in September 1979, when the Pope appealed to the men of violence to lay down their arms. The IRA replied by asking whether the Roman Catholic Church (and the Holy Father) had forgotten that the traditional church teaching included the right to legitimate revolt under its just war principles (Shanahan 2008: 93). The IRA at this point appears deeply on the defensive, as Shanahan notices, seeking to defend its campaign against the criticism of the Roman Catholic Church at the highest level.

So how did this interweaving of religion and nationalism affect chaplaincy in the British Army in Northern Ireland, and especially those chaplains who were Roman Catholic? There is a significant caption in the chaplaincy museum at Amport House, Andover, the British Armed Forces Chaplaincy Centre. It speaks of chaplains leaving Northern Ireland during the insurgency being exhausted emotionally, physically and spiritually. It is the only operation of the Royal Army Chaplains' Department (RAChD) since 1945 that has this particular caption, and the caption adds that this sense of exhaustion was probably appropriate. Some Roman Catholic chaplains went out of their way to build links with the nationalist community. In 1988 Fr (later Mgr) Kevin Vasey went to Army Headquarters in Northern Ireland as Senior Chaplain, where he worked to build links with the nationalist community that eventually resulted in the peace process. Another military chaplain, Fr David Smith, reflected on this period during the Troubles: 'from retired brother priests, one of the enduring themes appears to be that as RC priests, we "got it" from both sides: the Nationalists were suspicious of us since we were identified with the occupying force; the Army was suspicious of us since we were identified with the enemy. I'm not sure that the Irish took too much notice of the Holy Father on the matter of the wickedness of the IRA!'[8]

In 1972 a Roman Catholic chaplain was killed by the official IRA when they bombed the Aldershot headquarters of the Parachute Regiment. The role of a military chaplain in Ireland was never easy, but the truthfulness of their role was maintained. The fact that methods of enhanced interrogation were outlawed by the British prime minister in 1972 certainly removed a major challenge to their moral integrity. Military chaplaincy during the Troubles remained a ministry which sought to minister both to the units under its pastoral care, but also to the local community, of whatever political and religious persuasion. This was a challenging role which it had to endure, and there are many soldiers grateful for its ministry during 35 years of violence.

---

[8]   Personal communication to the author.

Counter-Insurgency and Interrogation in Afghanistan

The Afghan conflict is complex. It is a nationalist struggle concerned with freeing the nation from foreign occupation, and many are motivated by tribal rivalry. In this respect, Afghanistan is like Ireland in the 1970s–1980s. Nevertheless the explicitly religious dimension of the war cannot be denied. A struggle which has an intrinsic, and not merely secondary, religious dimension has to raise issues for military chaplaincy, which is by definition a religious body. Since the chaplain is a religious person, terrorism which is justified by religion involves a challenge to the chaplain. This can vary from the commonplace remark that 'religion is wrong, because it motivates terrorists' to the more sophisticated awareness that in a struggle which is seen as being between religions the chaplain's own faith has to become involved. Since the 1980s we have seen the rise of terrorism which is based on religious beliefs, especially from Islam.

Counter-insurgency work can be tactical, involving the regular army, including both patrols against the enemy and reassurance patrols. It can also be strategic, which involves increasingly the use of specialist military units. The nature of modern warfare is changing as many books on military operations make clear (Smith 2005). Chaplains who are posted to specialist military units have particular demands on them. There is an inherent secrecy about the work. In one way this is similar to chaplains to RAF bomber bases in the Second World War, who also lived with great secrecy. What is different today is that we live in a very open society bombarded by news, whereas specialist military units demand a high degree of confidentiality that cannot be revealed.

One chaplain had reflected hard on his role:

> Soldiers recognise that they are fighting people of faith, but this faith leads them into "criminal acts", which have no regard whatsoever for the Afghan people and innocent life. Total war is the challenge which we face … we are facing those who have absolutely no qualms about using total war, but we are adhering absolutely to the conventions of modern warfare which makes it very one sided sometimes. Also the faith which the Taliban express is very different from the local Afghans whom I have met. They wouldn't recognise the extremism of the Taliban … the big question is whether the desire for power imposing the Caliphate as their own political power base as a state on earth from the Taliban is really about faith or because they haven't been able to get into power anywhere else. Many of the Taliban are foreign fighters rather than Afghan (Croatians, Russian, some Westerners, and Pakistani). It would be valuable if there was some way within the Muslim world to look at the genuineness of the *madrassas* as religious schools. Those who teach can be illiterate and there is only learning by rote, not any in-depth study of theological reflection, but any such study would have to be from within the Muslim world … that is a hugely contentious and difficult issue. We (British forces) now have to deal with multi-faith insurgency and all that means but we are relatively clear that these are extremist jihadists

who have issues with the rest of the Muslim world because they see them as apostate for having sold out. Religion is part of Afghan life but we almost give it too much of a priority as the Taliban would wish.

The chaplain went on to say that soldiers also ask about the religious element of the war since the Taliban see themselves as extremist jihadists within the Muslim faith, and they want the establishment of the caliphate and sharia law. The chaplain is certainly asked about the religious element: '[soldiers] are intellectual and inquisitive people who do ask significant questions, usually very piercing questions, I have to say. They want to understand who they are fighting and why, for operational and personal reasons'. This can lead into questions about chaplaincy, and why chaplains respond the way they do. 'Where does our faith come from, and how does it affect us?'

It is not easy for chaplains who reject religious extremism to know how to respond to acts of violence inspired by a particular understanding of religious faith. Extremism is not the same as fundamentalism, because that term arose out of Western (especially US) conservative evangelicalism. Extremism in Islam turns not on the justification of acts of terror (because then the definition is self-justifying), but rather on Islamic understanding of hermeneutics, and the interpretation of the Qur'an. A faith can be seen as extremist if it rejects centuries of scholarship and interpretation which allow the understanding of religious truth to speak through the revelation of the divine being by means of sacred scriptures. Such a hermeneutic is called by the Muslim scholar Tariq Ramadan (2004) *ijtihad*.

Extremism has two aspects which are proper to this discussion. Firstly it is monolithic, and as such denies the right of minorities to exist. The belief that there is only one truth can quickly become the view that minority beliefs should be removed from a society in which the extremist belief is dominant. Secondly there is an attitude to modernity which is often apocalyptic, using the language of military struggle and violence in the belief that final victory is in some way guaranteed by the heavenly order. Neither of these aspects of extremism need be true of a conservative religious faith, which may often tolerate other beliefs (only asking to be left alone), and may be fearful of its future.

There is a strong challenge to the justification of terror and religious extremism by Al Qaeda in the two articles by Tim Winter (2010) and Achmad Achtar (2010) in the recent collection *Just War on Terror?* Winter shows that there is at least the possibility of drawing parallels between the condemnation of *hiraba* in the Qur'an and the condemnation of terrorism today (2010: 21). The issue raised by Winter and Achtar is that the military chaplain must now engage with the question of whether religions can sanction terrorism, and this requires that the chaplain now becomes deeply aware of religious faiths other than their own. It also raises the difficult, and controversial, issue of the strong under-representation of Muslims in the British Army. It is reported that there are over 20,000 Muslims in the US Army, whereas the number in the British Army would be far smaller than that.

Winter argues that the duty to work for peace on earth in Muslim theology can require the use of force. Unlike Christian theology there is no inherent assumption that the fallen nature of humanity renders political action self-defeating. The key question is whether the caliphate duty to make war on the enemies of God's peace requires offensive or defensive war. Quran 2:2:16 says 'Fighting is prescribed for you, though you dislike it' (Winter 2010: 13). Classical Sunni law, formulated three centuries after the death of the Prophet, decided the scope of jihad on the basis of Ishmaelite responsibilities to humanity. The Qur'an in this view justified offensive war against unbelievers not to convert them by force, but to broaden the spread of Islam, under which members of non-idolatrous religions could worship. This is the familiar medieval division of the world into the *Dar al-Islam* (House of Islam) and *Dar al-Harb* (House of War). However Winter argues that the signing by the Ottoman Empire in 1856 of the Treaty of Paris implicitly validated the existence of the nation state. Further the acceptance of the UN Charter by the Organisation of the Islamic Conference, to which all Muslim countries belong, again prohibits armed aggression under Article 2(4). So there is an implicit repudiation of the possibility of armed jihad by all Muslim nation states (Winter 2010: 16–17). Furthermore the strong Quranic condemnation of *hiraba* as an insurrection, which is defined by its intention to cause fear and helplessness (48:26 and *sura* 5, verse 33), means that for many Islamic jurists there is a link between *hiraba* and the state of terrorism. All this could mean that Islam does not justify terrorism at all (Winter 2010: 19–20).

Nevertheless many Islamic jurists and radical groups do not agree with this interpretation. For many radical groups *hiraba* is the oppression of regimes currently in power in the Muslim world. These pro-Western tyrannies rule by torture, and to oppose them is a religious duty. Maulana Abula'la Maududi (d.1979) in his writings justified an absolutist theocracy, and redefined jihad as a revolutionary struggle to seize power (Oliver-Dee 2009). Maududi in turn influenced Sayyid Qutb. For Qutb there is a radical inversion of the interpretation of *hiraba*, which leads to martyrdom or true freedom (Winter 2010: 21). The division within Islam is very deep. Christian chaplains in the military have long understood the principles of classical just war theory. It is now time to make cross-cultural parallels between Islamic, secular and Christian definitions of just war theory. This has begun to be discussed by political theorists, and chaplains, which is a promising sign.[9] It is very important that this debate is taken much further.

The chaplain who discussed his role with me went on: 'The chaplain is the subject matter expert in terms of ethics for the unit, and the chaplain sits next to the doctor and the lawyer as well.' Chaplains may not be informed of forthcoming operations (the need to know basis of their work) 'but if I am asked a question

---

[9]   See the unpublished essay for the Cardiff University MTh in Chaplaincy Studies by Peter King (2011) *Could the Use of Improvised Explosive Devices by Insurgents in Afghanistan be Considered an Act of Just War?* He cites (Silverman 2004). See also the Cardiff MTh dissertation by Mark Grant-Jones (2010).

I will answer it as fully as I can'. 'Much in Afghanistan is relatively prescribed legally anyway in terms of what they can and cannot do.' But the nature of face to face warfare is 'undeniably psychologically difficult … the problems come when they are no longer in the environment of their peers'. The fact that it is such a close-knit family means that attempts to help have to be handled very carefully. Chaplains will be asked to help if the troops feel there is a need, and chaplains are swiftly involved if there is 'an issue – we are not kept at arm's length'. Chaplains on operations are not restricted as to their movements, and the whole point of chaplaincy is that someone is cleared to the appropriate level to be a recipient of confidential information after an operation, as soldiers debrief. 'You have to win their trust and that trust is not given lightly … it takes much longer than in normal chaplaincy to win this'.

There is no role for a chaplain during operations, but in a Forward Operating Base chaplains could sit in during the planning of the next operation. What made chaplaincy to specialist military units different was the nature of the troops involved. The chaplain described them as 'much more wary', because of the job they had to do, but once they accepted that 'you were not pretending to be one of them, then my experience is that they have been very welcoming'. 'They have issues in life like everybody else, and they would need to talk about those.' During the Second World War, there was a Special Forces chaplain who was both a chaplain and a driver for the SAS behind German lines in 1944–5, called Fraser McLuskey, who won the Military Cross for his bravery.[10] His autobiography said: 'They liked to see their padre as a man of peace without the weapons that they had to carry. They wished to see in him a man of peace. For these men their unarmed padre was the symbol that the arms they must bear were dedicated to the cause of peace and to the service of God.' They also liked to have him with them on their expeditions, so he went with them whenever possible as a driver, ambulance man or interpreter (McLuskey 1997: 136–7).

Chaplaincy is closely involved with both teaching and embodying the moral dimension of the British Army (even if chaplains often discuss the extent of their involvement in this moral education) and the curtailment of human rights raises moral questions. Curtailing human rights legislation can lead to charges of hypocrisy against the British government, and the armed forces in particular.

Torture and Terrorism

The justification of enhanced interrogation is one of the most disputed areas in military operations.[11] There is a distinction that can be made between this and torture. The distinction does not merely turn on the degree of brutality involved,

---

[10]   See http://www.independent.co.uk/news/obituaries/the-very-rev-fraser-mcluskey -500565.html. See also the obituary in the *Daily Telegraph*, 19 August 2005.

[11]   This section draws heavily on Gross (2010).

since the impact will depend greatly on the person who receives the treatment. It also depends on intentionality. Torture is the way of regimes which repress dissent, terrorise the citizenry and stifle opposition. The intention is to prevent opposition from expressing itself. Torture is itself therefore a form of state-sponsored terror, and it often provokes terrorism in reply. Some nineteenth-century empires employed torture to subjugate and terrorise opposition, such as the security service in Tsarist Russia, and this provoked a campaign of assassination. One example of many was the murder by a bomb in 1881 of Tsar Alexander II by the terrorist organisation, The People's Will, who were themselves infiltrated and tortured by the security services.

Interrogational techniques which use coercion aim to elicit information to protect security. Such information may include blindfolding, sensory and sleep deprivation, water boarding, stress positions and noise. It goes beyond the standard use of police interrogation, such as isolation, psychological pressure and manipulation (including, but not confined to, the familiar good cop/bad cop scenario), and deception (Gross 2010: 127). Interrogation techniques have expanded greatly in asymmetric warfare. The intention is to gain information which is militarily important.

There have been repeated incidents of enhanced interrogation in the campaigns against insurgency by the British security services and military after 1945. As noted above, Prime Minister Edward Heath banned enhanced interrogation in Northern Ireland in 1972. There were much tighter safeguards following the abuse of detainees in Northern Ireland. Treatment banned included hooding, sleep deprivation, subjection to noise, and stress positions. The European Court of Human Rights (ECHR) in 1976, examining British responses to insurgency in Ireland, drew a distinction between the combined use of the techniques described above, which does constitute torture, and the individual techniques, which while inhuman and degrading did not occasion suffering of such an extent that they would be called torture. The ECHR here makes an important point, that even if the intention is to gain information and not terrorise the individual, the combined use of interrogation techniques can be so severe that it passes from the description of them as inhuman to the term torture. However this is a subtle distinction. Defenders of enhanced interrogation argue that the practices of disorientation are indirect, or passive, rather than being directly invasive techniques, such as beating. The empirical evidence of long-term harm on this point is inconclusive (Gross 2010: 130), but French describes how the aim of this interrogation is to break the will. So it can never be justified (French 2011: 171–6).

There have been times when counter-insurgency becomes out of control. The Baha Mousa inquiry, set up in May 2008 and which reported in September 2011,[12] heard this evidence:

---

[12]   See http://www.bahamousainquiry.org/.

> Lieutenant Colonel Nick Mercer, one of the army's most senior legal advisors, gave evidence to the Baha Mousa inquiry … [He] told the inquiry that shortly after the invasion, he had visited an interrogation centre near Basra operated by the army's joint forward intelligence team … He had warned that hooding and the use of stress positions were illegal, but was informed that it was "in accordance with British army doctrine on tactical questioning".[13]

The judgement by Sir William Gage, the judge who led the inquiry, was severe. In terms of chaplaincy he criticised a Roman Catholic chaplain, Fr Peter Madden, who was alleged to have witnessed the brutality of British soldiers. The chaplain was described as a 'poor witness' and Sir William said

> He ought to have intervened immediately, or reported it up the chain of command, but in fact, it seemed he did not have the courage to do either.[14]

Fr Madden has since left the army and become a parish priest. The report led to a discussion in *The Tablet* for several weeks after the publication of the report. Mgr Stephen Alker, the Principal Roman Catholic chaplain for land forces, defended Fr Madden and said the criticism was 'unfair'. He went on, 'the job of a Catholic chaplain is extremely difficult and demanding'.[15] Colonel Nick Mercer, who has since become a Church of England parish priest, wrote to say that he had known chaplains to be sacked for speaking out. Mercer was Command Legal Advisor to the First UK Armoured Division during the Iraq War. He himself had been silenced by the Ministry of Defence at a meeting of the International Committee of the Red Cross, although he had intervened in March 2003 at the start of the Iraq War to prevent brutality at the interrogation of prisoners at the Um Qsar interrogation centre.[16] Mercer gave another interview to the *Guardian* in November, where he was deeply critical of the British Army for a 'cultural resistance to human rights' and a 'moral ambivalence' about how British troops should behave.[17] In a further letter to *The Tablet* he said 'there is an institutional failing at the heart of this which extends even into the realms of the Christian church'.[18] The debate, and the allegations made by Colonel Mercer, showed that the British Army had still not learnt fully the lessons from Northern Ireland, which is a point he himself made in his *Guardian* interview.

A common ethical defence of enhanced interrogation that was made by the Bush administration was that of the lesser evil (French 2011: 158–60).[19] Terrorists,

---

[13]   Ian Cobain, *Guardian*, 1 July 2010.
[14]   *The Tablet*, 17 November 2011.
[15]   *The Tablet*, 24 September 2011.
[16]   *The Tablet*, 30 September 2011.
[17]   *Guardian*, 25 November 2011.
[18]   *The Tablet*, 30 September 2011.
[19]   The whole of chapter 7 (of French 2011) on torture is relevant.

who give information under interrogation, or even torture, remain alive. Their intended victims die a gruesome death. A utilitarian or consequentialist argument will try to weigh the two sides of the argument, including the possibility of mistaken subjects of torture, who are in fact innocent, but are simply associates of the terrorists themselves. The claim by some US intelligence officers five years ago was that the cost and fear of a large terrorist attack (such as 9/11) are so great, that one only requires a small possibility of interrogation yielding important information to prevent acts of terror, to argue that it should be adopted (Gross 2010: 134–5). Against this, French argues that the 'ticking time-bomb' scenario is inherently implausible, because it relies on knowing information which by definition is unlikely to be available (e.g. that one of those detained knows there is a bomb, and where it is) (French 2011: 169–70).

All this leaves the chaplain in a very difficult position. There is evidence that a Muslim chaplain at Guantanamo was effective in preventing enhanced interrogation. In January 2002, Brig. Gen. Michael Lehnert was given orders to prepare the Guantanamo Naval Base for the arrival of first detainees from Afghanistan and Pakistan. Lehnert was very careful to follow the Geneva Convention of 1949 with a special focus on Article 3.1c, which prohibits 'outrages upon personal dignity, in particular, humiliating and degrading treatment'. Lehnert also sent a request to the Pentagon asking that the International Committee of the Red Cross (ICRC) inspect the camp.[20] Lehnert worked closely with a Muslim chaplain. However Donald Rumsfeld, US Secretary of Defence, removed General Lehnert from his post and began a regime of harsh interrogation. According to Jane Mayer (2008), techniques under the next camp commandant Maj. Gen. Michael Dunlavey included 'harsher interrogation techniques', with water boarding, total sensory deprivation, being shackled in stress positions, 'psychological torment that includes religious and sexual humiliation', and the use of dogs to induce the extreme fear that Muslims have of them.[21] James Yee was arrested as a Muslim chaplain at Guantanamo, interrogated, and then restored to full duty. On his resignation from the army he was commended for his exceptionally meritorious service'.[22] He was interviewed by the *St. Louis Beacon* and said:

> I also believe that my role as a chaplain down in Guantanamo, raising concern about the abuse of prisoners that occurred when I was there, was a reason why I was targeted as well. The military is not a good environment where problems can be properly addressed. It's an environment where people are trained to follow orders, to do what you're told, don't question. If you go up against the chain of command, it's known you will lose your career. As a chaplain, though, I was someone who felt very strongly about faith and dedication to

---

[20]   See http://www.class.uidaho.edu/ngier/HumaneTreatment.htm.

[21]   See http://www.class.uidaho.edu/ngier/HumaneTreatment.htm.

[22]   See http://www.stlbeacon.org/issues-politics/nation/8871.

the ethical and moral values our nation upholds and my religion advocates. To me, it took precedence over whether my career would be destroyed. That's why I spoke out.[23]

The dilemma for chaplains remains acute. Gross argues convincingly that insurgency increasingly presents dilemmas of non-combatant immunity, which is met by reliance on intelligence and interrogation. That in turn leads to the enhancement of interrogation. However chaplains remain a moral witness against the crossing of a boundary which involves the innocent, who are also non-combatants.

Risk, Protection and Justice

In an unpublished article, the late Christopher Jones (who was an academic and Church of England chaplain at Oxford University for many years, and then advisor on criminal justice and terrorism to the Mission and Public Affairs Unit of the Church of England for an equally lengthy period) pointed to the increasing preoccupation with risk in contemporary societies. Precisely because standards of public and private health have increased beyond the imagination of past generations during the period since 1945, there is now a desire to eliminate the remaining risk factors. Governments are held to account and criticised for their failure to anticipate and protect against risk. Advances in technology and empirical knowledge lead to a desire to reduce all risks which still remain in human life. Christopher Jones wrote:

> These considerations indicate the inadequacy of viewing risk as a purely objective phenomenon, akin to the weather which is unaffected by our feelings about it (though the traditional view of the weather as beyond our influence has been shattered by the science of climate change). Risk is a feature of human interaction with the world – to adopt Marx's celebrated distinction, both in understanding it and seeking to change it. It is human beings, under particular social and cultural conditions, who apprehend and interpret risk, as well as adopting strategies to manage it. Beliefs about risk therefore reflect our map of reality, our social structures, our understanding of human behaviour and particularly our hopes and fears. (Jones 2006)

This is not to deny that the world (especially in the areas which the British Army has fought in during recent decades) can be a very dangerous place, However the growth of anxiety can become a powerful driver in threatening political situations, with similar potential for generating defensive or aggressive

---

[23]   See http://www.stlbeacon.org/issues-politics/nation/8871.

reactions. It may prevent rational discussion of emotive or difficult subjects, such as child abuse, or it may encourage dramatic or imprudent action in an attempt to dissipate it. The enormous growth of intelligence agencies and of special forces in recent years is in one way the logical and sensible managing of a high-level risk to the very well-being of our society. In another way it is the response of the all-competent, modern, bureaucratic state to those risks which create anxiety and fear in its citizens, and which therefore must be eliminated.

Jones, following Ulrich Beck's famous book *Risk Society* (1992), argues that the management of risk includes both emotional distancing and hostile labelling. Terrorists are described by an inherently pejorative term, in the same way as such terms as 'sex offenders', 'paedophiles', 'lunatics', 'psychopaths', and other such labels are deployed. Jones writes: 'The effect of such language is to create a sense of stigma and distance, which both expresses and maintains anxiety about the danger posed by these groups. Such processes of hostile labelling and emotional distancing are usually accompanied by social and physical distancing' (Jones 2006). Beck points out that the army, like the police, is now seen by society, and especially by politicians, as a protective institution, where protective professions exist whose main function is the assessment and management of risk (Beck 1992). This is not the place for a reflection on the increasing convergence of military and intelligence agencies (as shown for instance by the appointment of General David Petraeus, who was commander of NATO forces in Afghanistan, to be Director of the Central Intelligence Agency in June 2011), although this is very much the theme of Philip Bobbitt's book *Terror and Consent* (2008). What is important to stress is that the management of risk must be in accord with justice. Jones argues that justice is both process and outcome. 'As *process*, justice requires adequate and accurate information, opportunity for argument and testing of assertions, and a careful weighing of conflicting interests. As *outcome*, justice seeks to render to each what is due, to act proportionately, to correct unfair or damaging actions and to safeguard the fundamental interests of every person' (Jones 2006).

The theological interpretation of this is that Christians must resist the implicit distancing which the management of risk entails. Military chaplains are constrained in how they can behave, because they are uniformed persons, subject to the discipline of the British Army. They cannot simply engage in a simplistic manner with the indigenous population, as though they were not part of the military presence in Afghanistan. Nevertheless the theology of the incarnation is about drawing near, both by way of taking risks, and so giving ourselves freely to others, and by way of being risk-bearers, accepting the cost of being faithful to others. Christians worship a God who is the very opposite of being risk-averse, and who embraced the risks both of creation and of the incarnation. The challenge to any chaplaincy involved with security and counter-insurgency is very hard. Jones describes the ministry of Jesus as one who 'in imaginative openness to others … overcomes the alienating effects of fear and anxiety' (Jones 2006). Once again the chaplain is caught between the demands of the institution they serve and the demands of the gospel, and that tension is irreducible. How chaplains resolve that tension remains the burden of this chapter.

Conclusion

The development of British military operations since 1945 shows the growing prominence of terrorism as a feature of military campaigns. It is virtually certain that a conventional war, such as the invasion of Europe in 1944, will not happen again for many decades, if ever. Even the 2003 invasion of Iraq now seems to be no longer the norm for land-based operations. However warfare certainly remains part of the international relations of the United Kingdom. That warfare is usually a form of insurgency. Some (not all) of that insurgency is inspired by religion, and it is often accompanied by terrorism. How the military responds is one issue. How chaplains re-evaluate their ministry in the light of the military response to insurgency and terrorism is much more difficult. The most difficult challenge for a chaplain is when the military fails to live up to its own standards, as seems to have happened in Iraq.

The IRA campaign in the 1970s forced the churches, and military chaplaincy, to be far more morally aware about the dangers of counter-insurgency operations. After 9/11, the debate changes. Terrorism becomes intrinsically involved with religion, so the chaplain has to justify what the role of religion in relation to violence and terror might be. The chaplain remains, as ever, a moral witness against brutality. The Mousa inquiry leaves chaplains with a severe challenge.

The response to insurgency and terrorism will include the use of many specialist units. It also involves the questioning of detainees by intelligence officers through interrogation, and this remains as an issue for chaplains on operations. Military chaplaincy is a very impressive ministry, but when it accompanies counter-insurgency forces, it walks a cliff edge high up in the mountains, where the path is not clear, the danger of a fall is fatal, and the weather is often murky. Raising these issues, as I do, is not to criticise, but rather to admire this ministry, and to stress the need for great care and debate on the future journey. I hope this chapter will have helped inspire that debate to a greater intensity. Someone has to accompany the military along this cliff path, and that is why military chaplaincy will always be needed, in spite of the irreplaceable role of the army legal service, or the support of welfare organisations.

Chapter 5

The Robotisation of War:
An End to Military Virtues?

David Fisher

Two Images of War

In Book Twelve of Homer's *Iliad* two warriors, Sarpedon and Glaucus, Lycian allies of the Trojans, discuss why they should continue fighting the Greeks before the walls of Troy. Sarpedon explains to his friend:

> Man, supposing you and I, escaping this battle,
> would be able to live on forever, ageless, immortal,
> so neither would I myself go on fighting in the foremost
> nor would I urge you into the fighting where men win glory.
> But now, seeing that the spirits of death stand close about us
> in their thousands, no man can turn aside nor escape them,
> let us go and win glory for ourselves, or yield it to others.[1]

Sarpedon's reply has become the classic presentation of the heroic warrior's rationale for war.

Homer's view of war is heroic, but it is not romantic. Homer has an intensely realistic appreciation of the horror and pity of war. His heroes die, screaming in agony, their guts spilling out from their wounds.

War cuts short friendships and family ties. Shortly after Sarpedon's exchange with Glaucus, Sarpedon is brutally struck down by a spear thrown by Patroclus, and calls out in vain for help from his friend. Glaucus is, however, some distance away on the battlefield, having himself been badly wounded by an arrow. Hearing Sarpedon's call, he tears the arrow from his wound and rushes to his friend. He is too late to save him. But, with help from the gods, Glaucus succeeds in retrieving Sarpedon's mangled corpse from the melee and so protects it from further mutilation. Fighting on the battlefield may be glorious. But the glory can be won in excruciating agony and lead to agonising loss.

Homer is acutely conscious of the suffering war brings to innocents far from the battlefield. When cities are sacked all the menfolk are killed and the women and children led away into slavery. This is the fate Hector, the Trojan

---

[1] Homer, *Iliad*, XII, vv 322–8, translated by Lattimore (1961).

champion, bitterly foretells in Book Six of the *Iliad* will befall his beloved wife, Andromache, after the fall of Priam's city 'when some bronze-armoured Achaean leads you off, taking away your day of liberty, in tears'.[2] War for Homer is a savage and pitiless affair.

So why then do the heroes fight? Sarpedon's answer is that they take their place in the front line to win glory by risking death on behalf of their fellows and, in so doing, exhibit the supreme heroic virtue of courage. The ageless and immortal gods cannot win glory in this way precisely because they are immortal. When they fight they do not risk suffering or death. They cannot, therefore, show, nor do they need, courage. Without the risk of death, without the opportunity for courageous self-sacrifice, Sarpedon confides to Glaucus that he himself would not bother to fight. It is the very danger of war that paradoxically impels him to the front line.

Now let us look at a modern warrior at work. He is an airman at an air base deep in the Nevada desert in the United States. He is seated at a computer console where he is staring intently at a computer screen, clutching a joystick. By wiggling the joystick, he is directing a *Predator* Unmanned Aircraft System – a drone – armed with a *Hellfire* anti-tank missile. The drone has been launched from an airbase many thousands of miles away in Afghanistan onto a target just across the border in the Pakistan tribal lands. The target is a house where intelligence, gleaned by Special Forces, has reported that a meeting of Taliban leaders is taking place. When the drone reaches the target, the airman presses a button and a *Hellfire* missile is launched from the drone. The missile destroys the house. The drone's surveillance camera takes photographs of the rubble that is left. This will be later analysed by intelligence experts and collated with other reports to assess the damage caused. The airman's task for the day is now complete. He clocks off and goes home for tea with his wife and children.

This day's work is far from untypical. Armed Predators have been in use in Afghanistan since late 2001, initially from bases in Pakistan to attack terrorist targets in Afghanistan. Drones are now being increasingly used to attack terrorist targets in Pakistan from Afghanistan, including leadership targets. Of the 500 militants killed by drone attacks between the summer of 2008 and May 2010, 14 it is claimed were top tier and 25 mid- to top tier Taliban or Al Qaeda leaders (Entous 2010). *Predator* drones are now being replaced by the more capable *Reaper* system that can fly longer, faster and carry more weapons. Use of drones has grown exponentially from a handful of platforms in 2001 to approximately 1,000 deployed by the US Army in 2010, averaging 25,000 hours per month. RAF drones flew over 1,200 hours per month in 2010 in support of operations in Afghanistan (figures quoted in MoD 2011: paragraphs 403–4). Between 2009 and 2011 the Obama administration authorised at least 239 covert drone strikes by the CIA, more than five times the 44 approved by President Bush (Rodhe 2012).

The airman is not ageless and immortal but, like a Homeric god, his actions are without risk to him. War for him has become like a video game but with the crucial

---

[2]   Homer, *Iliad* VI, vv 454–5, translated by Lattimore (1961).

difference that his actions, unlike a video game, have deadly consequences in the real world. Like a Homeric god, he deals out death from afar with no risk of harm to himself, no grounds for self-sacrifice and no need nor opportunity to display the soldierly virtue of courage. His safe, aseptic world is a far cry from the deadly, blood-bespattered battlefield in which Sarpedon died.

Ethical Challenges from the Modern Battlefield

War has long since ceased to aspire to the heroic model, espoused by Glaucus and Sarpedon. This trend was accentuated by the industrialisation of war in the nineteenth and twentieth centuries. But at least until recently the constraints of the just war tradition have still been considered relevant to war. Even modern battlefields have furnished a field for the exercise of virtues, including the courage of the warrior so central to Sarpedon's vision. But has the nature of war changed so dramatically in the twenty-first century that the just war tradition is now outmoded? Are virtues no longer required on the battlefield?

There is no doubt that the nature of war has changed and is changing. Indeed, the experience of the messy conflicts and civil strife in the Balkans in the 1990s led General Sir Rupert Smith, one of the protagonists of the conflict, famously to declaim, 'For it must never be forgotten: war no longer exists ... We now are engaged, constantly and in many permutations, in war amongst the people' (2005: 403–4). If war no longer exists then it might, indeed, appear that the medieval just war tradition has lost its purchase. The Balkans conflicts heralded a new permutation of wars among the peoples rather than wars between sovereign states. The current war in Afghanistan certainly bears little resemblance to a classic industrial inter-state war of the kind exemplified by the two world wars of the twentieth century.

But it is mistaken to suppose that the 'new wars' will become the new immutable model for warfare. War, as John Keegan once observed (1999: 72), is a protean monster that regularly changes its nature. There is, therefore, no reason to suppose that the latest permutation of war will be its last. In any case, some recent wars still look like old wars (for example the First Gulf War fought between states in self-defence of the beleaguered Kuwait), while some of the 'new wars' bear uncanny resemblances to previous mutations of warfare. For example, the counter-insurgency campaign in Afghanistan bears a striking resemblance to the Malayan Emergency fought in the 1950s – a counter-insurgency campaign, that lasted from 1948 to 1960, that the British Army won.

It is also to misunderstand the nature of the just war tradition to suppose that it was predicated on a particular model of war – industrial, inter-state war – whose decline in popularity might undermine the validity of just war thinking. That tradition, whose origin goes back at least to St Augustine in the fifth century AD, pre-dated industrial war and has already survived many permutations of the protean monster. The just war tradition seeks to impose constraints on the application of military force, in whatever mode it is employed, in order to reduce the suffering that may thereby be caused. It is thus relevant wherever and however military force is employed.

But drones, it may still be insisted, have changed things. With the advent of drones and the so-called robotisation of war, warfare is now so different that the old concepts and categories simply no longer apply. War has transmuted into a video game, changed so radically that ethics just cannot keep up.

The New Ethical Challenge from Drones

So what is so different about drones? Some of the features of drone attacks are noted below:

- They kill both non-combatants and combatants. A New America Foundation report in March 2010 claimed that in the US-led drone attacks in Pakistan one out of three killed by drone attacks was a civilian (Iqbal 2010).
- Drones have enabled a new policy of assassination. Drones are the weapon of choice for implementing the CIA's alleged hit list of Al Qaeda and Taliban leaders. This included the killing of the Al Qaeda leader, Anwar al-Awlaki, a US citizen, in Yemen on 30 September 2011.
- Drones kill people at a distance, with ease and without risk to our own military. The operator is secure in his airbase in Nevada, many thousands of miles away from the military action.
- The drone operator, facing no risk to his own person, neither needs nor can exercise the virtue of courage. The heroic self-sacrifice of the warrior is no longer relevant. Indeed, it may be questioned whether any of the virtues are any longer required.
- Drones, which already operate semi-autonomously, reduce and may one day remove the role of the human agent.

Drones mark a new mode of warfare. They certainly are different. But how different?

The initial controversy over the use of drones arose from the high level of civilian casualties that appeared to result. This stemmed, at least in part, from the fact that the missiles with which drones were equipped, such as the *Hellfire* missile, had originally been introduced as an anti-tank rather than anti-personnel weapon. The ease with which modern weaponry can kill civilians is itself hardly a novel feature, as the city bombing in the Second World War demonstrated. There have also been improvements in the weapons and tactics for the employment of drones, which can be targeted now with much greater accuracy. The ability of drones to stay on station for many hours observing the tactical battlefield can increase the accuracy with which weapon attacks are mounted. Civilian casualties have, it is claimed, significantly reduced in more recent attacks (Entous 2010).

Drones have been used with deadly effect to kill Al Qaeda and Taliban leaders. But drones do not of themselves create a new policy of assassination. Enemy leaders can be killed with guns, witness the killing of Osama Bin Laden on 2 May 2011. Moreover, in so far as the Al Qaeda and Taliban leaders being targeted by drones are those actively posing a threat of harm, for example plotting attacks on innocents, the use of military force against them to prevent such attacks would not necessarily breach the just war requirements that only proportionate force should be used and non-combatant casualties be avoided.

Drones threaten death at a distance. But that too is not new. So did the RAF pilots in the Second World War, as did, on an even larger scale, the operators of inter-continental missiles in the era of nuclear deterrence. The drone operators, moreover, work in conjunction with Special Forces selecting targets for the drones on the ground. Such forces will themselves face the normal dangers of the battlefield and so need the virtues of the warrior, including courage. Nor is the reduction of risk entirely new – the NATO air operations in Kosovo in 1999 were conducted without the loss of a single NATO service person. Such risk reduction is also not in itself a bad thing. Heroic self-sacrifice may be the stuff of epic poems and war movies. But a military commander has a duty to conserve the lives of his own personnel. The maximised slaughter in the trenches of the First World War hardly ennobled warfare nor redounded to the credit of the generals who commanded it.

So perhaps drones are not that different after all? Yet they are surely different. The ethical challenge posed by drones stems less from the factors individually than from their combination and, in particular, from the way that, taken together, they make killing both easy and risk-free. The airman in Nevada can wipe out his target, with no risk to himself, nor even any physical effort – just the flick of a joystick. The worry is, therefore, that the ease and low risk with which death can be dispensed will encourage reckless behaviour by both politicians and the military, whether in initiating military action or in its conduct, deploying excessive force and killing from afar not just legitimate military targets but civilian as well. Drones make killing too easy and cost-free for the operator, just as in a computer game.

So how is such recklessness to be countered? The answer is not by conceding that the drone operator, or the political or military leaders who instruct him, may operate in an ethics-free zone. On the contrary, we need to insist on the crucial importance of ethical constraints, including the crucial importance of both the just war principles of proportion and discrimination. We need to ensure that the force used is both proportionate to the good to be achieved and that non-combatant casualties are minimised. The very ease with which the drone operator can breach these principles underlines their importance in constraining his behaviour.

The drone operator will need, moreover, not just to be taught in a classroom the just war principles imposing ethical restraint. He will also need to be trained, by precept, practice and personal example, in their daily application, so that ethical restraint becomes, for him, second nature, just as are the drills with which he wields his conventional weapons. He will need to acquire the habits of thought, feeling and action – in other words the virtues – that will enable him so to act, even amidst the many temptations to err. Just as the technology makes it easier for him to act wrongly, so will it be ever more important for him to have learnt the habits and skills – the virtues – to enable him to act rightly. In such ethical training modern technology, including video games and computer-simulated exercises, can be employed to good effect, so using technology to counter the ill-effects of technology.

So what virtues will the drone operator require? We suggested earlier that in the safe, aseptic world in which he operates with no risk to himself of physical injury or death, he may no longer require courage. But is that so?

Courage is the virtue we need to enable us to persevere in the face of difficulty or danger, not allowing fear to obscure our judgement of what needs to be done. Where the fear is of physical injury or death, it is called physical courage, which is the virtue exhibited by the warrior on the battlefield. The drone operator, operating without physical risk to him- or herself, may, indeed, not need the warrior's virtue of physical courage.

But there is another variant of courage sometimes called moral courage. This is the virtue needed to enable us to stick to our moral principles and to challenge unacceptable behaviour, even when subject to pressure, threats or abuse urging us to do otherwise. The fear to be overcome may not be of physical injury but of other harmful consequences stemming from such threats, although, in the extreme, this too may involve physical injury. Disobeying Hitler's orders could, after all, lead to death by beheading. Moral courage is an important virtue. To counteract the ease with which the drone operator can dispense death, he may have particular need of such courage to enable him to take the right decisions, despite the countervailing pressures and temptations to recklessness. Moral courage may be needed to ensure he targets only combatants and only with a proportionate application of force.

Indeed, it is arguable that, in view of the nature of current warfare where wars are undertaken more from choice than necessity and often driven at least, in part, by humanitarian motives, it is not just drone operators but our military more generally and, indeed, our political leaders, who need to be strongly encouraged to develop the virtue of moral courage so that they will challenge unacceptable behaviour. For, as has been demonstrated by the cases in 2003/4 of ill-treatment of detainees in Iraq – both by US soldiers at Abu Ghraib and British soldiers in Basra – the bad behaviour of a few soldiers can risk undermining the overall strategic – humanitarian – objectives of a campaign.

Such moral courage was critically lacking in the officers, including the medical staff and padre, who failed to do anything to stop the savage beatings and other abuse by British soldiers that took place in Basra on 14–16 September 2003. This abuse led to the death of Baha Mousa and serious injuries to eight other Iraqi civilian detainees held in British Army custody. Sir William Gage, who chaired the public inquiry into these events, expressed 'concern about the lack of discipline and lack of moral courage to report abuse within 1 QLR (Queen's Lancashire

Regiment)' (Gage 2011: vol. III, Summary of Findings, para. 203). He criticised the padre who 'must have seen the shocking condition of the detainees, and the deteriorating state of the TDF (Temporary Detention Facility). He ought to have intervened immediately, or reported it up the chain of command but, in fact, it seems he did not have the courage to do either' (Gage 2011: 112). One of the key recommendations of the Gage report is, therefore, that there is a need to devise better ways to teach moral courage to the military (Gage 2011: vol. III, pt. XVII, Recommendations, Recommendation 58).

The exercise of moral courage may at times appear to conflict with another virtue, in which soldiers are also rightly inculcated, that of loyalty to their comrades. Loyalty is a valuable quality for soldiers in wartime. It is the virtue that impels a soldier to return to the battlefield to rescue a comrade. But soldiers may also feel discouraged from challenging unacceptable behaviour as a result of loyalty to close comrades. This is, however, to misconstrue the nature and scope of the virtue of loyalty, which needs to be properly directed and not too narrowly focused that it becomes misplaced. This is what happened in the case of Baha Mousa where soldiers lied to the investigators to protect their immediate colleagues from prosecution. Their misplaced loyalty, and the 'wall of silence' from potential witnesses which it prompted, was rightly criticised by the British Army's own report into the incidents (MoD 2008: 12). Such loyalty was misplaced because it was too narrowly focused. The soldiers ignored the wider interests of the regiment and army in which they served and of the society in whose service they were employed, whose reputation they besmirched by their mendacity.

The drone operator will, therefore, need moral courage and will need to ensure its exercise is not impeded by loyalty to his comrades, a virtue he will properly cultivate but without allowing it to become too narrowly focused. In the exercise of his awesome responsibilities, he will also need the other cardinal virtues of justice, self-control and practical wisdom. He will need to learn the virtue of justice or respect for others, including respect for those who may be his enemies; and the virtue of self-control, so that he is not deflected by passion or emotion from discerning what is to be done and acting accordingly. Above all, he will need the virtue of practical wisdom – 'a habit of sound judgement about practical situations'[3] whose guidance will be crucial to enable him, amid the pressures of conflict and with time running out, to make the right decision in wielding the deadly force with which he is entrusted by society.

So the present generation drone operator will still need the virtues. Indeed, just war thinking and the virtuous habits needed to ensure their daily application on the battlefield, far from being outmoded in the era of drones, have become ever more necessary. This reflects, moreover, our wider experience of counter-insurgency operations in Afghanistan and elsewhere. For it has been an important lesson of

---

[3]   Geach (1977: 160). For a fuller discussion of the importance of virtues in the modern battlefield see Fisher (2011: esp. ch. 6). Some of the differences between moral and physical courage are discussed in Olsthoorn (2007).

the new counter-insurgency doctrine that ethical constraints, in particular, the protection of civilians, are a key to the success of operations (US Army and Marine Corps 2007). But what will happen as drones become ever more autonomous?

Future Drone Developments

The present generation of drones are only semi-autonomous systems, still subject to human control. Man is still firmly in the loop. They are, in the jargon, automated rather than autonomous systems. An automated system is defined as 'one that, in response to inputs from one or more sensors is programmed logically to follow a pre-defined set of rules in order to provide an outcome'. An autonomous system is, by contrast, one that 'is capable of deciding a course of action, from a number of alternatives, without depending on human oversight and control' (MoD 2011: 2–3). What if it were possible to produce a fully autonomous system, performing its own operations, with little, or even, at the extreme, no human supervision or control?

There are degrees of autonomy. The Israeli *Harpy* drone, for example, attacks any hostile radar activated within its pre-defined patrol area, the drone comparing the signal emitted to its library of pre-designated hostile emitters. Once launched, the drone carries out its radar-destroying activities without any further human intervention. The automated *Harpy* has thus a degree of autonomy. But its autonomous activities are still tightly circumscribed by a human controller who sets the rules which the drone is following.

The search is, however, now on for a fully autonomous battlefield system, with large sums of money being lavished on the quest. It is claimed that such systems will arrive in 'more than 5 years and less than 15 years' (MoD 2011: 5–4). It may, however, be open to doubt, whatever sums of money are expended, whether a truly autonomous system will ever be developed. For that would require a machine that thinks and, crucially, 'decides' for itself without any human input or control. The MoD Joint Doctrine Note that predicted the arrival of such systems in 15 years also wisely counselled that, while many systems may be called autonomous, 'as long as it can be shown that the system logically follows a set of rules or instructions and is not capable of human levels of situation awareness, then they should be considered automated' (MoD 2011: 2–4).

But in that sense it is difficult to conceive of any machine that would meet the test of full autonomy. For, a robotic system, however smart it may be, will necessarily have been designed and programmed by a human being and will be logically following a set of human-drafted instructions. In so far as it is still operating according to a programme or set of logical rules designed by a human being, it will still, in that sense, be an automated rather than a fully autonomous system.

Absolute autonomy may thus be a chimera. The search for a truly autonomous system may prove rather lengthier than is usually supposed, based as it is on a measure of conceptual confusion. Automated systems will, however, undoubtedly become smarter and the extent to which they can operate independently without requiring further human input will increase. In simple terms, the more autonomy the machine has the less control will be exercised by a human agent. Does such reduction or loss of human control matter morally? Machines do not get angry, nor do they feel fear, so perhaps entrusting them to operate freely on the battlefield would represent a moral gain.

But would it? Could a machine act as a moral agent on the battlefield? The two key ethical principles that need to be applied are those of non-combatant immunity and proportion. The application of both these principles on a confusing and fast-shifting battlefield requires fine discriminatory judgements often made in seconds. A robotic system might be programmed to distinguish between targets wearing uniform and those not. But application of the principle of non-combatant immunity requires distinguishing not just combatants from non-combatants but soldiers that are combatants from those that are *hors de combat* (for example, soldiers, still wearing uniform, who have surrendered) and are hence no longer legitimate targets.

The necessary moral appraisal also requires application of the principle of proportion to judge whether the force used is proportionate to the good to be achieved. Making such distinctions rapidly on a fast-moving battlefield, as NATO air operations in Libya in 2011 demonstrated, is difficult even for a human operator. It is very difficult to see how a robotic system could be programmed to make such fine ethical judgements.

It is also difficult to conceive of a robot exercising the virtues, which, we suggested earlier, a drone operator will require in order to enable him to act morally. Lacking emotions, the robot would certainly have no need of virtues such as physical courage or self-control. But nor is it clear that it makes sense to suppose a robot could exhibit moral courage – sticking to moral principles despite countervailing pressures – or practical wisdom, the judicious discernment of which moral principle applies to which practical situation. Moral rules provide us with the necessary guidelines while the virtues equip us with the requisite skills to enable us to flourish as humans. The relevance of such moral concepts to robots that lack humanity would seem questionable.

But if a robot cannot make ethical judgements and there is no human agent in the loop able to do so, the battlefield use of such weapons would be inherently indiscriminate and disproportionate, and hence immoral. The human agent who initiated the use of such systems would be guilty of morally culpable recklessness, with the less control exercised by humans, the greater the moral opprobrium. Such robotic systems would have a similar moral dubiety to anti-personnel landmines banned under the 1997 Ottawa Treaty. The concern with anti-personnel mines is that, once laid, they are no longer under human control, so posing an indiscriminate and disproportionate threat to anyone, including a child, who encounters them. Future robotic systems, in so far as they reduce human control over their use, would present similar moral problems.

Conclusion

The notion that the changing nature of war renders ethics outmoded is based on a false view of the nature of war. But it also crucially reflects a false view of the nature of just war thinking. Just war constraints are not tied to a particular model of warfare. They are about constraining the use of force, in whatever mode and by whatever means it is employed, to reduce the human suffering involved. The advent of drones and, even more their possible future evolution into more autonomous systems, far from outdating such ethical constraints, has rendered them ever more necessary both to constrain present use and to guide future development and deployment.

PART III
Chaplains and their Churches

The British Churches and their Chaplains: Standing Back to Back and Walking in Opposite Directions

Peter Howson

Churches' Ambivalence towards Chaplains

In 2004, the Methodist Church agreed to collaborate with the United Reformed Church in looking at the ethics of war. A joint working party was set up that led to the report, *Peacemaking: A Christian Vocation* (2006). The group was unusual among such consultations, in that it included a chaplain amongst its members, in this case the Revd Michael Parker, a Methodist army chaplain. An appendix to the report was entitled, 'What is war like? A chaplain's experience' (2006: 73). Rather than containing the view of a single chaplain, however, it was instead a collection of quotes from a number of sources, not all identified or necessarily by chaplains. The report noted its gratitude to Mr Parker for his insights but neither came to any conclusions as to how a chaplain might function as the directly authorised representative of a church on the battlefield, nor of how a church might use the insights gained by a chaplain. How did these two churches see the vocation of an army chaplain as part of gospel imperative of making peace? This was not dealt with in the report. As a result the chaplains from those churches remain uncertain about how their church views them when they are serving in Afghanistan.

This contemporary unwillingness by the churches to engage meaningfully with military chaplains is neither a recent phenomenon, nor one restricted to the Britain. Following a long and distinguished career as a chaplain in the US Navy, from the Second World War to the mid-1970s, Hutcheson commented:

> The chaplains, for their part, have much to offer the church at large. There are concerns for the whole church to which their experience would bring a special dimension: church-state relations; war, peace, and amnesty issues; civil religion; inter-racial ministries; ecumenical relationships; young adult concerns. Yet active duty chaplains are seldom invited to participate in church conventions or commissions dealing with these issues, or in the governing structures of their own denominations, to which they could indeed bring insights. (1975: 211)

His analysis was that much had changed in the United States as a result of the Vietnam War. For him the Second World War had been an era of close co-operation between churches and the chaplaincy. As I have argued elsewhere, the questioning of the contribution that chaplains made to the life of the church had begun as early as the 1950s (Howson 2006: 91). Whilst most, such as Burchard (1953), a collection of essays edited by Harvey Cox (1971) and Abercrombie (1977) focused on what had happened in the United States, Zahn in his study of Royal Air Force chaplains (1969), and Wilkinson in an article in *Theology* (1981) considered the British experience. These works were noted for a generally unfavourable attitude towards military chaplains. Some of this lay behind what has become the most accessible work on modern British army chaplaincy. Louden (1996) had the advantage of having served as an army chaplain when he wrote *Chaplains in Conflict*. He concluded of the work of the Royal Army Chaplains' Department (RAChD):

> The official goal of the RAChD – to make and sustain Christians – though its manifest function has been seen at the micro level to have been subsumed into a latent function of providing practical support for the specifically military objective of the host organisation. (Louden 1996: 120)

There has been something of a reaction to these views. In his important and lengthy history of the work of British army chaplains prior to the Korean War, Snape commented that the facts had been obscured by what he referred to as 'a mass of narrow and partisan writing on the subject' (Snape 2008: 362). In the conclusion of his book he argued that he had comprehensively demonstrated that the historical facts did not bear out any of the eight paradoxes identified by Wilkinson in his *Theology* article of 1981 (Snape 2008: 362–3). Zahn's work on RAF chaplains had already been examined critically from a theological perspective in an, as yet, unpublished thesis (Coleman 1994).

Whilst Snape, in his impressive body of work (2005a, 2005b, 2008) has examined both the religious experience of British soldiers, and the work of army chaplains, he only covered the period to the start of the Cold War. Little has been published to date about the relationship of chaplaincy and the churches that has existed over the last 60 years. This period is important because it covers, as Brown has suggested (2001), a time of rapid decline in Christian practice within Britain. This was to have subtle effects on the place of chaplaincy. There were also other forces at work that affected the way the churches saw military chaplaincy. Most obvious was the change in attitudes to the ethics of war brought about by the existence of nuclear weapons. It was these weapons of mass destruction, and the debates over their use, that were to lead to uncertainty about, and in some cases direct opposition to, the existence of military chaplains from within the British churches.

For many of the major British churches the recognition of the casualties and damage that would result from the use of nuclear weapons resulted in regular calls for their abolition. However such resolutions also needed to recognise that nuclear weapons existed, and that they were a part of a British defence policy that was carried out by the armed services of which the chaplains, who remained representatives of the churches, were a part. Failure to fully recognise this could lead, as with the General Assembly of the Church of Scotland of 1989, to the passing of two apparently contradictory deliverances on the same day. Main noted these in an article in the *Journal of the Royal Army Chaplains' Department* that surveyed attitudes to nuclear weapons within that Church (1992: 24). In the first it declared that:

> The church with increasing emphasis and urgency over the years declared its abhorrence of nuclear weapons and its perception that not only the use of them but possession and threat to use them are incompatible with the Word of God and with Christian revelation.

At the same time the second deliverance stated that:

> The General Assembly recognises the pastoral needs of those servicemen, servicewomen and civilians serving with the nuclear weapons programme.

The issue of how ministers who belonged to a Kirk that was opposed to nuclear weapons could serve as chaplains in armed forces that retained nuclear weapons reappeared in the report of the Committee on HM Chaplains to the 2002 General Assembly (Church of Scotland 2002). The presence of both US and British nuclear submarine facilities in the Clyde basin had, for many years, been a cause for complaint by some within the Church of Scotland. Since the end of the Cold War did not see the removal of all the nuclear submarines from Scotland the subject continued to appear on the agenda of the General Assembly.

As a background to the report there was a long and closely argued statement entitled, 'Delineating the Prophetic Voice of Chaplains to the Forces'. The report was not solely about army chaplaincy, indeed it was prompted by a demonstration in February 2001 at Faslane Naval Base, in which the then Moderator of the General Assembly had taken part. It did, though, contain references to army chaplaincy in support of its arguments. Its conclusions were also applicable to all military chaplaincy. It paid only passing reference to the kind of operations in Bosnia, Rwanda, Sierra Leone and elsewhere that had engaged the attention of the British Army since the end of the Cold War. It concentrated on a larger picture.

The report concluded with a restatement of the need, if it was to be 'authentic', for chaplaincy to continue to strive to be what it described as 'prophetic'. It was accepted that it was necessary for the chaplain who wanted to act in such a way to be responsible and to accept certain constraints on his freedom to act but at the same time the prophetic voice had to be what was described as 'genuine'. This required it to be both constructive and forward looking rather than merely keeping a tally of moral failures. The report concluded:

We suggest that retention of such a voice is crucial for the moral integrity of military chaplains, if they are not to reduce themselves to being merely the guardians of other peoples' protocols, failing thereby to be true representatives of their sending Churches and their faith communities. (Church of Scotland 2002: 6)

What was missing was any indication as to whether the Committee saw themselves as the body that was responsible for ensuring that the role they had outlined was fulfilled by Church of Scotland chaplains in the army. What the Kirk would be required to do if the chaplains had merely become guardians of other peoples' protocols was not discussed. The statement was also one-sided. It ignored the possibility that chaplains might be 'prophetic' within their own church in challenging the functional pacifism that had become so dominant.

This ambivalence within the Church of Scotland had also surfaced in its attitude to chaplains during both of the Gulf Wars. That of 1991 occasioned a sharp rebuke to the Church from its Committee on Chaplains to HM Forces. In its report to the General Assembly of 1991 it commented:

It remains a matter of regret to our chaplains and to our Committee that the broader scope of theological discussion in which they, and many others participated, did not appear to be reflected in the statements made between August 1990 and January 1991, which purported to reflect the mind of the Church. While chaplains and the Committee appreciated the statements of support that were made on the resumption of hostilities in January 1991, the sense of irritation that was experienced in the preceding five months was not so easily remedied. Whether it was intended or not, and the Committee is persuaded that it was not so intended, our chaplains were asked to prepare for a task that none wished to do, and asked to prepare dependent wives, husbands, children and parents in the light of statements that appeared to deny them the support of the Church … When it is widely stated that, "The Christians in Scotland are united in opposition to this war", and when it is stated that the war is both immoral and obscene, it is hard to escape the conclusion that your Church is suggesting that it is not supportive of you insofar as you are engaged in what is immoral and obscene. (Church of Scotland 1991: 308)

These were strong words from a Committee that had not previously been noted for speaking out on behalf of chaplains.

A similar tension had been visible for some time in the Methodist Church. Not everyone within Methodism was happy with the official policy of the Church on chaplains to the army. At the 1973 Conference, the Reverend Douglas Wollen, at that time a minister in the Poplar Mission Circuit, and a noted pacifist, raised two questions about the status of chaplains. As often happened, they were referred for an answer to be produced the following year. The Agenda for the 1974 Conference recorded the questions that had been asked:

The Reverend Douglas Wollen asked certain questions regarding chaplains.

> Their position as ministers who were also part of the military organisations, and, whether the pastoral care of men and women in the Forces could be separated from membership of the Armed Forces and done by civilian ministers working on a whole-time basis. (Methodist Church 1974: 201)

Discussions between a group of chaplains and members of the Methodist Peace Fellowship, chaired by the Reverend George Sails, the Secretary of the newly created Home Mission Division, that part of the Church with responsibility for military chaplains, were then convened in order to help the Conference frame a reply. Much of the discussion centred on the continuing debate about the use of nuclear weapons. Some general points were made. For the chaplains, the key issue was that of identification with those to whom they ministered. They were seen to be under the same discipline as the rest of the army. Nobody seemed to point out that, as non-combatants, they were far from being fully under the same discipline. Nor was any attempt made to either ask or answer the question as to what were appropriate orders for an Anglican Chaplain General to give to a Methodist chaplain to carry out his ministry. Important to the army chaplains was the issue of practicality. To minister effectively made it a necessity for them to be commissioned into the RAChD. Needless to say there was no general agreement. As the report commented:

> Some Christian pacifists were appalled that Christian ministers should wear the uniform of national armed forces. (Methodist Church 1974: 201)

But no serious splits took place within the Methodist Church as a result of these different positions. The report of the meetings concluded:

> All who shared in the discussions found that it proved a valuable exchange of ideas, and opportunity for sharing experience, and had revealed a depth of fellowship as brethren that surmounted the divisive nature of deeply held convictions. (Methodist Church 1974: 201)

It was acknowledged that it was not a simple matter. It was also accepted that the chaplains were not unaware of the nature of their position. As the report commented:

> Discussions on Chaplains in the situation of nuclear war made it clear that they were as well aware of the moral problems involved as any other thinking Christian person. They have wrestled with the problem and though their conclusion is not the same as that of members of the Methodist Peace Fellowship it is a considered and reasonable judgement. (Methodist Church 1974: 200)

Successive Secretaries of the Forces' Board did not engage in the discussions at later Conferences on motions about defence matters.

The continued opposition that chaplains faced from some parts of the Methodist Church was also well illustrated by the stance taken by the Reverend Dr Kenneth Greet, the Secretary of the Methodist Conference between 1971 and 1983. As a full-time administrator he had considerable influence within Methodism, and for many was its unofficial spokesperson. As Thompson Brake has shown, Greet, a well-known pacifist, had been given the additional honour of becoming the President of the Methodist Conference in 1980 (Thompson Brake 1984: 454). He used his position to draw attention to the threat that nuclear weapons posed to the world. Having completed his year as President he then became, in early 1982, the Moderator of the Free Church Federal Council. His inauguration coincided with the Falklands War and he took the opportunity to make clear his pacifist views about the way the crisis was handled. By chance, the 1982 Methodist Conference met in Plymouth in late June, soon after the fighting had finished. Thompson Brake described what happened:

> It was no surprise to observers of the Methodist Conference that it found time to set apart for a debate on the Falklands crisis, even though by this time the fighting had ceased. The Methodist Conference can scarcely ever refrain from passing resolutions on public issues. One thing which emerged during the bloody conflict in the Falklands was just how many "experts" there were ... This was particularly true of the self-styled spokesmen for the churches who knew no more about the situation than the average newspaper reader. (Thompson Brake 1984: 454)

He noted in particular the following, which he described as 'a cynical statement made to the Conference by Dr Greet':

> Exocet missiles have never been so popular as they are today – the sales of them will boom in the coming months. It is a victory of militarism – the thesis that international questions of the comparatively trifling kind that this war was about can somehow be settled in the name of justice by armed conflict. When the task force sailed to the Falklands the clock was turned back 50 years. (Thompson Brake 1984: 455, quoting the *Guardian* of 1 July 1982)

Against the background of such rhetoric it was no surprise that chaplains chose not to enter into the debate.

At one point, in the 1980s, a vigorous debate took place within the Roman Catholic community. It almost seemed possible that a radical change could have taken place in the way the Roman Catholic Church organised its chaplains. The 1985 National Conference of Priests in England and Wales saw a motion passed that requested a review of military chaplaincy. Writing in *The Times* the religious affairs correspondent, Clifford Longley, headed his weekly article, 'Status of

Armed Forces Chaplains may be Reviewed by Roman Catholic Bishops'. He summarised the debate thus:

> A call for the review of the status of Roman Catholic chaplains in the Armed Forces, particularly whether they should hold the Queen's Commission as officers, was requested by the National Conference of Priests at its meeting in Newman College, Birmingham, last week.
>
> They asked the Roman Catholic Bishops' Conference of England Wales to undertake this review, and the Catholic Bishop-in-Ordinary to the Forces, the Right Rev Francis Walmesley, said at the meeting that he would not oppose such a request.
>
> He clearly had strong misgivings, however. As Bishop he is not himself on the books of the Ministry of Defence. (Longley 1985b)

Longley noted that a previous resolution had recognised the right of those serving in the forces to enjoy pastoral care. The debate was, as he saw it, about how the status of chaplains, together with preaching and celebrating the sacraments, should be organised in the context of the army and the other forces. The mood of the Conference was that it should at least consider the possibility of what Longley described as 'the civilianisation of the forces' chaplaincy services'.

The Conference had taken place at a time of intense national discussion about the ethics of nuclear weapons. It had also been addressed by Monsignor Bruce Kent, the then General Secretary of the Campaign for Nuclear Disarmament. He had challenged the Roman Catholic Church in what he saw as its support for the state as against any advocacy of non-violence. He had told the Conference he believed that the bishops had been misled by government propaganda and, as a result, had not opposed the introduction of cruise missiles. Longley (1985a) believed that the majority of priests were not unilateralists. The 'review' was a way of dealing with what otherwise might have become a serious issue. Nothing further was heard of the proposal.

In other parts of the world challenges to military chaplaincy were to come from other directions. As van Niekerk has shown (2002: 349), it was also in 1985 that the first of what was to become a series of questions about the theological understanding of Dutch Reformed Church participation in chaplaincy within the South African Defence Forces appeared. The debate, which was to continue for much of the next five years, had nothing to do with the morality of weapons of mass destruction. The most serious attack on the chaplaincy came in 1990, when two former National Service Chaplains, the Revds Marious Maree and Lourens Erasmus, wrote an article that appeared in the Dutch Reformed Church magazine, *Kerkbode*, of 22 June 1990. Van Niekerk summarised their criticisms as:

A chaplain could do wonderful work and feel free to preach his prophetic message in a war situation, but his military status hindered the defusing of increased tension in South African society. In the present system the chaplain found himself in a paradoxical position, namely in a situation of violence where he was proclaiming a message of radical reconciliation. They felt that the inclusion of chaplains in task forces during anti-insurgency operations added to the chaplain's inability to act as an impartial peacemaker in the conflict situation. (van Niekerk 2002: 352)

There followed a debate in the following issues of *Kerkbode* with the Major General Naude, the Chaplain General of the South African Defence Forces, defending the position of the serving chaplains. It was only with the end of the apartheid regime, and the change of administration in South Africa, that the debate came to an end. Although chaplaincy existed during both world wars it was only after 1945 that it had been placed on a firm footing within the South African military. In his history of South African military chaplaincy van Niekerk has shown (2002) that despite its relatively short history the chaplaincy has made considerable efforts to define both the role of a chaplain and the relationship with the churches.

As a result of the war in Vietnam, there was considerable criticism of chaplaincy in the US Army during the 1960s and 1970s. The main challenge to its continued existence as a uniformed state-sponsored organisation came, however, from another direction. In the volume of the history of the US Army Chaplain Corps that covers the years 1975 to 1995, a section is entitled 'The Constitutional Challenge' (Brinsfield 1997: 120–31). What started as an academic exercise by two students at Harvard Law School soon progressed into a lawsuit. The first motion was filed in a District Court in New York on 23 November 1979. The students, by now qualified lawyers, continued their case through a series of appeals until 31 January 1986 when, with costs mounting, they agreed to drop the case, but on the understanding that they did so '*with prejudice*'. The central argument of their case was that by funding military chaplaincy the US government was violating the First Amendment of the US Constitution. The fundamental principle in that Amendment was that the Congress was not to make any law respecting the establishment of religion. Crucially it also banned the Congress from prohibiting the free exercise of religion. The courts were willing to accept the motion as valid but, to the relief of the Chaplain Corps, ruled that Congress was acting properly by providing military chaplains since these ensured that members of the military community would have the opportunity to exercise their right to religious freedom. One of the conclusions that helped decide in favour of a uniformed chaplaincy was:

the inability of the Wisconsin Evangelical Lutheran Synod to provide effective ministry during the Vietnam War. Civilian ministry, as envisioned by the plaintiff, would be even further negated without the substantive military logistical and transportational support provided by the Army for religious support to soldiers. (Brinsfield 1997: 128)

The outcome of the case led to the recognition that if the chaplaincy was to survive further legal challenges it had to ensure whatever it did could be justified as contributing to the free exercise of religion within the military family. As a result the Chaplain Corps looked at all its programmes and activities to ensure that they conformed to this principle.

Both the South African and American experiences showed that a serious external challenge to army chaplaincy resulted in thought being given to both the nature of the chaplain's role and also how the military chaplaincy related to the civilian churches. The British experience has lacked any such major discussion. Evidence from seminars in the Master in Chaplaincy Studies at Cardiff has shown that a number of service chaplains have been uncertain as to who they represent, and what their role should be in situations such as Afghanistan. Over the last 60 years two movements, the first within the churches and the second in the army, have been taking place in opposite directions leading to this position of uncertainty among chaplains serving in the complex ethical scenarios of twenty-first century conflict.

As has already been shown there has been a tendency for many within the hierarchies of British churches to display less than full support for chaplaincy. This is in part due to the fact that many, like their American counterparts, had become what may best be described as 'functional pacifists'. At least one American commentator on Christian ideas about the morality of warfare (Johnson 1999) blamed the American churches' over-concentration on nuclear weapons, in terms which could equally apply to those in Britain, for their failure to recognise what else was happening in the world. Referring to pastoral letters issued by the American Catholic Bishops in 1983 under the title, 'The Challenge of Peace', and by the United Methodist Church in 1986 as, 'In Defense of Creation', Johnson noted:

> The analysis of these pastoral letters, as well as most of the response they generated, paid no attention to the empirical reality that other sorts of conflict, not involving nuclear weapons and not directly involving the superpowers, had in fact become the characteristic of "modern war". Thus the two pastoral letters, along with much of the other ethical analysis during the 1980s, turned away from the particularly difficult problems posed by insurgency, covert activity, civil war, and ideologically charged conflict that held central place in policy planning for low-intensity conflict. (Johnson 1999: 12)

This over-concentration on the issue of nuclear morality led to the churches' apparent failure to recognise the existence of other situations required the application of moral thinking to warfare. This was to have important consequences during the 1990s.

Johnson argued that one such outcome was the development of a belief that war was of its essence so evil that the only legitimate position that a Christian could take was to oppose it in all its manifestations. As he commented:

> How is it possible to "be peaceful in warring"? For much of contemporary thought this is an oxymoron: peace can have nothing to do with the violence of war. Such dichotomization of the two concepts follows both from a pacific aversion to all violence as evil and, ironically from the diametrically opposite position that the conduct of war ought to know no limits except those of necessity. (Johnson 1999: 211)

The apparent inability of British churches to grasp what was happening when, during the 1990s, states began to 'fail', meant that they had little to offer their chaplains who from Bosnia, to Sierra Leone, to Afghanistan found themselves deployed to such situations. Equally the churches appeared to lack any mechanism to use the experience of the chaplains to help understand this new world order.

Church Oversight of Chaplaincy

One of the reasons for this has been that the churches have allowed not only their own internal chaplaincy networks to be sidelined but have also failed to maintain their collective oversight of army chaplaincy. Despite the unilateral act of the army that had created an Army Chaplains' Department in 1796, the churches had, from the start, believed that it was with the civilian officials rather than military officers that they dealt on matters of policy. This had come to be formalised during the First World War by the creation of an Inter-denominational Advisory Committee on Army Chaplaincy Services (IAC). Made up of representatives of each of what became known as the 'sending churches', it was chaired by the Permanent Under Secretary at the War Office. The Chaplain General was not a member and only attended by invitation. As recently as the early 1960s it was involved in discussions as to where the administration of army chaplains should lie when the War Office was abolished. Elsewhere (Howson 2006: ch. 6), I have shown that although it became accepted that the Adjutant General might *manage* army chaplains they reported to the 2nd Permanent Under Secretary in the new Ministry of Defence. It was for that reason that, unlike the position in the other two services, the Chaplain General's Department in the War Office became, in 1964, Ministry of Defence (Chaplains (Army)). Despite this success the Advisory Committee failed to continue to meet.

During the 1950s, the IAC had met at least annually. It continued to do so until 1963, when it held its 93rd meeting on 21 January. The file (Minutes of the IAC TNA WO 32/14820) then notes that further meetings were held 'in December

1964 and on 10 May 1968, but that no records were available'. In a letter from the Adjutant General (D/AG 6 August 2004), I was informed that this was then the last meeting of the IAC. The apparent failure to meet again may have reflected the more settled nature of the army, and the apparent lack of matters to discuss. At the same time, it is possible that subsequent Chaplains General preferred not to work through a formal committee structure, relying on informal briefings to Church representatives instead. The existence of such briefings was confirmed in the letter from the Adjutant General's Secretariat referred to above. It should be noted that these meetings, which began in 1987, were both informal and without record. This course of action left the churches, and the RAChD as their representative, poorly placed to come to a common mind on the nature and shape of army chaplaincy. It also meant the loss of a common memory to which reference could be made.

Reviewing the 'Spiritual Needs' of the Army

At the same time as the influence of the churches over army chaplaincy was waning, in the second change that of the army was beginning to increase. If the 1990s, with the upheaval brought about by the end of the Cold War, was a period where everything was considered for review, it is no surprise that consideration should be given to army chaplaincy. What was surprising were the methods used and the conclusions that were reached. After a failed attempt in the early 1990s to subsume the RAChD in to the new Adjutant General's Corps, in 1998 the Adjutant General announced a study into the 'Spiritual Needs' of the army. The task of compiling the report was given to Brigadier Ian McGill. The aim was:

> To state the need for spiritual values in the Army (collectively and individually) and how these values may be fostered. (McGill 1999: para. 5)

Ostensibly, this was not a report about the Royal Army Chaplains' Department. However, having decided that the army had spiritual values, the report then assumed that it was the role of the chaplains to inculcate them. Such a supposition meant that it inevitably became a review of the RAChD. The values that McGill described were not seen as mere abstracts. The opening paragraph of the report made it clear that, 'The Army needs to instil values which underlie its military ethos in its officers and soldiers during training and nurture these values throughout their service' (para. 1).[1] In its introduction the report recognised that, 'the British Army's values, standards and ethos are founded on our Christian history, culture and civilisation' (para. 3). This meant, amongst other things, that it needed to 'encourage a structured development of the RAChD, together with a better means of linking the RAChD's contribution to the Army overall, in conjunction with

---

[1] This and the following quotations are taken from McGill (1999).

the help provided by welfare agencies' (para. 3(c)). The chaplains were seen as existing to provide a function that would meet the needs of the army.

The tone was set in the introductory chapter. There was an underlying assumption that the army could define the task for the RAChD. The report noted the importance of the task that it had been set by commenting:

> The last time there was a formal attempt to address chaplaincy in the Army was the Creedy Report in 1920, which focused exclusively on the RAChD in the light of lessons from the First World War. Since Creedy there have been periodic adjustments in the RAChD's strength, in line with the fluctuating size of the Army, but no overall analysis of its worth nor a serious attempt to reconcile chaplaincy resources to commitments. (Para. 1)

The reference appeared rather more apposite to the Report into the RAChD published in 1923 (War Office 1923), rather than to the earlier Creedy Report (War Office 1920). The lack of detailed historical analysis was further demonstrated by McGill's choice of examples of good chaplaincy practice. Recognising that chaplains might have concerns about a role in 'oiling the wheels of combat effectiveness', McGill commented:

> But perhaps the role models provided by the Reverends Studdert-Kennedy and Hardy [*sic*] during the First World War are the clearest examples of the worth and value of a chaplain. (Para. 59)

Their importance was seen in the way in which they identified with the men to whom they were chaplains, principally by sharing their risks in the front line. For McGill, the value of such identification seemed to be the way it inspired the soldiers to be more effective. There was no realisation that these examples of best practice by chaplains were from a different era. They came from a time when the place of the church in society was more significant. They referred to chaplains who ministered to soldiers recruited for a war that had been fought with a large number of casualties. They also, although the report did not mention it, came from an era when Church Parades were compulsory.

The biggest drawback of the report was its failure to define the exact purpose of chaplains in the army. Having set itself a task that included collective spirituality, it then made no reference to how that concept worked in the army. It restricted itself to a notion of spirituality that had echoes of Christianity but was ultimately to be defined by the army. This may have been due to the rise in the popularity of generic concepts of spirituality. It is of interest that no specific mention was made of non-Christian religions within British society and their possible involvement with the army. All the report said was:

> Spiritual values are not exclusively about religion. Nor should they be compressed either into moral behaviour or into an ethical code, although they are

closely related to both. Everyone has spirituality, whether they are firm believers
in God, agnostic or atheist. Most officers and soldiers in the Army are not overtly
religious. Many are 'neutral' rather than active supporters of Christianity, but
because British history, civilisation and culture has been based on Christianity
for so many centuries, the standards, beliefs and ethos of the British Army are
founded on the Christian faith. Furthermore, spiritual values require the Army
to consider what the individual requires of the Army as well as what the Army
requires of the individual. They are bigger than an individual's needs and they
contribute to the overall endeavour of the Army. (Para. 23)

Having defined spiritual values to his own satisfaction he then attempted to
indicate the relationship of chaplains to them:

Chaplains, especially if they are good communicators and team players, are a
unique resource in promoting and safeguarding a particular kind of spiritual
rooting. However, while the RAChD's contribution is more radical and far
reaching than any secular spirituality, it is the chain of command which has a far
greater responsibility for the Army's motivation and standards. (Para. 33)

The reference to being team players was presumably in the context of the
army posting in which a chaplain found himself. A chaplain who was a good
communicator and who used his skill to stand out against the wishes of a
commander would find himself in difficulties. If the difference of opinion was on
a matter of 'spirituality' then there appeared to be no safeguard for the chaplain.
Support might come in the particular status of a chaplain. The report recognised
that chaplains were 'owned' by their respective sending churches, noting that they
were 'welcomed' into the army. This gave them a unique independence (para.
47). Quite how the differing views were to be reconciled never became clear
from the report. Having established that chaplains were beneficial for the army
in its quest for spiritual values for individual soldiers, the report then turned to
the future organisation and establishment of the RAChD. Here, the central theme
of the report was the proposal that 'The Army should provide every deployable
major unit and formation headquarters with its own chaplain, as well as every
training unit' (para. 88). This conformed with the idea that chaplains were of most
use to the army when in close contact with soldiers. In saying this, McGill was
unconsciously echoing a sentiment expressed by Sir George Turner in his report to
the IAC in 1956 when he commented:

The job of the chaplain is to be in close proximity to the troops, and every
chaplain who is confined to a Headquarters on administrative work is one less
chaplain available to perform the primary functions of the chaplaincy service.
(War Office 1956)

Where Turner differed from McGill was in his belief that such a move would also make it easier for soldiers to 'consult with chaplains of their own denomination'.

The report recommended that, as a start towards achieving the aim of a chaplain with each unit, those in other roles should be redeployed. It was recognised that this had implications for the command of chaplains. One of these was that the parallel administrative structure that existed for Roman Catholic chaplains, created in 1919, should be removed, not least because it would make more chaplains available to be posted to units. The report noted in its recommendations, 'That it is highly desirable that the Roman Catholic chaplains should join the RAChD under the same arrangements as the other denominations of the Unified Department' (McGill 1999: para. 37). The reasoning in the report that lay behind this was less direct. It merely remarked that the gradual process towards closer convergence between the two branches of the RAChD should be 'strongly encouraged' (para. 49). It failed to be a second 'Creedy', in that it did not suggest the structures that would be required to ensure that the changes it had proposed took place. It did however have a wiring diagram for a possible future Ministry of Defence (Chaplains (Army)) that included the Principal Roman Catholic Chaplain (Army) in a subordinate role to the Chaplain General and abolished the post of Deputy Chaplain General (Annex C). As well as removing the parallel command system the report noted that the whole command and control system was considered 'unsatisfactory' by many (para. 50). The inference was that the posts in the static headquarters could be removed and their functions either carried out by the Ministry of Defence (Chaplains (Army)) or by others in the chain of command. This raised an important question, which was not answered, as to how the rights of the sending churches over their clergy would be safeguarded. It also raised a question as to how chaplaincy would be provided away from major units in such a way as to meet the needs of all members of the army. The previous system of a pooled establishment under the control of the senior chaplain had always been flexible. The plan to post rather than attach chaplains to units suggested that this flexibility might not be present in the future. The plan also seemed to place a high value on the role of the chaplains as individual practitioners in the area of spiritual need, rather than as part of either a church or an integrated chaplaincy service.

The report was in the end muddled. It was forced to recognise fully how chaplains were different from other members of the army in the allegiance they owed to an organisation outwith the army. At the same time, it regarded the army as having the task of setting the agenda for chaplains. It also failed to set out a clear role for the chaplain, even though it had noted that 'there exists a degree of uncertainty and confusion about the role of chaplains' (para. 57). At the same time the report had as a central theme that chaplains were there for the military and not the church. This tension was obvious when it commented:

> The role of the chaplain raised a number of comments during the study; perhaps unsurprisingly as a chaplain's first loyalty remains to the Church, not the Army. Nevertheless, a directive from the CG and through the chain of command

> which ensures that commanders and chaplains understand the chaplain's role
> would help remove misunderstanding and would focus the chaplains' efforts.
> The priority for a chaplain to be with soldiers, rather than involved with church
> affairs, needs restating. The image of chaplains is crucial to their credibility and
> effectiveness. (Para. 79)

The report appeared to have been trying to provide something for all parties. It was generally welcomed by the churches. Unlike the reports of the 1920s, it was not presented to the IAC for formal discussion. As has been noted above, that body had already effectively ceased to meet. Individual churches made their own responses. Thus the Committee on Chaplains to HM Forces of the Church of Scotland commented favourably in its report to the General Assembly of 2000. It noted that it 'strongly endorsed' the work of the RAChD and recorded that:

> Such a positive and appreciative report, coming from an external source, came
> as a considerable encouragement to the Royal Army Chaplains' Department.
> (Church of Scotland 2000: 18/4)

The Committee returned to a further consideration of the report in 2001. It noted that it was now being implemented. It further noted that there was a distinction in Brigadier McGill's thinking, between broad spiritual values and the narrower band of specifically religious values, which in some cases sustained Christians and in others the subscribers to other faiths (Church of Scotland 2001: 18/5). The Committee believed that within this distinction, what is described as 'the perceived need for spiritual values, and the vocation of Christian chaplains to nurture the responsibilities and changed behaviour which is a response to the preaching of the Christian gospel', McGill had endorsed the work of the RAChD. If so, he had done so without any reference to how differences would be resolved when the two positions were not aligned but opposed. The Committee then went on to consider the position of those with spiritual needs whose religious values were rooted in one of the major non-Christian religions. It drew attention to the experience of the US Army, arguing that it provided some pointers as to how a situation, which in Britain remained fraught with unresolved problems, might be resolved (Church of Scotland 2001). In doing so it made no mention of the established churches within the United Kingdom and how that affected the shape of army chaplaincy. No voices within the chaplaincy were raised on the matter at all. No doubt chaplains were blinded by the continued lack of any need to provide for the spiritual requirements of the handful of members of other faiths spread throughout the army.

The other churches made no public response to the McGill report. For the Roman Catholic Church the report signalled that the army was no longer prepared to accept a dual system that it had identified as wasteful in terms of resources. The implications in terms of chaplaincy meeting unspecified 'spiritual' needs, which it was for the army to define, rather than 'religious' requirements that were the responsibility of the churches, does not appear to have been commented upon by anyone.

Within the next five years army chaplaincy had changed in significant and important ways. The most significant was the introduction of an 'all souls' ministry through the integration of the two parts of the RAChD. This has led to the posting of chaplains to individual units without particular reference to their denomination background. Whilst this has the attraction of simplicity (*The Tablet* 2010), it has diminished the connection between the chaplains and their churches as, particularly in the case of Roman Catholic chaplains, they no longer had immediate contact with all the members of their denomination and thus lacked the overview that they had previously. The decision was also made, with considerable publicity, to appoint 'Faith Advisors' as Civil Servants. These were to come from the Islamic, Buddhist, Hindu and Sikh communities. Instead of using the previously used method of appointing such individuals as 'Officiating Chaplains' a new category was created. Quite how they were to relate to the existing faith communities in their dealings with the Ministry of Defence was not set out. It is of note that neither the Jewish rabbi responsible for the armed forces nor any of the Christian leaders, such as the two bishops to the Forces, had been given such status. An 'Advisory Group' was set up but since it was to advise the Chaplain General it lacked the status of the former IAC. Crucially it moved the locus of authority for chaplaincy from the civil to the military side of the army, something that the British churches had always been keen to avoid in the past.

So, British chaplains serving in Afghanistan find themselves with an uncertain relationship with their own church and in a responsibility structure that, whilst seeking to unite church and army, is at best unclear and inevitably ambivalent. As such they have been placed in a difficult position when it comes to interpreting the morality of war espoused by their church, in their dealings with the army, whilst at the same time finding equal difficulty in offering any understanding of the changing nature of modern warfare to the church that ordained them. It is thus no wonder that, as a number of the pieces of work produced for the Master of Theology in Chaplaincy Studies at Cardiff University have shown, there is a considerable degree of confusion in the minds of some chaplains.

To help the chaplains in their difficult task there needs to be recreation of a structure that recognises the understanding that they inhabit two spheres of authority; that of the church or faith group to which they belong, as well as the army. This is true both of those who are employed as commissioned chaplains and also of those who serve either as faith advisors or as officiating chaplains. Unless this happens the danger is that chaplains will lose their independence and become so identified with the military community that, at least for Christian chaplains, there is no ability to offer any form of prophetic ministry. The easiest solution would be the restoration of some form of advisory committee for the representatives of all faith groups that is not responsible to any military officer but is chaired by a senior Civil Servant. This ability to engage at the highest level within the Ministry of Defence would both give chaplains the sense that they were not under military command for more than administrative matters, and also encourage the churches to see chaplains as not merely members of the military. The alternative would be to follow the suggestion made, in 1985, by the Conference of Priests and move to a chaplaincy which had civilian status and was under direct control of the church. This was not without historical precedent as it was the system followed by the Wesleyan Church from the creation of their Forces Board in 1860 to the outbreak of the First World War in 1914 (Watkins 1981). Whether this would prove to be the most appropriate system for the modern army is questionable, but clearly something needs to be done to identify more appropriately the relationship that chaplains serving in Afghanistan and elsewhere have as members both of a faith community and of the military. It might then be possible for serving chaplains, or those recently retired, to be able to contribute to works such as that which reviewed the involvement of the Church of England in British foreign policy with its subtitle of 'Christian Engagement with the Modern World' (Blewett et al. 2008). But then the principal editor, described as a member of the Royal Army Chaplains' Department with experience in Bosnia and Iraq, found no place in the work to comment on either his own experience or that of the many other Anglicans who have served as chaplains.

Chapter 7

'O Hear Us When We Cry to Thee':
Liturgy in the Current Operational Context

Jonathan Ball

Setting the Scene

Writing in the *Church Times* of 12 November 2010, the Revd Stuart Hallam, a Royal Marines chaplain, reflected on his operational tour of duty with 40 Commando Royal Marines in Helmand Province 2007–8, and in particular on the death of Lieutenant John 'JT' Thornton after his vehicle hit a mine:

> For two hours, JT fought for his life, but the odds were stacked against him. Eventually, the consultant said: "There's nothing more we can do for him, Stu. It's over to you now." I thanked them for all they had done, and prayed for them, and then I gave JT the last rites.

> I was unable to take JT's funeral. But we routinely have a service of repatriation for the dead at Camp Bastion. It is a poignant affair, and in many ways, serves as a funeral for the lads. The service takes place at sundown, and the whole of the camp's personnel assemble at the airhead, forming up in a hollow square.

> JT's friends carried him on to the parade. During the service, there is a two-minute silence, and the Last Post. Then the Hercules flies in and reverses into position directly behind us – an impressive sight.

> Finally, JT was carried aboard for his journey home. The most poignant moment for me was on board the aircraft, when all the lads knelt around their friend's coffin to say their final goodbyes. I prayed: "Go now from your Corps family, to be with your earthly family, in the love of the heavenly family, Father, Son and Holy Spirit."

These words encapsulate both a description of the use of formal and informal liturgy on operations in Afghanistan, and also some of the dilemmas and questions surrounding its use. It is clear in this example that the chaplain has a defined role, at least in the hospital: he is expected to perform his rituals as and when necessary. He has an assumed mandate to the departed soldier, and prays for the theatre staff who sought to save the soldier's life. It can be seen that ritual and formal repeated ceremony – to whose format service personnel become accustomed – serves to substitute other formal ceremonial.

Chaplains are aware that during the formal parts of liturgy, there are nevertheless moments of informality which themselves, in turn, become ritualised. Creative and full participation is frequent by non-chaplains and senior officers, while formal liturgical words are created by the chaplain, which to the layman have an origin and authority indistinguishable from those which come from approved denominational texts.

The dilemmas are closely allied: to what extent should the military chaplain assume the consent of personnel to be objects of prayer in a way which a civilian counterpart in a peacetime context could not possibly take for granted? To what extent can or should military ceremonial and ecclesiastical ritual be permitted to have blurred boundaries, and at what point does ecclesiastical ritual cease to be what it is meant to be and become military ceremony (and can the chaplains collude with this)? And to what extent can an oath of obedience which includes a promise only to use authorised services and forms of words be ignored should it appear expedient on pastoral grounds?

This chapter seeks to ascertain what Christian liturgy is being used on operations today, and to assess the dilemmas it raises in the context of the make-up and attitudes of the majority congregation; liturgical reform both within and outside the military and its effect on liturgies used, and on the ownership of liturgy by the non-committed.

This assessment is undertaken in the light of the offerings of liturgical scholarship, the most significant among these for the purposes of this study being Ronald Grimes' definition of the purposes and effects of liturgies:

> Every liturgy attempts to answer every question, to declare, "This is the way things are." Of course, it does so in the words of a specific tradition. A liturgy tries to focus all things through a few things. (In Bradshaw and Melloh 2007: 141)

Finally this chapter seeks to ascertain whether the high intensity of the operations in Afghanistan have impacted on the 'ownership' of religious liturgy by military personnel.

The Wider Context

Church Decline

The decline in Christian religious practice has continued apace, if not accelerated, through the last two decades of the twentieth century and the first of the twenty-first: Robin Gill cites Brierley/MARC Europe censuses which claim that weekly attendances across the Christian denominations in Great Britain fell from 12 per cent in 1979, to 10 per cent in 1989, and 8 per cent in 1998 (Avis 2003: 24);

in 2000 70 per cent of those aged over 50 had been baptised in the Church of England, whilst less than 20 per cent of newborns were baptised in that year. This meant that in 2001, though 72 per cent of English and Welsh, and 65 per cent of Scots claimed to be Christian in the National Census (falling further in 2011 to 59 per cent), the numbers of baptised Anglicans in the English population fell below 50 per cent for the first time since the Reformation (Avis 2003: 97). Grace Davie has aptly coined the phrase 'believing without belonging' as applying to the UK population (Davie 1994). The implication of this is that the churches are losing their place in civic culture. Kieran Flanagan comments:

> Whereas in the past, pietism and civil powers enforced an interest in religious practice, now there seems to be a creeping indifference. Indeed, it could be said that liturgy, or religious ritual, is intrinsically boring and uninteresting for many. (1991: 24)

Youth and the Church

Christian belief declined faster in the 18–24 age group (from which the armed forces primarily recruit) than any other, and professed disbelief grew faster in that group than in any other: between 1981 and 1990 belief in God declined from 59 per cent to 45 per cent, whilst disbelief in the afterlife grew from 39 per cent to 52 per cent, and professed atheism grew from 28 per cent to 38 per cent (Avis 2003: 26). Savage et al., drawing on Leslie Francis' research into the beliefs of 33,000 13–15 year olds in the 1990s, surmise that the post-baby boom generation, 'Generation Y' (born since 1982) has particular characteristics which may be major reasons for this, principally that society shapes its members first and foremost by the need for them to play the role of consumers:

> Generation Y is the first 100 per cent consumer generation … We are what we buy … The central value of such a society has moved from progress to choice: the absolute right of freedom to choose … Belief in God is an optional matter, a consumer choice. (2006: 144)

It follows in their opinion (2006: 158) that telling Generation Y what to believe will not work, though the abandonment of compulsory church parades in the army as far back as 1968 showed that Generation X (those born between 1962 and 1982) was not so dissimilar: perhaps what is new is their argument that Generation Y has implicitly placed itself at the heart of the person, in the place of God (2006: 162–3).

However, telling the Christian story in a way that raises questions about the participants' own stories ('What sort of person do I want to be?'), is suggested as a key skill for clergy, with Jesus' use of parables providing an important model. In the context of military operations in Afghanistan today, liturgy provided and used by chaplains can do precisely this, because all the personnel addressed are in the same situation facing identical challenges; and so the statistics are open to defiance at least in theory.

Both in Generation Y and older people, the discrepancy between profession of belief and regular formal religious practice reflects the fact that spirituality has a better press than religion:

> Religion tends to be associated with what is publicly available, such as churches, mosques, Bibles, prayer books, religious officials, weddings and funerals. It also regularly includes uncomfortable associations with boredom, narrow-mindedness and being out of date, as well as more disconcerting links with fanaticism, bigotry, cruelty, and persecution. It seems that in many people's minds religion is firmly caught up in the cold brutalities of history.

> Spirituality is almost always seen as much warmer, associated with love, inspiration, wholeness, depth, mystery and personal devotions like prayer and meditation. (Hay and Nye 1998: 6)

But this does not necessarily indicate hostility towards the church. In Francis' study 73 per cent said they would want to get married in church, and 54 per cent that they wanted their children to be baptised or christened, whilst many recognised that church can have a positive impact on those who attended, even if not for them personally:

> "Church gives people peace"; "It provides a place to show their devotion in public"; "It gives a sense of unity with other believers, a sense of community and mutual support"; "It helps people to live better lives". (Savage et al. 2006: 15)

However, lack of overt religious sensibility does not appear to result in young people feeling disenchanted, alienated or lost in a meaningless world. Instead, the data collected by Francis indicates that they found meaning and significance in the reality of everyday life, which the popular arts help them to understand and imbibe. In other words, they see no need to place ultimate significance elsewhere beyond the immediate experience of everyday life; there was no obvious need for what Savage et al. call transformative spirituality, or a 'God-shaped hole' – though there was a basic, formative spirituality running through the young people's engagement with the world.

They coin the phrase 'Happy midi-narrative' to describe the storyline of young people's worldview, using the term to distinguish it from the concept of a meta-narrative, a story about how the world works, often with a goal. In contrast they conclude that young people operate on a more modest scale of here and now. But this is not individualistic, rather communal on a small scale (my friends, me, my family: a midi-narrative). 'Happy' refers to the fact that central to young people is the belief that the universe and the world are essentially benign: difficult things happen but there are enough resources within the individual and his family and friends to enable happiness to prevail (2006: 37).

They conclude that the distance between the worldviews of the church and Generation Y means that there needs to be a prior mission to young people, involving primary focus on who they want to become rather than on what they should be doing, and on individual formation rather than on moral decision-making.

Arguably this is precisely what may be effected through use of formal and informal liturgies and prayers for soldiers on operations in Afghanistan. The RM chaplain Stuart Hallam writes of his Royal Marines: 'My experience tells me that they have a real need to explore and express their spirituality as they operate in the most extreme of conditions – and as they contemplate life and death on a daily basis' (*Church Times*, 12 November 2010). In other words, the intensity of military operations begins to challenge the midi-narrative and to focus soldiers' thoughts on the purpose of their lives and their potential.

The Afghan Context

Captain Doug Beattie MC, a soldier of 30 years' service in the Royal Irish Regiment and its predecessors, epitomises an attitude towards religion typical of Generations X and Y found across the ranks, and especially amongst so-called Late Entry officers who have been commissioned from the ranks after progression to Warrant Officer. He writes of meeting with Afghan Muslims on operational tour in Helmand:

> Despite resorting to religion to get me out of my predicament it was not a subject I wanted to discuss much further … And as an Irish Protestant I knew better than to get on to religion … I have never been religious. At least not in the sense of having much time for the Christian church … To me the Bible might be a good read but not something to live my life by and certainly not something to evangelise about. Which is different from saying that I don't believe in God. I think there is an omnipotent presence, an all-powerful being, but not one who can only be reached through a priest at Sunday service. (Beattie 2009: 186)

And yet, paradoxically, when telling of the medal parade for his unit, 1st Battalion The Royal Irish Regiment, on 17 October 2008, the first thing he mentions, and quotes in full, is the Regimental Collect prayer (Beattie 2009: 313).

It would of course be a crass and indefensible generalisation to argue that Beattie's view sums up the attitude of the majority of military personnel towards religion: as in every walk of life there is a range of stances and levels of profession, from those who are committed to their faith, through those who have a vague belief in God and are content to accept a Christian framework in which to locate this, and those who tolerate the institutionalised religion represented by service chaplains, to those who are hostile.

When compared with the UK Census statistics, there is a much higher proportion of those who profess to be Christians within the military: in 2008, 93 per cent in the army were registered as Christian (as against less than 1 per cent other world faiths and 6 per cent declared atheists, agnostic or having no faith). In other words, any assumptions made on account of the statistics presented by Brierley/MARC Europe are directly contradicted. A number of reasons can be mooted for this discrepancy, including the increased likelihood of death, peer pressure, habit or even some kind of insurance bargain with God, but it will be argued here that the first reason does indeed ensure that there is more ownership of liturgy even amongst normally non-practising Christian military personnel when on operations.

It is not just that soldiers are forced by the harshest fighting for British soldiers since Korea to focus on their own destinies. In a loose Minute to the Director of Personal Services (Army) on Pastoral issues dated 12 May 2010, the then Chaplain General the Venerable Stephen Robbins CB wrote:

> There have been a noticeable number of commanders, soldiers and families discussing with their chaplains what can only be described as "fearfulness", particularly prior to deployment to Afghanistan. This is not altogether surprising … In the case of those in command positions these fears are not so much about their personal safety but their responsibility for their soldiers and how they will cope if their soldiers are killed especially in instances of multiple casualties.

This has led both to deliberate and unintentional changes in officer training at the Royal Military Academy Sandhurst (RMAS). The intentional changes include a formal lecture on the morality of killing given by one of the chaplains alongside a regular officer, indicating a shift from the idea that only the chaplains deal with the ethics of killing and PTSD, rites of death and remembrance, to an assumption that all officers will be involved. There is also a lecture from the College Adjutant to officer cadets directing them to become familiar with forms and styles of worship, since 'at least half of you' will be speaking at the funeral of one of your soldiers. College Prayer services are put together by cadets, where it is noticeable to the chaplains that cadets stay with familiar and traditional forms of worship, reflected also in the negative reaction across the services to the CCBI 2005 Remembrance Sunday service as against the tried, tested and arguably more partisan 1968 service – perhaps because the former includes an extended liturgy of penitence which grates with those who fought what they took to be a just cause on the nation's behalf.

The outgoing Senior Chaplain Canon Jonathan Gough reported in 2010 that changes in the educational process, which is now more project-based, has unintentionally led to a greater breadth of understanding, where spirituality is seen as integral to life rather than as represented solely by organised religion. In this context questions about meaning, purpose, belonging and destiny surface much more easily.

Most significantly, the Commissioning Service which precedes the Sovereign's or Commissioning Parade has now assumed greater importance than the parade, principally because of the promises written into the Liturgy, whose introduction states boldly:

> In this house of prayer we place our private lives and corporate into the care of the Lord our God. May the pages of the Academy's history being written with the story of our lives, be worthy of the traditions we inherit and pleasing in the sight of God.

The service continues:

> The Call to Service

> *The Chaplain:*

> Would those who are commissioned or whose commissions are to be confirmed please stand.

> The Collect of the RMAS

> *The College Commander:*

> Almighty God, whose Son, the lord of all life, came not to be served but to serve; help us to be masters of ourselves that we may be the servants of others and teach us to serve to lead; through the same Jesus Christ, our Lord. Amen

> *The Chaplain:*

> You have heard the Collect of this Academy, [*sic*] by serving to lead will you show the courage and devotion to duty that will be expected of you as an Army Officer?

> *Officers:* With the help of God I will serve to lead.

> Will you be loyal to your superior officers and to your soldiers both in peace and on operations?

> *Officers:* With the help of God I will serve to lead.

> Will you be a person of integrity, having respect for others of whatever creed or colour and treat your soldiers with equity?

Officers: With the help of God I will serve to lead.

Will you, by the discipline of your life, be an example of sacrifice and service to your soldiers and to all whom you meet in your duties?

Officers: With the help of God I will serve to lead.

May God confirm and fulfil in you this life of service and leadership.[1]

From the point of view of chaplains, this new intense context has led to renewed concentration on the provision of chaplaincy, liturgy and worship rather than welfare support. During 2008–9, during 3 Commando Brigade's operational tour in Helmand, the principle was established (as it had been in 1916 on the Western Front) that chaplains should be based as far forwards as possible, and spend the majority of their time in Forward Operating Bases, Patrol Bases and at checkpoints, meaning not so much the provision of formal worship far forward (though this was the effect), but that chaplains were not always able to move easily or even at all to other bases where formal worship might be needed. This is reflected in the Operating Instruction sent by the Revd Andrew Totten MBE, Senior Chaplain of 16 Air Assault Brigade, to his team of chaplains in July 2010 prior to his Brigade's Deployment in September:

> 2. Chaplains will provide spiritual support as required, underpinned by religious services (both denominational and Military) …

> 3. Consideration should be given to holding pre-deployment services, at sub-unit level where necessary. In addition to the Brigade-level Homecoming service, a date and location should be set as soon as possible for any unit-level homecoming services.

> 4. In addition to their daily devotions, chaplains will lead at least one act of public worship each week …

> 5. As it is a winter tour, chaplains will plan for the religious ceremonies associated with Remembrance and Christmas. There may also be significant regimental battle honours or saints' days requiring religious input.

> 6. Religious elements also attach to the different stages of the repatriation process …

---

[1]   RMAS – Royal Memorial Chapel – Commissioning Order of Service. Used by permission.

7. Chaplains should ensure that prayers and simple orders of service are available for junior commanders to lead worship, particularly acts of remembrance, in the absence of the chaplain.

17. Copies of the AFOS and PB (JSP 587) will be issued to all personnel for use during deployment. A plastic card imprinted with the Brigade Collect and the 23rd Psalm will also be issued to all personnel.

Liturgy in the Military Context

Edward Shils has argued that ritual and belief are intertwined and yet separable, since it is conceivable that one might accept beliefs but not the ritual activities associated with them, concluding, 'beliefs could exist without rituals; rituals, however, could not exist without beliefs' (in Cutler 1968: 736). However, in the military context, it may be that rituals are tolerated or even supported without the underlying belief, either because there is no substitute for a ritual that is seen to serve an important and mutually supportive purpose, or because there is a parallel belief which can sustain the same ritual.

The Purpose of Liturgy in the Military and Operational Context

Liturgies in current operational contexts are intended to serve a number of purposes, though it may be that different individuals and groups intend differing purposes.

Firstly, Catherine Bell argues that 'the simplest ritual activities are seen to "fuse" a people's conceptions of order and their dispositions (moods and motivations) for action' (1992: 27). Certainly, commanders might well see them as motivating soldiers to perform better in their duties, whether it is because they are more certain of the justice of their cause, or because they have been built up in self-confidence through affirmation by the supportive message of Christian faith for the individual and for the body of the church.

Secondly, Ronald Grimes (in Bradshaw and Melloh 2007: 139) asserts that ceremony invites the participant to surrender idiosyncrasies and independence to a larger cause, for which one is willing to fight, die or pay homage:

> ceremony has imperative force; it symbolizes respect for the offices, histories, and causes are condensed into its gestures, objects and actions ... Ceremony is manifestly competitive ... [and] both expresses and creates "our" solidarity as opposed to "theirs".

It is arguably for this reason that chaplaincy is principally tolerated by the military, along with its ability to bolster morale. Meanwhile, the sending churches tolerate the toleration for the sake of presence where there is need. Napoleon asserted that the moral component of war was three times as important for success in war as the physical and intellectual components; this certainly might explain the support for the official propagation of religion within the military when on the face of current trends this might seem wholly anachronistic. Michael Sledge argues that the unique nature of military service is responsible for this:

> Morale is one product of the passionate bond that soldiers form with their fellows, a bond rarely experienced in civilian life. Combining the camaraderie of a football team, the dedication to task accomplishment of a dot-com start-up workgroup, the sense of separation of a cult, the unit preservation of a police department, and the love of a family will yield a cohesive force that still falls short of the ties that bond military members together. (Sledge 2005: 15)

Thirdly, Clifford Geertz, Greg Bateson and Claude Levi-Strauss see ritual as designed to address fundamental conflicts and contradictions in the society in question. This might well represent the view of the chaplain, who seeks to make sense of the insensible that is war, and the differences between peoples, and so give peace of mind to soldiers – though undoubtedly worship has also a pastoral priority.

Fourthly, Grimes (1982: 12–13) defines liturgy as any ritual action with an ultimate frame of reference: it is closely related to magic, on the one hand, when participants are attempting to manipulate the transcendent; and to celebration, on the other, when participants focus more on the encounter with the transcendent than on the outcome. This might well represent the view of soldiers who may see worship as a means to harness the support of a higher power; and their participation as a bargaining counter which (hopefully) ensures survival. Doug Beattie MC, writing of his first operational tour in Helmand, confirms this:

> I was lucky to have made it out of there. Almost every step of the way I had been terrified. I'd prayed to God, made pacts with the devil, done anything that might keep me safe and allow me to return to a loving family, and a future. And guess what? It had worked. Despite everything, I had made it out of that Helmand hell. Lady Luck had been on my side. (Beattie 2009: 8)

These four definitions concern the intentions of individuals, and indeed psychologists would most likely focus on ritual behaviour as it serves the needs (usually unconscious) of the individual. But Mark Searle points out (in Bradshaw and Melloh 2007: 11–12) that sociologists and anthropologists, on the other hand, look at the way ritual serves collective needs, such as the maintenance of group solidarity, the rehearsal of group values and worldview, the maintenance of social distinctions and categories and the containing of social conflict. Functionalist views of ritual often portray it as maintaining social cohesion and cultural coherence in the face of various kinds of threats. But most importantly for the military context,

Searle argues that religious ritual is 'said to enable people, collectively as well as individually, to face the boundary situations of human existence'.

Undoubtedly there is a need for a chaplain in any act of worship to balance the needs of the community with the needs of the individual despite any pressures from commanders for the community to be seen as having priority in every circumstance.

What is Going on?

The Revd Stuart Hallam's description of Lt Thornton's repatriation ceremony cited at the beginning clearly shows the blending of informal ceremonial with religious rite with blurred boundaries which may seem incongruous to the outsider but which appear seamless to those in the military including the chaplain. Kieran Flanagan comments:

> Differing forms or styles of rite produce contrasting effects in the way the social is arranged to capture the holy. Informal rites serve to heighten a sense of fellowship of the kingdom being present in a way that binds all together in a common hearing and feeling of God's presence … These communal feelings of the Divine make the participants oblivious to detail, but yet aware of what it facilitates. Later memory might settle on the pattern of the table-cloth, or the cadences of the bidding prayers, or the rather fat, red candles burning brightly. There is an almost apologetic, perhaps accidental quality to liturgical detail remembered. It was not what the transaction was about, but what emerged and was unintentionally marked in memory when the social was domesticated for holy use … Attachments to aspects of the rite are generated through habitual use. If these are believed to "work", a brand loyalty to a particular liturgical style will be developed. (1991: 33)

But it is not just informal rites used in Patrol and Forward Operating Bases which have – because they have been remembered, or 'worked' – caught on. Formal rites of the church, such as the anointing of each soldier, have been used at whole unit parade services prior to deployment in Iraq and Afghanistan, while use of prayers of confession principally at smaller gatherings or with individuals have assisted soldiers in coming to terms with using authorised lethal force either when there has been no question about using it, or in the frequent grey areas which warfare brings and when much depends on spur of the moment decisions. These have had a profound effect on the Generation Y recipients, not so much as demonstrations of formal commitment to the church, but – on the part of some – as a mark of God's promise of blessing on them and on their being marked out for a special task, or – on the part of others – as a taking on of a quasi-insurance policy in the hope of safe return. As Flanagan also argues:

> Rituals bear subjective meanings in a ceremonial format. They handle a
> distinctive phenomenon and the actors involved in their reproduction have a
> tacit set of assumptions that governs what is intended to be revealed and to be
> understood ... A collusion is required in the use of the social apparatus that
> allows the rites to repeat and to re-present their incredible messages in a credible
> manner. (1991: 6)

In the military context this may mean that the chaplain may consciously be
saying one set of words and performing an accompanying set of actions, knowing
that the personnel taking part may be reading in a different set of assumptions. Each
tolerates the other: the chaplain is tolerated as the subject matter expert for ritual,
the chaplain tolerates the other assumptions for the sake of the gospel – the church
is present and its rites are performed, being objectively sufficient in themselves. In
most contexts this goes unnoticed, but there are significant dilemmas of which the
chaplain is – or ought – to be aware.

Dilemmas for Military Chaplains in Leadership of Worship

Because chaplains are part of their institution, they can understand its language,
ethos and modus operandi, and because they are subject to similar pressures,
can empathise with its members. But because the chaplain remains an outsider,
she or he is also able to challenge the institution. However, the longer chaplains
remain within the organisation, the more inculturated they become, and less able
to challenge it; from this it is a short step to using religious language and ritual
to consecrate the secular purposes and actions of the organisation. Awareness of
these tensions is critical to the Forces chaplain because of how she or he is seen by
his or her host organisation. The army certainly sees its chaplains as being there to
serve its own needs, rather than the purposes of God or the church (McGill 1999:
14, para. 50).

Are services saying that God is on our side? Biblical passages, particularly
from the Old Testament, can easily be allegorised or interpreted in any way the
reader wishes. The outbreak of the Second Gulf War in 2003 brought a sharp
attack on military chaplaincy and the worship they offer by the Revd Dr Giles
Fraser in the *Guardian* on 26 March:

> TV pictures show chaplains asking God to bless the soldiers. As they do so,
> helicopters, full of troops, buzz overhead. There is a difference between blessing
> the soldiers and blessing the battle itself, but it's a slender one.

Doubtless passages such as Deuteronomy 20:2–4 (where Moses instructs the
people of Israel to have a priest assure them God will fight on their side and give
them victory, before they go into battle) and Joshua 6:2–5 (where priests blowing
trumpets lead Joshua's army around the walls of Jericho) were in his mind, as well
as the excesses of clergy in the World Wars.

But not to offer worship would not least mean not doing what chaplains are uniquely qualified and expected to do. More so they would not have been responding to specific needs: to be put right with God, to pray for family, to ask for protection, and not least the need to be assured that what is about to be done is right.

Such an absolutist position as Fraser's – which he has subsequently abandoned – is challenged when Christians within the armed forces demonstrate that in an imperfect world where wars take place, Christians can do their utmost to ensure that they are fought as humanely as possible, with every opportunity taken to lessen the consequences of conflict. This has to guide the chaplain in the choice of content of acts of worship.

But it is an irresolvable dilemma, not least because the so-called sending churches do not give guidelines or make known their expectations of their forces chaplains, who can become totally isolated from their sending church. So what model of church is this? Certainly not a gathered community: the chaplain is more like Paul on his missionary journeys, travelling perhaps with only one companion, preaching to those who have an altar to an unknown god (Acts 16:17–23).

Liturgical Provision by the Churches

Liturgical reform in the mainstream churches has of course been inherited by the three armed services: in the army context, early Church of England Series 1 and Series 2 reform, in the 1960s and 1970s was reflected in a new Field Service Book in 1968 which coincided with the end of compulsory church parades in the Army. According to Queen's Regulations, the only compulsory act of worship a trained soldier can now be ordered to attend is Armistice Day/Remembrance Sunday; though this is widely ignored by commanding officers who order attendance at acts of worship on numerous regimental occasions. Furthermore, there is little resistance to repatriation ceremonies since these constitute a tribal farewell as well as a Christian act of worship, whilst remembrance services within a wholly military context may be perceived by outsiders more as a cult of the dead.

Wider reform in the Methodist Church, URC and Church of Scotland together with the publication of the Alternative Service Book in the Church of England in 1980 led to the publication of a further Field Service Book in 1982. This included Eucharistic rites of the sending churches as well as an ecumenical field service along with hymns and readings. Chaplains were obliged (as they still are in theory) to use the texts of their own sending church, and apart from the Field Service, there was no ecumenical provision. Interestingly the Royal Marines chaplains did produce their own unofficial prayer book which did include an unauthorised ecumenical Eucharistic rite.

The increasing Tri-Service nature of operations from the Balkans (1993) through Afghanistan (2001) and the Second Gulf War (2003) led to the publication of a Tri-Service Armed Forces Operational Service and Prayer Book in 2006: it includes personal prayers, a format for a Service of the Word, Bible readings, communal prayers, prayers for the dying, a shortened form of burial service (including at sea), a service of remembrance, hymns and short orders for Jewish, Hindu, Buddhist, Muslim and Sikh burial services which have been approved by the Ministry of Defence chaplains appointed to care for their communities in 2005. Eucharistic rites were deliberately not included because of the variety of options now open to chaplains due to latest liturgical revision: chaplains are expected to use the rites of their own sending church. The Prayer Book was intended, and is, more a personal resource for non-chaplain personnel.

Liturgical Provision from Unofficial Sources

The Revd Brian Elliott, a Church of England army chaplain from 1977 to 2010, pioneered a website (www.labarum.org) in 2003 as a resource site for chaplains, offering tailor-made services of the word, Eucharistic rites and remembrance liturgies. His work epitomises the approach of chaplains to liturgies created for personnel, which are not created *ex nihilo* but rather see existing forms and words adapted for appropriate use. For example, Elliott wrote a version of the naval hymn *For Those in Peril on the Sea*, with re-written second and third verses, one for land forces and one for air forces, sandwiched between the traditional first and last verses to provide a sung Tri-Service prayer for use on operations and at home:

> Eternal Father, strong to save,
> Whose arm doth bound the restless wave;
> Who bid'st the mighty ocean deep
> Its own appointed limits keep;
> O hear us when we cry to Thee,
> For those in peril on the sea.
>
> O Christ, the universal Lord.
> Who suffered death by nails and sword,
> From all assaults of deadly foe
> Sustain Thy soldiers where they go;
> And evermore hold in Thy hand
> All those in peril on the land.
>
> O Holy Spirit, Lord of grace,
> Who fills with strength the human race;
> Inspire mankind to know the right,
> Guide all who dare the eagle's flight;
> And underneath Thy wings of care
> Guard all in peril in the air.
>
> O Trinity of love and power!
> Our brethren shield in danger's hour;

From rock and tempest, fire and foe,
Protect them wheresoe'er they go;
Thus evermore shall rise to Thee,
Praise from the air, the land, the sea.

W. Whiting (1825–78) alt. Elliott [2]

One might well ask if the blurring of boundaries between soldiers of Christ and soldiers of the Queen is acceptable. Elliott's site proved to be the genesis of a book launched on the wider market in 2006, *They Shall Grow Not Old*, a book of resources for remembrance. It is traditional in language and praxis, but imaginative in application to context, reflecting the approach of many service chaplains in theatres of operation as they constructed appropriate services not simply for regular worship or remembrance, but for one-off high-profile services marking the end of operations in particular theatres such as Bosnia and Iraq.

There has never been any significant effort at Service level to encourage or produce so-called Fresh Expressions of Worship so much that they become formal liturgical provision, though individual chaplains have frequently used imaginative combinations of music, word and image. Instead it has been more the case that individual chaplains, like Elliott, have taken initiatives in use of more formal and traditional forms. The Revd Andrew Totten, then Senior Chaplain of 16 Air Assault Brigade, simply composed a new Collect for his Brigade's tour in Helmand Province from September 2010 to April 2011 whose phrases were intended to provide both a manifesto for and a reminder of how the operation was to be carried out; it was done in consultation with commanders to enhance ownership not just of the words of the prayer, but of the intended lessons in its phrasing. Totten submitted the following rationale for the new Collect:

1. A military collect should distil the ethos of its regiment or brigade. The existing prayer has a few good phrases, but gets lost in sub-clauses.
2. As an iconic fighting formation, the Brigade is reminded by the collect that peace must always be its final goal. Acting wisely and justly are key steps on that path.
3. The collect recalls the four cardinal virtues of wisdom (or prudence), justice, temperance, and courage. To these classical virtues, St Paul added the theological virtues of faith, hope, and love (1 Corinthians 13). Paul starts that passage with the words 'and now I will show you the most excellent way' – hence the ending of the Collect (as an implied bridge to the Christian virtues).
4. That mention of excellence, following the earlier reference to humility, resonates with SF ethos.

---

[2]   Verses 1 and 4 by W. Whiting; verses 2 and 3 by Brian Elliot. From Brian Elliot (2006). Used by permission.

5. The collect is written in iambic pentameter – basically ten syllables to a line. That's to echo Shakespeare's war rhythm ('Cry havoc and let slip the dogs of war', 'now is the winter of our discontent'), with the hint that there's a deep warrior ethos that the Christian message seeks to transform. It should also make the collect easier to say and remember.
6. Despite all this guff, it's also hopefully something to which the troops can relate.

The Chaplain General approved the Collect:

> O Lord, the author and lover of peace,
> from whom all wisdom and justice proceed:
> we humbly beseech thee to remember
> members of 16 Air Assault Brigade.
> Keep us bold in deed and true in spirit;
> lift us with courage on wings like eagles;
> and show us now the most excellent way;
> through him who loved us, Jesus Christ our Lord.
> Amen.

The Brigade on tour comprised some 9,000 personnel; a supply of thousands of credit-card sized versions of the Collect backed with the 23rd Psalm had been almost exhausted prior to deployment; they were frequently used throughout the tour. Notably both the Collect and the Psalm were written in traditional 'Book of Common Prayer' language, appending an authority and solemnity which proves popular. Chaplains report that it is not just public school-educated officers who prefer more traditional liturgies and hymns, but soldiers with little or no formal church adherence, to whom the phrases of formal liturgies constitute a worthy tribute to the service of the living or courage of the fallen, with the poetic mystery of words not quite understood adding to the sense of the 'band of brothers' meeting together in the noble cause that is the service of one another if not the nation.

Use of the 23rd Psalm in particular has resonated with personnel on more than one recent Helmand tour, with its forming the foundation for sermons to soldiers based on its authorship by a warrior king who knew what it was to face death in hand-to-hand fighting of the kind that has been evident in Helmand.

Repatriation and Memorial Liturgies

Formal liturgy, whether from the established churches or constructed by service chaplains on or for operations, has been particularly important in helping soldiers to come to terms with the death of their comrades, and then assisting them to move on. The efficient functioning of a military unit of any size is hugely dependant on this, as Michael Sledge explains in a study of US practice regarding military deaths:

John D. Canine likens the death of a member of society to the action of a mobile: "When one part of the mobile is moved, all the other parts move in response." The death creates an imbalance that begs for resolution. One obvious reason is that the duties previously performed by the dead must be reassigned among the survivors. However, there are more obscure forces behind the creation and nature of this imbalance.

When a person is alive, his physical self and his social self proceed on parallel, if not identical, tracks, and the two are often viewed as one. However, at death the tracks begin to diverge, for the body, if not embalmed, will decay rapidly. The social status of the deceased, however, tends to remain with the living for a more extended period of time. Hallam, Hockey, and Howarth describe this state as "socially alive but biologically dead". This duality of identity creates a dissonance in the minds of the living, who in order to achieve "closure", must recognize and accept that the new physical status is irreversible; hence, they must establish a new social identity for the dead that is harmonious with it ... Without this process of resolution, the social self of the dead continues to occupy space on the track that is normally assigned to the living. (Sledge 2005: 21–2)

Since the First Gulf War of 1991, when bodies of British soldiers have been routinely repatriated rather than buried in the country where they fell, there has been a standard repatriation ceremony where bodies are loaded onto a transport plane or immediately prior to being transported to the airhead. However, the intensity of the Helmand conflict led in 2008, during 16 Air Assault Brigade's second tour, to the emergence of vigil services instigated by the Senior Chaplain the Revd Nick Cook, since not all a fallen soldier's comrades can accompany a coffin to the airhead or be available at the time of the coffin leaving.

There was a simple format to these vigils:

1. A few opening sentences of scripture.
2. An introduction explaining that all were gathered in the presence of God to remember the fallen, pray for the bereaved, and seek the comfort and peace of God.
3. A scripture reading by the senior officer present.
4. A eulogy by a representative of the cap badge.
5. An act of remembrance incorporating the Laurence Bunion poem *For the Fallen* said by the senior soldier present, last post, silence, and reveille.
6. A prayer of commendation.
7. The losing unit's Collect, read by a cap badge representative.
8. [For 16 Assault Brigade] The Brigade Collect, recited by all from the Collect card.
9. The Lord's Prayer, said by all.
10. The Blessing.

These simple services took place at locations ranging from a patrol base to HQ Task Force Helmand at Lashkar Gah, but the main gathering was at Camp Bastion, where thousands might be on parade.

Orders for such services were adapted during 52 Lowland Brigade's tour (2008–9) by the Senior Chaplain the Revd Mark Grant-Jones with the intention that they could be conducted in the absence of a chaplain. This pragmatic decision was based on the realities of difficulty of movement for chaplains, although one chaplain on the 16 Air Assault Brigade tour 2010–11 arrived at one Company location immediately prior to a vigil to be told that he was not required, though he could talk to the soldiers afterwards if he wished; again the boundaries between Christian liturgy and military ceremony are porous, and the latter can under such exceptional circumstances mutate into something resembling quasi-Nordic cult with a hint of Valhalla awaiting the fallen warrior.

19 Light Brigade's tour in mid-2009 saw the deaths of 78 soldiers – the highest number during any tour in the last 10 years – leading to Vigil Services at the Brigade Headquarters at Lashkar Gah gaining a remarkable momentum of their own under the guidance of the Brigade Senior Chaplain, the Revd Dr Philip McCormack MBE. At these services, whose text was entirely based on the Christian scriptures and which took place the evening prior to every repatriation of bodies, the then Brigade Commander, Brigadier Tim Radford, insisted that he would read the scripture reading when he was in camp, while a eulogy using the Christian name of the fallen would be given immediately afterwards by one of the soldier's comrades of whatever rank. It quickly came to be considered an honour to be asked to read the regimental or corps collects of the fallen. Exactly the same ceremony was carried our regardless of rank or nationality; the Danes and Estonians adopted this form for their fallen; and it was noticed by the US personnel attached to the British-led Helmand operation that no such ceremony existed in the US areas of operation.

The actual repatriation ceremony takes place in the early hours of the morning afterwards. This comprises a short ceremony at the hospital chapel for the bearer party, with a short reading and a few prayers, followed by a move to the airhead and the Ramp Ceremony. The chaplain then leads the bearer party between lines of soldiers into the hold of the aircraft. Engines are running, so nothing is audible save to the immediate party in the hold, but again it takes the form of a few sentences of scripture, a prayer of commendation, and a blessing once the chaplain has descended the ramp, facing back into the hold, immediately before the tailgate is closed and lights extinguished.

Implications

The experiences of and use of chaplains since operations in Helmand commenced in 2006 suggest that the profile of chaplaincy has been transformed: partly this is due to the conscious relocation of the chaplain to the front line, something which slipped away in the context of the invasion of Iraq due to difficulty of movement.

But I would argue that it is primarily the intensity of the conflict which has led to a resurgence of the power of formal liturgy, whether carried out in small patrol bases with half a dozen soldiers, or in Camp Bastion with thousands. This transformation has seen clear blue water put between welfare workers and chaplains, with the significant expectation that chaplains are present to provide religious things to soldiers, and to equip officers and soldiers with religious resources for those occasions when they are not themselves available. And it is evident that these resources and services are much in demand, not least in forms which can assist soldiers who wish to deal in some way with the guilt of what they have done in the name of the nation.

The continued extremely poor support of the churches which send chaplains to the armed services is therefore in this context all the more deplorable. Support is urgently needed both in order to ensure that the chaplaincy services remain able to carry out a prophetic role within the armed forces and are not overwhelmed by the sheer call to service need, or to act as multipliers of military efficiency through the bolstering of morale; but also to resource chaplains in the liturgies they are able to provide, which to date to a large extent are imaginative in use though based on long-established forms.

The huge take-up and power of the liturgies referred to in what is a mostly male population and masculine culture should also send a clarion call to the church saying that its worship is still something that can appeal to men if delivered sensitively and appropriately; in a context where women outnumber men in the Church of England in most parish churches by some 2 or 3:1 and where this gap is widening, it is clear that there is a feminisation going on which will see men opt out of the church before long.

Conclusions

I began this discussion by quoting Ronald Grimes' definition of the purposes and effects of liturgies:

> Every liturgy attempts to answer every question, to declare, "This is the way things are". Of course, it does so in the words of a specific tradition. A liturgy tries to focus all things through a few things. (In Bradshaw and Melloh 2007: 141)

Chaplains in Helmand do indeed endeavour to give meaning to whatever happens on OP HERRICK be it victory, defeat, injury, death, or causing injury and death, and in particular to assure individuals of their acceptance by God, and of his love for and blessing of them.

But more than declaring, 'this is the way things are', their liturgies are concerned with offering to God the way things will be from now on; and with building bridges between God and personnel who rest uneasy in deep uncertainty, asking many questions, some of which are undergirded by fear: what will happen to me – will I live, or die? And if I die, what will happen to my body? And if I live, will I be horrifically scarred in body or mind? Will I crack and let my friends down – or will I crack and do something terrible either here or back at home? What will happen to us now he or she is dead or injured? Are we succeeding – and what does success mean? And if we are, is it worth the price? Or are we losing – and if we are, why go on? Will life ever be normal again – will my relationships with my family and friends be damaged forever? And perhaps the question most unspoken of all: why do we do this – and is it right?

It is to the chaplain and the words he or she uses that the task of giving answer falls, and the challenge includes the chaplain wrestling with the age-old pressure to declare that God is on our side, and instead to pose the question through word and worship, 'Are we on God's side?'

In the extreme context of Helmand, such demands mean that there is little time and space for the niceties of ascertaining consent at leisure prior to leading worship. Similarly there can be no precious demarcation of what is purely religious and what might possibly be construed as pure military ceremony. And it would be risking the loss of credibility within the prime (military) community to observe the niceties of oaths taken at ordination only to use forms fully authorised by the sending churches.

The chaplains who have served in Afghanistan have simply got on with the task in hand, and that there has been an overwhelmingly positive response to their ministry indicates they have made the right choice. The Forces might well consist of those in Generations X and Y who cannot be forced to believe and may indeed turn away from the support of the church on return to normality (if such is possible); but it is clear that many have indeed taken ownership and been well-served by the liturgies offered them on tour and immediately on return.

Chapter 8

Just War: An Ethic of Principles or a Principled Ethic?

James Coleman

Introduction: Just War and International Law

> I do not bring with me today a definitive solution to the problems of war. What I do know is that meeting these challenges will require the same vision, hard work, and persistence of those men and women who acted so boldly decades ago. And it will require us to think in new ways about the notions of just war and the imperatives of a just peace. We must begin by acknowledging the hard truth: We will not eradicate violent conflict in our lifetimes. There will be times when nations – acting individually or in concert – will find the use of force not only necessary but morally justified. (Obama 2009)

This quotation indicates one of the main themes of President Barack Obama's Nobel Peace Prize acceptance speech in December 2009. In essence Obama used the opportunity to defend then current and recent American military action and, by extension, similar actions on the part of both NATO and UN forces. In so doing he appealed to traditional just war thinking, even while acknowledging the complexities thrown up by interventionism, the challenge of peacekeeping, international terrorism, perceived threats to global security, the problem of civilian casualties, and so on. Such issues are well known to any student of just war theory, but it is significant when 'the Commander-in-Chief of a nation in the midst of two wars' (as the president described himself) should resort to the language and concepts of just war on an occasion more usually seen as a celebration of peace. It is true that in the second half of his speech he went on to describe three ways to 'build a just and lasting peace', including exerting sanctions on those countries which flout international law, sharing a commitment to upholding human rights and, thirdly, promoting development as a means of combating poverty and disease. In each case, however, Obama also indicated that war might be necessary, albeit as a last resort, concluding that 'we can understand ... there will be war, and still strive for peace'.

Of particular interest for this chapter is the fact that while religion and faith are mentioned at a number of points in the speech there is no reference to God, beyond mention of wrongs being done in the past 'in the name of God'. Obama does speak of 'that spark of the divine that still stirs within each of our souls', but this is merely to reflect the language of post-modernist secularism. As such this chapter will argue that just war theory has in many cases been cast adrift from its Christian theological underpinnings which, in turn, threatens its contemporary usefulness.

A similar, what may be termed 'secular', use of just war language has been evident in the ongoing Chilcot Inquiry into the Iraq War of 2003. One obvious example was provided in the evidence given on 29 January 2010 by the former prime minister, Tony Blair (Blair 2010). Much of the hearing that day revolved around the legality of the invasion of Iraq in March 2003 and the judgement prior to the invasion given by the then Attorney General, Lord Goldsmith, to the effect that the military action was indeed justified. While the details lie outside our current scope we need only note here that Blair, himself a lawyer, clearly felt it important that the weight of law should support the invasion. Moreover, when the former prime minister returned to the inquiry to give further evidence almost exactly a year later, the legal question again occupied much of the four-and-a-half-hour session (see Blair 2011a). In a statement prepared a week ahead of this second session Blair described how the US government had been committed to a policy of regime change in Iraq since a decision of Congress in 1998, but noted his own resistance to this approach without first gaining the support of another United Nations Security Council Resolution sanctioning such action. He gave two reasons for this stance: it would be helpful in realising his goal of building a broad coalition; and the advice received from the Attorney General to the effect that 'such a fresh resolution was obligatory for reasons of international law' (Blair 2011b: 5). At the same time his statement shows that he saw such a resolution as giving Saddam Hussein 'one final chance to comply; and [to] make it clear if he didn't, then we would act, if necessary by force. In other words: change of heart or change of regime' (Blair 2011b: 5).

Given Blair's insistence on finding a legal basis for the invasion of Iraq, this last statement is quite astonishing. Article 2 of the United Nations Charter specifically states:

> All Members shall refrain in their international relations from the threat or use
> of force against the territorial integrity or political independence of any state, or
> in any other manner inconsistent with the Purposes of the United Nations. (UN
> 1945: ch. 1, Art. 2, para. 4)

It is true that this is later qualified by Article 51 which acknowledges 'the inherent right of individual or collective self-defence' (UN 1945: ch. 7, Art. 51), but this is in the context of facing an armed attack. While the arguments continue around the legality or otherwise of embarking upon military action against Iraq specifically with regime change in mind, it is sufficient to note here that even after the United Nations Security Council had passed that desired resolution (UN 2002: Resolution 1441) the legal issues remained far from settled.

Resolution 1441 did, however, eventually help to convince the Attorney General that the involvement of the British armed forces in any invasion would be in accord with international law. There has been considerable discussion about both the extent to which his view may have disagreed with that of the international community and the fact that this later opinion seems to have represented a considerable change of mind, but this does not detract from the importance of such a judgement in the former prime minister's thinking. Yet while legality is indeed one of the criteria in just war theory, once again the lack of any theological input is striking. Equally striking is that during his second appearance before the Chilcot Inquiry, Blair was at one point quizzed over the apparent discrepancy between what he had said in public about British commitment to possible military action and the advice he had received from Lord Goldsmith. In response to the panel he sought to draw a distinction between making a political point or a legal point (see Blair 2011a: 71, line 7, to 76, line 6), leading his interlocutor to challenge the claim to be able to 'distinguish when ... speaking to the House of Commons as Prime Minister between making a political point and a legal point when ... making a point about a legal interpretation of UN resolutions' (Blair 2011a: 73, lines 19–23).

It can be conceded readily that politicians may not be the ones best placed to make theological judgements, but when they deal with ethical matters it is hard to see how they can make good decisions if done in a manner which is purely functional. Yet this is precisely what tends to happen when discussing just war theory; and the effect is multiplied many times over in the popular media. There is, in short, an increasing tendency to resort to just war language in all sectors of society, while at the same time seeking to reduce the tradition to the status of little more than a checklist. Recognising that many of the principles of just war theory are enshrined in international law it is deceptively easy to argue that, in seeking to determine the legitimacy of any decision to resort to arms, all that is required is to appeal to such law for verification. Disarmingly simple and attractive though this might be, the discussions leading up to the Iraq War prove conclusively that such an appeal to law is likely to generate as many problems as it seeks to address.

Despite these difficulties there are many who still wish to approach the subject of war, and just war especially, purely from a legal standpoint. Thus Nabulsi (2006) argues strongly that justice is entirely a legal concept, with a concomitant emphasis upon justice in war also being seen through this particular lens. Indeed she seeks to draw the boundaries even more tightly by stating her conviction that 'the main rule to establish in being able to set standards of justice in war is: who is a legitimate combatant' (Nabulsi 2006: 44). Unfortunately this emphasis upon legitimacy further isolates just war theory from any theological foundation. Nabulsi in fact contends that what she terms 'a modern concept of justice *in* war' was formulated precisely 'to be ideologically neutral' (Nabulsi 2006: 44), but how realistic is this? On the contrary, to adopt this argument is to so divorce just war theory from theology that it is doomed to failure. For Nabulsi the fundamental challenge is to identify who merits being called combatants – and whether or not they are legitimate – but this is an extremely narrow 'focusing down' of just war thinking.

In formulating her thesis Nabulsi traces the development of this legal approach from the pioneering work of the Dutch jurist Hugo Grotius, whose seventeenth-century *De jure belli ac pacis* laid the foundations for much of today's international law, including such law as it relates to the conduct of war. As Nabulsi indicates (2006: 45), Grotius was concerned with trying to establish a pragmatic middle way between opposing 'philosophies of war and peace ... [which] were [either] ... too excessive [or] too absolute in the extent and limits they sought to place upon war'. In other words, up to that point many had either adopted a laissez-faire attitude to war where one party was seen as entirely just and the other as entirely unjust, leading to unrestrained action on the part of the so-called 'just' belligerent; whereas others adopted an approach so conditionally constrained that war could rarely be seen as just, if ever. The irony here, of course, is that in pressing for this middle ground based on a framework of legitimacy, the ground was laid for the subsequent development of just war theory as being increasingly dependent upon the legal test alone. As Nabulsi observes (2006: 46), 'Grotius' method of seeking moderation, *temperamenta*, was crucial, and laid a foundational stone for the nineteenth-century Grotian tradition of the laws of war'. Above all the inevitable outcome of his views was a diminution of the place and importance of the individual citizen, and the elevation of the place of the state. Concluding her analysis of the influence of Grotius, Nabulsi writes:

> Sown by Grotius, the seeds of the distinction between the rights of states and armies and the subordinate position of civilians – expressed in the legal dichotomy between lawful and unlawful combatant – germinated in the later nineteenth century and remain with us today. (Nabulsi 2006: 48)

There is some debate about the extent to which Grotius actually achieved his aim of establishing a realistic middle ground regarding what properly constitutes justice in war, but the relevant point here is that, in attempting to address the ethical and moral concerns raised by warfare, Grotius clearly believed the answers were to be found entirely within the rule of law. Thus we see how justice increasingly came to be seen as purely a legal concept and, while it would be naïve to argue that juridical justice does not contain any ethical dimension, it would be equally naïve to ignore the old adage that it is the victor who determines what is right and, therefore, 'just'. This is to reiterate the oft-repeated criticism of that view which regards 'might as right', and simply appealing to a legal test is no guarantee against falling into such a trap. Indeed, to return to the Chilcot Inquiry and the statement prepared by Blair in advance of his second appearance, he noted that prior to 2003 as prime minister he had been involved with four previous 'major military actions', described simply as 'Iraq 1998, Kosovo, Sierra Leone [and] Afghanistan'. He stated that in all four 'there had been legal issues [especially] in Iraq 1998 and Kosovo [where] the legal bases were highly disputed' (Blair 2011b: 11). He then concluded this part of his statement with these telling words:

> In my experience the more disputed the politics, the more disputed the law. That is why international law continues to be the subject of fierce debate and development. (Blair 2011b: 11)

To summarise this part of the argument, while we can accept that it is an obvious good that international law should try and curb the excesses of war – both in the proclivity to go to war and the methods used for waging war – arguably that same appeal to, and reliance upon, international law has also done a disservice to just war thinking or, at least, to the notion that the church has anything relevant to offer in this matter. 'Let the law decide' might well be the mantra of the secularists, media and politicians, even while each tries to appeal to just war criteria to further their own agendas. The irony that this is often the very criticism aimed at Christians who try to engage in the debate need not go unnoticed.

The Adequacy of Just War Theory

All that being said, it is true that just war theory does seem to offer a set of discrete principles, easily described and tested, and here it will be helpful for the sake of clarity to state briefly the usual criteria which apply. Classically there are two sets of standards to be met – those which relate to the conditions for going to war in the first place, *jus ad bellum*, and those concerning the right conduct of war, *jus in bello*. Reed (2004: 35ff.) outlines seven principles of *jus ad bellum*:

1. Any conflict must have a *just cause.*
2. The decision to engage in war must be taken by a *legitimate authority.*
3. There must be a *right intention* behind the decision to engage in conflict.
4. There must be a *reasonable chance of success.*
5. War must only be entered upon as a *last resort.*
6. *Proportionality of ends* must be observed – i.e. Will the good anticipated outweigh the evil involved in waging war?
7. The *aim* of any conflict must be that *of restoring peace* as soon as possible.

As for *jus in bello*, Reed notes two primary concerns:

1. *Discrimination* must be observed in the waging of war – i.e. every effort should be made to avoid direct or intentional harm to non-combatants.
2. *Proportionality of means* should be exercised – i.e. the warring parties should only use such force as is necessary to secure the ends which are envisaged.

It is immediately apparent how these principles appear to offer *in themselves* an ethical framework which is helpful for discussing the evils of violence and warfare, especially when other factors are also taken into account, such as the authority of the United Nations and the place of the Geneva Conventions. Yet just how useful in practice is the just war tradition? In a strongly worded critique of the 1991 Gulf War, Zahn (1991: 366) states his conviction that 'a good case can be made that most, if not all, of the just war conditions were ignored or violated'. In fact such is his suspicion of just war theory generally that he clearly wishes to disregard it altogether, as shown when he remarks:

> Though I do not accept the validity of the just war tradition as a source of Christian moral guidance, I feel obliged to play the rhetorical game … it is a game. Were the conditions of the just war ever honestly applied to an actual war, they would lead to behavioural conclusions identical to those required by the pacifism to which I personally subscribe. Real wars, alas, are never put to that test. (Zahn 1991: 366)

Zahn is making two different, but related, claims. Firstly, he is arguing that the just war tradition has never been applied to an actual conflict in an honest or meaningful way, thus invalidating claims that any war is somehow justified. Secondly, he argues that even were we to appeal to just war theory, it would merely serve to prove the moral and logical impossibility of trying to justify conflict under any circumstances. In short, for Zahn, the notion of just war is suspect as a source of moral guidance and, even when appealed to, is usually perverted by those wishing to advocate their own views.

It would be easy to dismiss Zahn with his own criticism about indulging in rhetoric, but we cannot ignore the implication that, once again, whenever referring to just war theory it seems that its interpretation is entirely at the mercy of the interests of the party employing the arguments. In Zahn's case however he at least tries to comment theologically and concludes:

> The technology of modern war has brought us back to the choices faced by Christians in their pre-Constantinian commitment to pacifism and non-violence … What is more urgently needed is a new (perhaps resurrected?) theology of war. Putting aside learned discourses and *summae* of the past, theologians might – like Augustine – "start from scratch". (Zahn 1991: 368)

To 'start from scratch' can, of course, only ever be aspirational, for we cannot undo either that body of international law to which we have already referred, nor the fact that many Christians, believing that war and violence is one inevitable consequence of unchecked sin, are prepared to countenance the use of arms. But Zahn is surely right in his call for a new theology of war, one which will take account of the sheer complexities now facing the international community today. As one helpful contribution to what this new theology of war may encompass some time will now be taken to examine the ideas of Bonhoeffer, particularly those indicated by his well-documented participation in the plot to assassinate Hitler, as discussed by various writers.

Bonhoeffer and a Theology of War

Taking as his starting point a lecture on Christian ethics given by Bonhoeffer in 1929, Green (2005) notes that the then young Lutheran pastor originally 'had a very conventional attitude to war', describing it as 'sinful and murderous' even while being prepared to justify it 'in terms of the love owed to one's own people, one's Volk' (Green 2005: 33). Although Bonhoeffer was to become a very committed pacifist over the next two to three years, at this stage in his life the lecture revealed, according to Green, 'not the voice of a pacifist', but one declaring 'a volkisch, nationalistic, lebensraum philosophy' (2005: 34). Thereafter Green outlines the development of Bonhoeffer's emerging pacifism, arguing conclusively that such was the depth of his commitment to this new-found ethic that he, in turn, was influential in encouraging others to follow suit.

Without discussing the details of Green's arguments it is sufficient for our purposes here to note his assertion that 'for Bonhoeffer, the Christian peace ethic is at the centre of the gospel' (2005: 39). Stassen (2010a: 194) agrees, describing 'the core of [Bonhoeffer's] ethic of peacemaking as commitment to following Jesus Christ', a commitment based on a particular reading of the Sermon on the Mount and an understanding of 'servanthood to Jesus Christ in Christian community' consequent upon such a reading. Kelly (2010: 215) reinforces the point, when he states categorically that 'one would miss a central feature of [Bonhoeffer's] Christian spirituality if his strong peace ethic were ignored'.

The obvious question which arises out of all this is simply stated: how could Bonhoeffer, such a committed pacifist and Christian, possibly bring himself to actively participate in a plot to assassinate someone, no matter how evil that person might be? At this point Green introduces the notion of tyrannicide as 'a specific ethical tradition', indicating that 'Karl Barth pointed to Aquinas, Calvin, Beza and Knox as some of the theologians who allowed that tyrannicide might be done in obedience to God's command in conditions of extreme public emergencies' (Green 2005: 42).

While there are similarities between just war theory and this tradition of tyrannicide – Green gives just two examples, the principles of last resort and legitimate authority – Bonhoeffer's justification for tyrannicide is based upon 'core theological beliefs, rather than … the sort of principles found in the just war doctrine' (Green 2005: 42). Summarising a lengthy passage in Bonhoeffer's *Ethics* (pp. 257–89), Green points out that for Bonhoeffer participation in tyrannicide involved a 'free, responsible action [which] arises from a christological foundation: the incarnate Christ resists the tyrannical despiser of human beings; the crucified Christ opposes the worldly success of tyrants; and the resurrected Christ rejects the idolisation of death' (Green 2005: 43). The action which follows has four elements to it, the first three of which involve 'vicarious representative action', a correspondence with reality, and a freedom 'modelled on God's freedom for humanity and embodied in freedom to love the neighbour and serve the community' (Green 2005: 43). The fourth element – and the one which is arguably of most interest for our present discussions – states that the 'free responsible action [involved in tyrannicide] requires willingness to take on guilt'. Here Green quotes Bonhoeffer's own words:

> The man who acts out of free responsibility is justified before others by dire necessity; before himself he is acquitted by his conscience, but before God he hopes only for grace. (Green 2005: 43)

This is a hugely significant statement for it points to a way of dealing with violence which simultaneously recognises the reality of sin and guilt, the existence of evil, and the grace of God, all while dealing with the uncertainty of life as it is encountered. As Green (2005: 44) argues convincingly, 'For Bonhoeffer ... Christian ethics is not about wielding principles that we have in hand; Christian ethics is, ultimately, about doing the will of God. And the will of God is only to be found in concrete reality'. Writing in a similar vein Elshtain (2010: 51–2) poses the question as to when one might disobey the state and argues that, for Bonhoeffer, such a question could only be answered on a case-by-case basis thus explaining 'why he refused to write up a kind of tick-list for the moment when disobedience kicks in' (Elshtain 2010: 52). As Green rightly observes, Bonhoeffer's commitment to the will of God carried a degree of risk – not so much a risk to one's safety (although that was very real for Bonhoeffer) – but rather a risk to one's standing before God. Bonhoeffer himself referred to this as 'a free wager of faith' where a willingness to risk becoming guilty through any 'free responsible action' itself rests on the grace of God 'who promises forgiveness and consolation to the person who becomes a sinner in that action' (Bonhoeffer, *Letters and Papers from Prison*, quoted in Green 2005: 45).

Here we can now return to our earlier discussions about just war theory, and especially to those critics who wish to dismiss it as irrelevant because it does not seem to 'work'. As we have seen this largely arises when it is reduced to the status of a checklist, for then it becomes far too dependent upon subjective interpretation. While accepting that the tradition of tyrannicide is not the same as that pertaining to just war, Bonhoeffer's example provides valuable insights, two of which are particularly important for our argument.

Firstly, his life and example shows that it is possible to hold to an ethic which is far more than just a set of principles. As Stassen remarks (2010a: 195), 'Most English-speakers use the word *pacifist* to mean a person opposed on principle to violence in any form, especially in war. But Bonhoeffer explicitly opposed an ethic of principles; his "pacifism" cannot be a principle of non-violence'. He then adds that even 'the leading pacifist theologian, John Howard Yoder, criticised an interpretation of Bonhoeffer that equated pacifism with moral absolutism' (2010a: 195). As his involvement with the attempted coup d'état revealed, Bonhoeffer's peace ethic nevertheless enabled him to be committed to a course of action which, at one and the same time, was commensurate with his Christian faith and yet still far more dynamic than trying to adhere to any so-called 'objective' checklist.

The second insight to be gleaned from Bonhoeffer's example is simply that his is a stance which recognises the realities of the world, and especially the existence of sin and guilt, as well as the equally substantial realities of grace and forgiveness. His is not a kind of reworked Niebuhrian Christian realism, but a determination to live out faithfully that call to commitment and obedience to Christ which he regarded as implicit in the Sermon on the Mount, along with a willingness to embrace the risks and dangers which inevitably follow such radical discipleship. As Jenkins (2010: 252) points out, for Bonhoeffer the usual understanding of ethics 'stands for the attempt to acquit oneself, to safely extricate oneself from ambiguity'. He then adds this compelling thought:

> That sort of ethics shuts down theological creativity, insulates oneself from reality, from neighbours, and from God. Bonhoeffer confronts that tendency with the irruption of command: Might not God call us beyond conscience, beyond good and evil, beyond our own selves? (2010: 252)

Some may feel that Bonhoeffer's willingness to risk becoming guilty, along with the accompanying emphasis upon grace, is to invite irresponsible, even unethical action, since dependence on God's grace will effectively 'cancel out' any wrongdoing. Yet quite apart from Bonhoeffer's clear commitment to peace, as well as his readiness to hazard all for the sake of his Christian beliefs, to make such a charge would be to ignore the teaching of Romans 6:1–2: 'What then are we to say? Should we continue in sin in order that grace may abound? By no means! How can we who died to sin go on living in it?' (NRSV). Worth noting is the fact that, far from condemning Bonhoeffer's part in the attempted coup, Stassen (2010a: 204) regards his action as 'an act of peacemaking, akin to humanitarian intervention or the "responsibility to protect", which the ethic of just peacemaking affirms in carefully limited conditions'.

This theme of just peacemaking will be taken up shortly, but before doing so it is helpful to ask the question: what might be the implications of all these discussions for the future development of just war theory? Doubtless there are many which could be identified, but at this juncture let us note just three. Firstly, by reorienting the debate around the themes of sin, guilt and grace the relevance of the Christian voice can be re-established alongside the powerful claims of the lawyers, politicians and military leaders. Moreover, when such pronouncements as are heard from the church currently tend to favour a view of pacifism which leaves little or no room for military action, Bonhoeffer's example potentially challenges the church to embrace a far broader analysis than seen in recent years.

Secondly, and following on from the point just made, it would be as wrong to try and present Bonhoeffer as giving support to war and violence, as to think he can be absorbed wholly into the pacifist 'camp'. Despite his participation in the failed attempt to kill Hitler, he remained firmly wedded to the importance of the principle of last resort. 'Free responsible action' demands that all possible avenues are explored thoroughly before taking up arms, and this is a message which needs to be restated whenever the justification for military involvement is being considered. Arguably this precondition should even be operative when considering military interventionism, such as in peacekeeping operations, for there is no doubt that the mere presence of a foreign military force increases the likelihood of violence escalating.

Thirdly, Bonhoeffer's thoroughgoing commitment to peace points us to the argument of many students of just war theory today, that a new category is required, namely that of *jus post bellum*. It is true that the conditions for a just peace are implicit in the criteria for *jus ad bellum*, particularly the condition stating that the aim of any conflict must be that of restoring peace as soon as possible. Yet as McCready (2009: 67) mentions, 'Historically, in the run up to war, considerations of what should happen after the war usually gets lost in the shuffle'. Following a number of others, McCready is of the view that 'postwar [*sic*] planning has often been, at best, superficial – although post-war considerations are implicit in pre-war ethical analysis' (2009: 67). When this is overlaid with the sheer intensity and complexity of military operations today, the necessity for this third category of *jus post bellum*, to reinforce the ethical commitment to peace-making, becomes unavoidable.

Jus Post Bellum: Engaging with Peace

In considering what needs to be done to define this new category, McCready gives an important warning when he states that 'the purpose of a *jus post bellum* category is to increase the likelihood of a just and lasting peace, not provide an additional topic for academic papers and conferences' (2009: 68). However this still leaves unanswered the question concerning what criteria would constitute an effective *jus post bellum* and, as this chapter has already argued in relation to the other just war categories, McCready (2009: 72) warns against an approach which 'looks too much like a checklist'. Nevertheless he offers three possibilities for consideration (2009: 74) – right intention (the aim of establishing a more just society); retributive justice (which seeks to punish violations of the laws of war by either side); and, 'the obligation to re-establish political, economic, and social stability in the defeated nation(s)', even if this requires financial contribution from the victor. In other words, 'after the fighting is over the victor may not simply declare victory and walk away' (2009: 74).

It is fair to say that these are precisely the conditions under which many current military operations are carried out, notwithstanding the need and preparedness to use force in fighting one's enemy. There is, in fact, a growing awareness of the place and importance of peace-making and peacekeeping – both within the military community and beyond it – and it is therefore appropriate that in thinking about *jus post bellum* we do so in relation to these two key areas. As Dixon so aptly comments:

If just war is to be applied in a flexible but holistic way, and not with the legalism that seems to have taken it over, decision-makers and commanders need to balance conflicting factors with the end state always in mind. The best do this already. And the post-war situation that should be in sight in almost any such conflict – however distant a goal it may seem – is a just, reconstructed society at ease with itself: a reconciled society. (2009: 145)

In working towards this reconciled society Stassen (2010b: 89–113) suggests seven steps of just peace-making. In so doing he recognises that in today's pluralistic world if any ethic is going to command a public hearing it will need to be '*both* (1) an *explicitly Christian ethic* with a strong scriptural base and (2) a *public ethic* that appeals to reason, experience, and need and that cannot place the same emphasis on Scripture and prayer that an explicitly Christian ethic can' (Stassen 2010b: 93–4, original emphasis). These 'seven steps or axioms' (2010b: 94) are as follows:

1. *Affirm common security* – i.e. recognise 'that our security is inextricably interwoven with the security of our adversaries; whether we like it or not, we have a security partnership' (2010b: 94).
2. *Take independent initiatives* – i.e. be prepared to take actions 'directed towards transforming the reaction of the adversary', so that such independent initiatives 'make our defensive intent and our desire for détente credible' (2010b: 99). One clear example the author offers is that of refusing to engage in an ever increasing arms war, leading to unnecessary stockpiling of weaponry which signals an offensive rather than defensive attitude. He accepts the need for deterrence to be maintained through a sufficiently robust policy, but suggests that deterrence often 'tips over' into a situation where 'distrust increases the danger of accidental war' (2010b: 99).
3. *Talk with your enemy* – although self-explanatory, Stassen warns against situations where 'sometimes governments negotiate for show … offering terms designed to be rejected by their adversaries'. As he rightly states, 'This is not the talk and the listening of conflict resolution' (2010b: 102).
4. *Seek human rights and justice* – noting that 'the lack of human rights is itself the absence of peace', Stassen argues that the 'relative deprivation of human rights is the major cause of violent rebellion' (2010b: 103). Later on he acknowledges that for many in the west 'human rights' are often defined too narrowly; suggesting that in the United States, for example, emphasis is often placed upon 'the freedoms of speech and press, religious liberty, and freedom from torture or arbitrary imprisonment but [people] de-emphasise economic rights to health care, housing, food and jobs' (2010b: 138). Without commenting on the detail of this, we can see readily how this effect can be greatly multiplied on the world stage where many face deprivation of the worst possible kinds imaginable.

5. *Acknowledge vicious cycles: participate in the peace-making process* –
   although this follows on closely from the preceding steps, here Stassen
   has in mind the specific challenge represented by the nuclear arms race,
   deploring how 'these technological developments continue despite the fact
   that they are out of step with political reality and make life precarious'.
   He also notes the huge economic costs of such development, as well as
   the environmental and health consequences created by 'nuclear testing and
   uranium production processes' (2010b: 106).

6. *End judgemental propaganda, make amends* – i.e. be prepared to
   'acknowledge to others that we have caused hurt and want to take actions
   to do better' (2010b: 107). Stated simply this is about publicly recognising
   that rarely, if ever, is any party to a conflict entirely blameless, even the so-
   called 'innocent' party. Again it would be possible to discuss this in greater
   detail, but it is fair to say that certainly in regard to war-fighting history
   shows that wrongs are just as likely to be committed by those reluctantly
   drawn into the conflict as a defensive measure, as by the original antagonists.

7. *Work with citizens' groups for the truth* – i.e. 'participate in groups with
   accurate information and a voice in policy making' (2010b: 109). This
   step is really about transparency on the part of policy-makers and being
   genuinely open to public consultation while, for their part, citizens are
   enjoined to seek ways to actively engage with such consultative processes.

In comparing both McCready's three possible criteria and Stassen's seven
axioms there is, inevitably, a reasonable degree of overlap. Less clear is quite
how some of these ideas could be codified into clear principles to be applied by
the international community *post bellum*, although this may be an advantage
given our earlier discussions about the legalism now surrounding traditional
just war theory. At the same time it needs to be noted that several of these
suggested conditions indicate a prior need for attitudinal changes on the part of
the international community and, where vested interests resist such changes, the
force of law is likely to be needed to underpin the steps required to implement a
true *jus post bellum*. Bugnion hints as much when, while talking about the need for
humanitarian laws to be observed during conflict, he writes:

> With respect to recent conflicts, there has been a general feeling that substantive
> rules did indeed exist but that major crimes nevertheless occurred owing to utter
> failure to respect those rules. Special consideration should therefore be given to
> strengthening the mechanisms for ensuring the law's implementation. (2004: 53)

While appreciating the sentiments being expressed here (along with the fact
they can apply equally to *jus ad bellum* or *jus post bellum*), the risk with this call
for a reinforcing of international legal processes is that, once again, important
ideals could be reduced to a mere checklist. This particular concern will be
addressed shortly in the final part of this chapter when we come to look at the role

of chaplains vis-à-vis just war theory, but before leaving this brief discussion of *jus post bellum* one more observation needs to be made and that is to do with the place of non-governmental organisations (NGOs) both during and after conflict.

In a short paper presented to the same Royal United Services Institute conference as that attended by Bugnion, Yates (2004) challenges the perceptions about the Afghanistan conflict presented to the conference by British and American government speakers. In particular he questions the claim that stabilisation had been successful, pointing out that 'stabilization is not merely a matter of moving from bombs to bread. It is much more complex. Warlord, rather than democratic, politics continues' (Yates 2004: 139). Given that the conference took place in 2002,[1] and that the fighting is still going on in Afghanistan over a decade later, as this book is published, his critique seems remarkably prescient.

Speaking as an NGO worker and member of the UK-NGO Military Contact Group, Yates argues for due recognition of the work of NGOs both during and after war, and for an appreciation of the special expertise they bring to war-ravaged areas. In order to facilitate this it might be necessary for the military to either withdraw from any involvement in relief operations, or to avoid involvement in the first place, and to recognise that NGOs are frequently 'better equipped, experienced and demonstrably motivated by impartiality and humanitarianism' (Yates 2004: 140). Echoing these thoughts, another conference speaker and NGO worker, Tim Aldred, pleads for '"space" for humanitarian action to take place', highlighting that NGOs 'do not simply turn up at the end [of war]; [they] are engaged *throughout* a conflict' (Aldred 2004: 149, original emphasis).

In offering their perspectives Bugnion, Yates and Aldred are making an important contribution, not just to any discussion about what passes for humanitarian provision during and after conflict, but to the whole debate surrounding just war. They are surely right that NGOs have a long track record of working in some of the most arduous and dangerous places in the world, whilst their claim to impartiality is often their only protection. As far as *jus post bellum* is concerned, therefore, it seems entirely reasonable that their presence should be given every support by the international community, including by any military forces responsible for overseeing the transition from *in bello* to *post bellum*.

This chapter began with a discussion about the growing secularism surrounding just war theory today, frequently leading to a point where the tradition tends to be reduced to the status of a legal 'tick test'. In order to reverse this trend we have argued for a rediscovery of the theological roots which have historically been foundational for just war thinking, although it is recognised that there are those who feel the theory is no longer relevant given the type of conflict (including international terrorism) which is increasingly prevalent throughout the world. However using the example of Bonhoeffer we have argued that it is still valid

---

[1]   Although the conference took place in 2002 the proceedings were not published until 2004, hence the apparent discrepancy between the conference date and the related bibliographical entries.

to appeal to just war thinking, for this does not necessarily mean denying either one's own peace ethic or a general commitment to making and keeping peace. Nevertheless it is undeniably true that the changing nature of the threat now facing the international community requires a constant reappraisal of just war theory, including giving attention to what might be required by a new category of *jus post bellum*. In order to give all this some practical focus, we will now turn to the last part of this chapter and consider how everything that has been discussed thus far might coalesce in the praxis of current British military chaplaincy.

Implications for Military Chaplaincy

Before actually looking at chaplains per se, it will be useful to begin with the concept of the 'strategic corporal' (Krulak 1999). Based on a fictional account of military involvement in a humanitarian programme, Krulak coined the term to denote how, in future operations, it is increasingly likely that decisions will need to be made quickly on the ground by relatively junior personnel. Moreover, given the presence of embedded media such decisions are also likely to be broadcast far and wide, possibly affecting the planning occurring at a more senior, strategic level. Two years earlier, in a speech to Washington's National Press Club on 10 October 1997, Krulak also introduced the idea of 'three block war' to indicate his belief that, again in future operations, service personnel will more often than not find themselves simultaneously engaged in war fighting, conducting peacekeeping operations and assisting with humanitarian initiatives, all within a limited physical environment roughly equivalent to not much more than three continuous city blocks.

   While these ideas have not been universally adopted throughout the military world, it is enough to note here that they still enjoy a measure of currency within the British forces, at least within the army. Both ideas are, for instance, part of the lexicon used during officer training at the Royal Military Academy Sandhurst, and certainly the importance of equipping junior soldiers to exercise leadership on the ground is viewed as a significant task. To this extent at least the term 'strategic corporal' is useful shorthand for what is coming to be expected of junior personnel in the face of operations progressively characterised by asymmetric fighting, insurgency and terrorist activity, frequently taking place within a hostile and constrained urban environment, where almost every movement is subject to the searching scrutiny of the world's media.

   The challenge, of course, is equipping soldiers to face these newly emerging responsibilities and, as Krulak (1999) discerns, 'an emphasis on *character* remains the bedrock upon which everything else is built', before adding that 'the really tough issues confronting Marines will be *moral* quandaries, and they must have the wherewithal to handle them appropriately' (original emphasis). Although said of American marines and before such events as the terrorist attacks on the twin towers on 11 September 2001, or the subsequent war in Afghanistan, his remarks retain considerable resonance today.

Krulak's comments, in fact, serve to remind us of the importance of seeing military personnel as moral beings, and the need for them to be encouraged to be personally morally responsible for their actions. In discussing classical just war theory O'Donovan (2003: 16) mentions that modern critics often disparage the idea that 'the common soldier could and should presume the justice of his [*sic*] prince's decisions until persuaded otherwise'. However he argues that this notion came into being 'precisely to allow *more* scope for the soldier to exercise judgement *about his own actions*' (2003: 16, original emphasis), since he would be unable to make an informed decision about the justness or otherwise of a war, not being party to all the relevant information. O'Donovan concedes that the time could come where even the most junior soldier would know enough to lead him to recognise that a conflict could no longer be supported, in which case 'at that point he must extricate himself from it as best he could' (2003: 16). Whatever the merits or otherwise of O'Donovan's argument, the demand for individual moral responsibility is again paramount.

Writing in a different context, Sherman says much the same thing when, speaking of the warrior's need to guard against *unbridled* anger or a desire for revenge, she states:

> To be a soldier, defending principle, abiding by rules of engagement, cognizant of the constraints of just war and just conduct in war embodied in such documents as the Law of Land Warfare or the Geneva Conventions, in fact requires a principled response to the demands of warfare. To act out of frenzy or rage, [or] to systematically dehumanize the enemy in the way that anger toward an enemy often requires … [is] to risk breaking the moral framework of war. (Sherman 2004: 121)

Thus in a few brief sentences Sherman recognises that war can and should have a moral framework, that those engaged in it are morally responsible for their own actions and, lastly, that while the presence of anger in war fighting is readily understood, that ought not to be allowed to lead to seeing one's enemy as any less human than oneself.

In trying to hold all this together, different armed forces have adopted differing programmes of moral and ethical training. For example, in recent years the British Army has adopted a 'Values and Standards' programme, which seeks to instil six core values of courage, discipline, respect for others, integrity, loyalty and selfless commitment, underscored by three key standards enjoining soldiers to exhibit behaviour which is always lawful, appropriate and totally professional (British Army 2011). Both formal and informal methods are used to pass on these core values, but once again we can see that the key concern is that service personnel are helped to form those qualities deemed to be essential for the demands of military life.

Here we come to the particular contribution of chaplains, for although they have always been involved in the formal delivery of character training programmes of one kind or another, arguably that is the least significant part of their influence when thinking about just war. Quite simply, if our armed forces personnel are to be morally equipped to deal with the peculiar challenges which have been outlined above, especially those faced in the heat and stress of high intensity operations, then they need to be able to see what this looks like in actual practice. Given that just war demands an ethical framework, and that recognizing the humanity of all can help avoid demonising the enemy, there are clear parallels here with the gospel message. Moreover, in the person of the chaplain it is possible to offer an example of living out the morally responsible life, grounded in the call to human community represented by the Christian church.

Lest critics argue that any participation by chaplains in the just war debate is to render them morally compromised by association, we need only recall our earlier discussion of Bonhoeffer, and how his example points towards a principled ethic which allows active participation, not just in the discourse surrounding war, but in the actual theatre of war itself. As was seen this involves risk – both of a moral and physical nature – and, ultimately, there is a danger of becoming guilty by working through one's commitment to a chosen course of action. Nevertheless the risks must be faced for, as Bonhoeffer himself said (with no little humility), 'We have learnt a bit too late in the day that action springs not from thought, but from a readiness for responsibility' (Bonhoeffer 1964: 158).

For military personnel caught up in the reality of fighting, and who frequently have to do things far beyond the experience of most people, the possibility of guilt should not be underestimated, nor the difficulty of dealing with it in a way which truly restores the individual again. Chaplains, however, having themselves shared the same physical and moral risks, not to mention the environment within which war takes place, are well placed to offer the grace of God revealed in Christ who, despite knowing no sin, was made to be sin 'so that in him we might become the righteousness of God' (see 2 Corinthians 5:21, NRSV). It is also important to note this verse is set within a context of teaching about reconciliation, for those who have been reconciled to God are in a better position than most to seek reconciliation with others, since they have personally experienced both guilt and forgiveness. Here we recall the words of Dixon quoted earlier, asserting that the aim of any war ought to be the restoration of 'a just, reconstructed society at ease with itself: a reconciled society' (Dixon 2009: 145). By their presence and ministry, chaplains point to such a reconciliation, not as some vain hope, but as a realistic possibility when grounded in faith in God.

Yet – and again as seen when discussing Bonhoeffer – there is the equally real danger of offering a forgiveness which is too easy. Not only might this fail to address deep-seated needs in those who have been caught up in war, but it could actually discourage them from facing the reality of sin in their own conduct *in bello*. And once that is allowed to occur, it is but a small step to regarding oneself as entirely right and 'just', and the enemy as entirely wrong and 'unjust'. Even if this stops short of actually demonising the enemy (in which state one is more inclined to do whatever one wishes to the 'demonic' other, since the other is now seen as inhuman or sub-human), such an attitude would hardly be conducive to reconciliation of any kind.

In his seminal book *Exclusion and Embrace*, Miroslav Volf (1996) takes as his central theme the embrace which God offers to all through the sacrifice of Jesus upon the cross; an embrace, moreover, which was offered even 'while we still were sinners' and 'enemies' of God, needing to be reconciled to him (see Romans 5:8–10). Far from dehumanising or demonising the enemy, Volf argues powerfully that 'if we believe rightly in Jesus Christ who unconditionally embraced us, the godless perpetrators, our hearts will be open to receive others, even enemies, and our eyes will be open to see from their perspective' (1996: 215).

Here again chaplains have a great deal to offer, not only in terms of setting an example of openness to one's former enemy, but also in reminding those to whom they minister that 'all have sinned and fall short of the glory of God' (Romans 3:23, NRSV). Needless to say this truth requires sensitive handling especially when dealing with any who have seen friends and colleagues killed in conflict, but it is still a truth which, once comprehended, paves the way for a recognition of the other as someone equally in need of forgiveness. One helpful way in which such openness could conceivably be encouraged might involve including acts of confession and repentance in any post-tour services of thanksgiving, for the moment one's stance becomes that of confession, rather than bellicose triumphalism (however muted), the potential for reconciled relationships is increased.

Undoubtedly difficult though it is, Jesus' command to love even our enemies (see Matthew 5:44, NRSV) challenges the all too common desire for revenge, whilst still accepting the reality that enemies do exist. However the gospel message, along with the example of Jesus' own sacrifice, together remind us that we are also called to work for reconciliation, perhaps all the more so in the hardest of circumstances such as those presented by war. To help others recognise this is arguably the greatest challenge faced by chaplains when trying to work out the implications of just war theory, but this is precisely where the tradition offers the most realistic hope of enabling a conflict to aim for justice. As O'Donovan (2003: 96) says, 'We learn to conceive of just war as force put under the discipline, and in the service, of justice', thus picking up a point made in his preface in which he states that 'this tradition is in fact neither a 'theory', nor about 'just wars', but '*a proposal for doing justice in the theatre of war*' (O'Donovan 2003: vii, original emphasis).

Without labouring the point the justice being referred to here, of course, goes far beyond that defined solely by reference to law, for it rather alludes to God's justice which seeks the good of all. Interestingly this thought is echoed by some non-Christian writers, such as Tim Winter, currently the Shaykh Zayed Lecturer in Islamic Studies at Cambridge University. He writes: 'In the developed theologies of war in Judaism, Christianity and Islam, to take up arms is not simply to protect oneself or one's ethnic group. It is to defend the precious principle that there should be justice in creation' (Winter 2010: 9). Although it is well beyond the scope of this present chapter to consider what similarities might or might not exist between just war theory as we have been discussing it and similar traditions in other religions, this brief comment at least indicates the possibility of the principles of just war having a broader appeal than may often be supposed. At the same time, and mindful of conflict situations which frequently cross different cultures and religions, we do well to note Winter's concluding remark that 'no amount of just war theory can bring peace, if there is no heroic empathy with the Other' (Winter 2010: 24).

Just war theory has, inevitably, undergone many changes through the centuries, and critics sometimes seize upon this aspect to dismiss it out of hand. For them the idea that the tradition has to be constantly reworked merely shows that it cannot be trusted – it is, quite simply, too insecure a concept to be regarded as a reliable guide for moral choices about war. Yet far from dismissing it there is a strong case to be made not just for its retention, but for its rediscovery within the mainstream of theological enquiry. That it has offered a framework for meaningful discussion about war since the time of Augustine, and still continues to do so, is testimony to its very real usefulness. However we have also seen that any tendency to reduce just war theory to a mere checklist ought to be resisted firmly, for this is to strip it of its dynamic potential. The best way of ensuring this does not happen is to reassert its central Christian aspect, pre-eminently seen not in the sinful crusading spirit of former ages, but in the example of the one who gave his life on the cross in order to bring about true peace and reconciliation. This message lies at the very heart of the Christian gospel, and it is a message which service chaplains have the privilege of conveying to the entire armed forces community.

Chapter 9
Moral Engagements:
Morality, Mission and Military Chaplaincy

Andrew Todd with Colin Butler

Introduction

In building on previous chapters, this chapter will offer a critical overview of the distinctive moral role of British military chaplains, in order to understand how this is an aspect of their 'mission'. That last word is chosen deliberately, recognising the special conditions under which military chaplains operate. As was signalled in Chapter 1, they are engaged in mission both in an ecclesial sense, and in the military sense, and the word provides a theological point of entry into consideration of the ambiguity of the role of chaplain, and the necessary tension with which the chaplain lives, between the call to live out their faith and the responsibility to contribute positively to the life of their unit.

The approach taken will address chaplains' own discourse relating to their multi-dimensional moral role, drawing on new evidence from the research project which gave rise to this book. In particular the chapter will investigate the way in which, in the research data, chaplains construct their role in negotiation with the military discourse of morality and ethos, which forms an essential dimension of the context in which they operate; and in their day-to-day interaction with military personnel. In evaluating this discourse, the chapter will seek to identify how chaplains deploy particular ethical language and/or approaches; and the significance of this contribution to moral debate and practice and the practical ethics of war. Of particular significance will be the distinctive, and often unrecognised, contribution which chaplains make in the military context by working between moral systems from different settings: that of the military, of wider society and of faith communities.

The chapter will then locate the moral role of the military chaplain within wider frames, offering a new theoretical perspective on the role and its wider significance. Drawing on, and extending, the work of Gadamer and Habermas, it will argue that the role is essentially hermeneutic – about interpreting different traditions in relation to each other. This critical role suggests a particular understanding of the 'mission' of chaplaincy, that the chaplain is not so much a missionary to the military, as someone responsible for discerning where God is at work within that context. This understanding gives rise to the critical and highly significant question: how is the mission of God (the *missio Dei*) to be discerned in the midst of armed conflict and the use of lethal force? This question is critical both for chaplains, as they participate in the 'mission' of the armed services; and for the churches who sponsor chaplains, and whose members serve as military personnel alongside them. The chapter will argue that the question demands a positive engagement with the moral purpose of the military from the churches, rather than a more passive, functional pacifism (cf. Reed 2004: 73) which is currently more prevalent.

Prior Question – What Kind of Actor?

As part of this evaluation of chaplaincy it is worth asking, as a preliminary, what kind of 'actor' the British military chaplain might be. This is significant both in terms of contextualising their role, and in understanding their scope for manoeuvre within the military context.

One way of establishing what kind of actor the chaplain is, involves delineating the lines of accountability which exist as part of the governance of military chaplaincy. Taking British Army chaplains as the example, within the frameworks set by the Army, they are the subject of dual command. They are commanded, or controlled, primarily by the Royal Army Chaplains' Department (RAChD) and secondarily by the commanding officer of the unit with which they serve. So whereas chaplains are commissioned and hold equivalent rank to other commissioned officers, which makes them appear to be straightforwardly part of the state's military arm, the reality is more complex. Chaplains' ultimate military command structure being provided by the RAChD places the chaplain, in a formal sense, outside the chain of command. In practice however in unit life they receive both appropriate direction to allow them to function and also clear requirements that they are expected to fulfil. These two aspects nonetheless generate a degree of independence within the military structure, which is significant for their moral role. This status is perhaps reinforced by other ways in which the chaplain is set apart, for instance as someone who is not only a non-combatant, but who also does not bear arms.[1]

But the question of chaplains' accountability is more complex still. For while chaplains are answerable as officers to the army, they also remain accountable to their 'sending churches'. They must remain in good standing with their church and are not infrequently required to report to it.[2] If churches are reckoned to be

---

[1]   Other non-combatants, such as doctors, do bear arms for the purposes of self-defence.

[2]   Currently, all commissioned chaplains within the army are Christian. Sending churches include: Anglican, Roman Catholic, Methodist, Baptist/URC/Congregational, Church of Scotland/Presbyterian, Elim or Assemblies of God. See http://www.army.mod. uk/chaplains/career/1223.aspx [accessed: 5 April 2010]. Representatives of world faiths other than Christianity are appointed as Civilian Chaplains to the Military by the MoD, see http://www.raf.mod.uk/chaplains/whoweare/worldfaiths.cfm [accessed: 5 April 2010].

amongst non-state actors (see, e.g., Ryall 2001), then chaplains are in some sense non-state actors within a state operation. Once again, this is significant for an understanding of the contribution to military morality made by the distinctive figure of the 'padre'. This is an aspect of the contextualisation of chaplains' voices, and of the construction of their particular moral discourse.

The Military Discourse of Morality

The British armed services generally have a policy of maintaining a distinct, cohesive military identity, rooted in a commitment to 'traditional' values (perceived as greater than that to be found in contemporary society), including a Christian heritage (Deakin 2008). This was developed in relation particularly to the British Army in the last decade of the twentieth century and the first decade of the twenty-first.[3] Key documents included: an internal paper, *The Discipline and Standards Paper* (1993); (McGill 1999); (MoD 2000a); and (MoD 2000b).[4] At the heart of the development of a distinct army 'ethos' lie the core values of the army: courage, discipline, integrity, loyalty, respect for others, selfless commitment. This is in keeping with military doctrine that holds that the effectiveness of the armed services is directly dependent on their morality. In this understanding there are three components to fighting power: the 'conceptual' (the thinking behind the ability to fight), the 'physical' (the means, or resources, to fight) and the 'moral', which is defined as follows:

> The Moral Component has three fundamental elements: the motivation to achieve the task in hand; effective leadership from those placed in authority; and sound management of all personnel and resources. Together they produce the will to fight. (MoD 2000b: section 0108)[5]

Lest the picture seem too clear, it ought to be said that moral reasoning within the military context is quite diverse. Evaluation of military behaviour includes a rules-based approach, reinforced by the concept of discipline and obedience, but also one which evaluates actions on the basis of outcome (as in the consequentialist Service Test, which offers the criterion of the contribution a soldier's behaviour makes to military effectiveness). And the moral reasoning implied by the development of a military ethos is also ambiguous. On the one hand it may look like an example of the development of corporate values – encouraging soldiers to sign up to the army 'way'. On the other hand the aim may be more far-reaching – to encourage the development of the virtuous soldier, for whom the core values act as virtues.

---

[3]   The army process is mirrored by similar debate and evolution of core values in the other two services.

[4]   For a fuller discussion see Mileham (2008).

[5]   See http://www.abnetwork.org/articles/military-covenant/ [accessed: 15 April 2011].

However, the ethos outlined above in turn constructs the organisational role of the military chaplain. The overall role is defined in terms of providing: spiritual leadership; moral guidance; and pastoral care.[6] The moral role has a formal component. In each service there is an expectation that chaplains will contribute to moral training, to the formation of personnel in the core values of their service. Chaplains are therefore involved in character training in initial (Phase One) training of recruits, and in continuing training which focuses on the core values of each service.[7]

It is recognised that the moral role of the chaplain also has its informal dimensions, which include responding to the questions of soldiers and acting as a critical friend to commanding officers. This is frequently described as acting as the 'moral compass' of the services; and is identified as an indirect, if key, aspect of the moral component of fighting power.

The organisational role of the chaplain is therefore constructed in terms of their contribution to the distinct moral identity of the armed services, and is embedded within military policy and doctrine. This raises the question (central to this chapter) about whether chaplains simply legitimate the military moral status quo. However, the ambiguity, discussed above, concerning the kind of 'actor' that a chaplain is, recontextualises this question. It encourages the observer to explore: the extent to which military chaplains' religious identity and affiliation generates room for manoeuvre in their engagement with military protocols and expectations; and the kind of power that places within the hands of the chaplain. To pursue this exploration we turn now to consideration of chaplains' own understanding and accounts of their moral role works.

Investigating the Moral Practice of Military Chaplains

During 2009 and 2010 the Cardiff Centre for Chaplaincy Studies[8] carried out a series of research workshops involving army and air force chaplains, together with interested academics, to investigate 'military chaplaincy and the ethics of conflict', with the support of a small grant from the British Academy. As part of the workshops, the perspectives of participants (especially those who were, or had been, military chaplains) were gathered on the moral role of chaplains. This section of the chapter draws directly on that exercise. The quotes are taken

---

[6]   See http://www.army.mod.uk/chaplains/role/default.aspx [accessed: 5 April 2010].

[7]   In the army this continuing role is governed by the protocol MATT6, and focuses on rehearsing the core values of the army.

[8]   The Centre is a partnership between Cardiff University and St Michael's College. It exists to research chaplaincy and the issues it raises, and to offer education and professional development to chaplains. See http://www.stmichaels.ac.uk/chaplaincy-studies.php. It delivers an MTh in Chaplaincy Studies to military chaplains under contract to the MoD (as well as to chaplains in other domains).

from participating chaplains (or former chaplains) reflecting back the voices of military personnel and their own voices, casting light on how they construct their role in dialogue with others. The section will consider: moral questions asked of chaplains, especially in relation to the contexts in which those questions may be located and their interaction; questions asked about the chaplain; and the nature of chaplains' responses. This will provide a basis for discussing the implications of the research for understanding the moral role of chaplaincy.

Moral Questions Asked of Chaplains and their Contexts

A number of questions illustrated well the breadth of questions that come to military chaplains' ears. They also indicated that many issues raised by military personnel might well be raised by anyone in contemporary UK society. These included questions about sex and relationships ('is it right to pay for sex?', 'is it right for gay/lesbian couples to have married quarters?'), drugs and alcohol ('why are people out for drugs, but not for drink driving?'), and pay and conditions ('what is "robust man-management", what is bullying?'). These questions position military personnel, and chaplains, as members of contemporary society, not just of the military sub-culture. They also illustrate the breadth of the dialogue relating to moral issues in which chaplains are involved, and locate that dialogue within the broader pastoral relationship between chaplains and personnel.

However, there were indications of particular military policies giving rise to specific moral questions. The policies include: the services policy of giving the same rights to same-sex couples in a civil partnership, as to those who are married; and a 'zero-tolerance' policy towards drug taking, reinforced by random drug tests. These responses to policy were, however, little different from responses to equal opportunities, or drug, policies in other organisations.

In terms of moral reasoning the questions construct a picture of moral dialogue between chaplain and soldier (whatever the attention paid to replies!). Chaplains perceive an expectation that they will respond to questions such as: what justification is there for a different policy in relation to alcohol, than that in place for illegal drugs? What agenda lies behind policy on bullying? What is the religious perspective on sex?

Other questions, identified by chaplains as being asked by military personnel, develop a picture of a tension between the military ethos, and the moral mood of wider society. These included questions such as: 'why is this not a nine-to-five job?', 'when I put on uniform – have I sold out on individuality?'. A number of further questions explored loyalty, including issues of loyalty to 'mates', or a spouse, alongside loyalty to the army, or to orders.

A tension, which chaplains also talked about during the research workshop, is apparent here: between what happens during the working week and what happens at other times (as it were, on 'Saturday night'). Chaplains commented on different moral codes operating in these different areas of soldiers' lives. For example, the difference might be between sexual ethics driven almost entirely by self-interest and pleasure in the setting of a Saturday night out, and a strong commitment to the well-being of fellow soldiers during the week. The limited effect on moral reasoning of a strong espoused corporate ethos is seen in the tension between 'the uniform' and individuality; in the questions about whether the army is a job or a whole-life occupation; and in the questions raised by the core value of 'loyalty' for participation in different social contexts: army; marriage; amongst 'mates'.

Further, chaplains' accounts suggest that they are at home engaging with both contexts for moral discourse, not just that provided by the military ethos, but also that which has a wider cultural currency; and they are open to discuss questions which explore the boundaries and overlap between moral domains. The ambiguity of the chaplain's role appears to create an opportunity to which military personnel respond. In research conducted by the Cardiff Centre for Chaplaincy Studies during 2010 (Todd and Tipton 2011), prison chaplains were identified by prison staff as symbols of the world outside the prison important within the system. It would seem that military chaplains too have this symbolic role which shapes their moral engagements. This compares well with McCormack's proposal (2005) that the chaplains' moral role be characterised as that of an 'external voice' at work within the military context.

The above pattern sets the context for questions asked of chaplains that are more likely to be occasioned by deployment to a theatre of operation and the experience of combat. Some questions reported by chaplains are about the immediacy of this setting: 'Was it right that I killed that man?', 'I got a real thrill about killing – what do I do about it?', 'Can I be forgiven (for killing)? ... by whom?', 'Can I find peace for failing to save soldiers, or civilians?' (a Commanding Officer's question). Clearly these raise a range of issues, including the theological. The question of killing people highlights the possibility of action which may be justified in terms of necessity, but still carries with it guilt that needs to be assuaged (as is discussed by Coleman elsewhere in Chapter 8 of this volume).

Other questions reveal a different order of moral reflection, in relation to particular conflicts (e.g. Iraq or Afghanistan): 'Should we pull out?', 'Would the deaths [of our colleagues] be in vain if we do?', 'What is victory?', 'Why haven't we got the kit we need?', 'Why aren't we allowed to defend ourselves as we see fit; in relation to: shooting back; use of landmines; treatment of prisoners?', 'Why are the rules of engagement so one sided?'.

All these questions indicate an awareness of the political context of military operations. Not surprisingly, in a world where military personnel are often aware of media representation of their actions, and of the questions arising, in the midst of combat, media questions become part of the dialogue with the padre. The questions offer a picture of the tension between military values (loyalty, commitment to each other), together with the culture of honour to which those values give rise (seen in the honour given to those who have died), and the critical questions asked of those who have taken the political decision to commit the armed services to this campaign, and who decide on the manner of its execution. Perhaps most poignant is the personal question that sits at the heart of such a tension: 'My mother says I should leave the army, I've done my bit, should I tell them I'm not fit?'.

Chaplains present, through their identification of particular questions asked of them, an identity which is built on dealing with the moral tension between participation in the ethos of the services and awareness of society's evaluation of that role. Two questions arise. Firstly, how does this expand understanding of why (according to chaplains' perceptions) such questions are asked of the padre? Secondly, how comfortable are chaplains in negotiating this complex moral territory?

Questions Asked about the Chaplain

Some clues to the first of the two above questions are furnished by chaplains' presentation of questions asked about their own role. These demonstrate the chaplains' view that their status and identity is a talking point, the source of misunderstanding and suspicion, but also valued. Religion appears to be at the heart of such questions: 'How can you be a vicar and in the Army?'. Questions explore such issues as the difference between chaplains and other officers (and whether this is justified); and whether chaplaincy offers value for money. A particular recurring issue has to do with chaplains being unarmed.[9] Reactions to this vary from amazement, to suspicion (because other personnel must therefore carry the burden of protecting the chaplain), to valuing the fact that the chaplain does not carry a weapon. Indeed, there is some evidence that the unarmed chaplain has a totemic status – soldiers want to be where the padre is, to travel in the same transport as s/he does.

A similar ambivalence is seen in how military personnel respond to religion in general. While participating in religious ritual (such as a repatriation ceremony), they will be critical of religion: 'religion cause wars'; 'religion is part of problem we're here to solve'.

What the above views suggest is that, while the response to the chaplain's religious status and identity is complex, it is nonetheless significant. At least in chaplains' minds, their being religious is part of the reason why moral issues are brought to their door. This is seen not only in the specific questions about religion, but also in the theological dimension of some other reported questions considered above.[10] This is, in one sense, an obvious conclusion! However, it is

---

[9]   As indicated above, chaplains are non-combatants. This does not require them to be unarmed (chaplains from other countries operating under the Geneva Convention are armed for the purposes of self-defence); but this is the current practice of the British armed services.

[10]   The picture of why chaplains were the focus for moral questions was expanded elsewhere in the research. Chaplains' direct responses to this question highlighted: the significance of their pastoral relationship with personnel, and their availability; their view that personnel valued the moral framework that chaplains were able to offer; and the way

relevant when considering the room for manoeuvre generated by the chaplain's dual accountability both to the military, and to their faith community. It confirms the significance of the chaplain being a non-state actor in a state operation. It also provides a particular nuance to the suggestion that the chaplain acts as a symbol of the outside world – it is important that the chaplain symbolises the role of religion in a wider social context, albeit a version of that role which is not highly prescriptive about moral behaviour, but supportive of individual wrestling with moral questions.

The Nature of Chaplains' Responses

We turn next to the question of how comfortable chaplains are in negotiating such complex moral discourse. In the research project a number of questions asked of chaplains were designed to provoke reflection on how they dealt with moral issues discussed with them. In many ways the picture that emerged was in keeping with chaplains acting as a catalyst for the discussion of moral issues (rather than as a source of prescriptive moral judgements).

Thus chaplains' responses are characterised by: reflecting the question back – asking what the soldier thinks about the issue; unpacking what a core value, such as respect, might mean; exploring with personnel the range of different views on a subject, such as abortion; offering information which expands understanding of the issue. At the same time, chaplains are alive to the close relationship between their moral and their pastoral roles. They seek to discern the interplay between moral and underlying pastoral questions; the extent to which they are being invited to reinforce prejudice; whether personnel are looking for advocacy from the padre.

But at some points chaplains identify ways in which they offer a distinctive viewpoint. They were conscious of raising questions that did not represent a moral issue or dilemma for other members of the armed services. For example, chaplains might raise questions about honesty and money that could be met by a very different outlook to the chaplain's own. And there are questions that chaplains have to ask that aren't being asked, for example about racism, or about setting the moral tone.

A further nuance of chaplains' self-understanding emerged from a conversation on training that focused on the non-voluntary nature of military moral training and the chaplain's involvement in this. The discussion of this theme paid particular attention to the chaplain's representative role and offers a picture of chaplains wrestling with this function; and of their not wanting to be defined by it. Ball captures this angst well, pointing to 'the challenge of [chaplains] being used as force multipliers or moral police through Core Values teaching' (2006: 48); and to the accompanying temptation, that 'the Core Values training can be seen [by

---

in which they were seen as having some 'wisdom', rooted in their being different, and represented the ethical expert.

chaplains] as a bargaining chip to maintain freedom to operate, influence and power' (2006: 57).

Thus for participants in the research workshops, involvement in moral training was an opportunity to say 'you matter' to soldiers, rather than just to communicate the army view. Training provided the opportunity to ask: 'how have you improved? How have you gone downhill?'. Chaplains themselves identified the ambivalence of their role – which is both representative and 'anarchic', maintaining that soldiers are glad of a critical perspective on the army. Participants suggested that the moral role of chaplains includes: being human; being subversive; being the clown.

The word 'subversive', used of military chaplains' moral role, particularly captured the attention of workshop participants. For example, it was regarded as a better word than 'prophetic'.[11] They discussed whether chaplains have permission to be subversive, concluding that they did. They further maintained that the chaplain's subversive role is part of the way in which military accountability works, providing checks and balances, not least for the Commanding Officer. This was a way of working that society has forgotten. Some questions remained about the 'subversive' role: whether it is tacit; and whether permission to exercise the role comes from: the RAChD; the army as a whole; the Christian tradition ('the gospel'); or the church.

It would be reasonable to conclude that 'subversive' acts as a label for the tension between the chaplain's commitment to the military and their perceived responsibility to speak the truth as part of their job. But the word sits a little oddly as a designation of what is, at heart, a supportive role, internal to military structures. Indeed other chaplains to whom Todd put this designation, during his involvement with ethics education offered to all British Army chaplains, found the term quite problematic. The import of the word is perhaps clarified by a later comment, that the subversive role is about discipline; that a key principle for the chaplain is about developing self-awareness which removes, or reduces, the need for imposed discipline to generate moral behaviour (because it increases self-discipline).

Understanding the Moral Role of Chaplaincy

The above exploration of how chaplains present their moral role as a dialogue with military personnel provides a basis for evaluating the kind of moral reasoning in which chaplains perceive themselves to be involved. Chaplains clearly give more weight to some of the possible approaches to morality provided within the military ethical discourse, less weight to others. There are few signs of chaplains

---

[11]   One of the traditional models of chaplaincy, used in different settings including the military one, is drawn from Christian theology. It identifies the chaplain's roles as those of: priest (attending to the ritual dimension of culture); pastor (offering pastoral care); and prophet (being prepared to speak out, or act as the advocate of those whom the chaplain serves).

themselves offering a rules-based approach to ethics. Rather they are open to discussion with military personnel that explores the issues that arise from the rules (as in the case of a zero-tolerance approach to drugs). And in the discussion of their role in non-voluntary training, the emphasis given to self-discipline makes their approach to rules-based ethics explicit – for chaplains imposed discipline is a poor substitute for a morality that has been internalised. This approach to rules is very much in keeping with chaplains' organisational status and identity. They are officers, but are not expected to give orders; they are under command, but in a way which locates them outside the chain of command. They use rank sparingly, preferring other forms of address, such as 'padre'.[12]

It would be wrong to conclude that chaplains are therefore straightforwardly consequentialist in their discussion of moral questions. Certainly they do spend considerable time with military personnel weighing up the consequences of actions, both those that belong clearly within the working, or operational, context, and those that have more to do with 'Saturday night' behaviour. This points to a role that is situational, not least because the moral goes hand in hand with the pastoral. But chaplains are clearly not afraid to introduce particular norms into their pastoral moral reasoning. They will work with the armed services' own norms, especially the core values (unpacking the nature of 'respect' for example). They will also draw on faith-based norms (perhaps in relation to the issue of abortion). And they will deploy norms that derive from contemporary society (such as that of equal opportunity in the face of racism). But they are careful as to how they offer such norms – the overall tenor of their approach is very much facilitative, rather than prescriptive; characterised by the skilful question, rather than by the dogmatic statement.

In working with the army's norms, it appears that chaplains feel the need to locate them in a wider frame than just that offered by military doctrine. On other occasions chaplains have commented that the core values are not inevitably the continuation of a Christian heritage, as the documents surrounding their evolution might suggest. And in their engagement with personnel, chaplains will make explicit connections with their own tradition. Further, the discussion about being 'subversive' in the context of training suggests a clear emphasis in the mode of working with military core values. Chaplains are critical of them when they operate as a tick list of corporate values.[13] Chaplains want personnel to inhabit the values. In chaplains' understanding of their contribution to the moral component of fighting power, core values appear as virtues, characteristics of the virtuous warrior, who is changed by living those values (cf. Totten 2006).

Against this background of moral reasoning, chaplains present particular aspects of their role that focus on armed conflict. Clearly they work with some of

[12]   Or 'Father' in the case of Roman Catholic Priests.

[13]   In the army this applies in relation to the regular rehearsing of the core values under the provisions of MATT6. Chaplains are concerned that this can become an exercise in paying lip-service.

the questions raised for military personnel that would come under the heading of *jus in bello*. The questions noted above connect with the issue of the proportionality of the means of war, and to a lesser extent, with those to do with discrimination between combatants and non-combatants. But chaplains also appear to be working with an implicit critique, perhaps to be found in the media, of decisions about entering into a particular conflict, that would be evaluated according to *jus ad bellum* criteria. For example, the question about the nature of victory raises further questions about both whether chances of success were properly evaluated, and whether the aim of bringing about peace through military engagement had been fully thought-through.[14] Such discussion, involving the deployment of the kind of moral reasoning outlined above, is at the heart of the chaplain's involvement in the practical ethics of war.

That such questions are dealt with in conversation with the chaplain returns attention to the critical role of military chaplaincy. *Jus ad bellum* questions are sensitive ones within the military context, amongst those whose role is to implement the decisions of the executive. Too much questioning of the political decision-making that gave rise to operations has the potential to destabilise the military community; undermining their identity as the servants of the state entrusted with the task of exercising lethal force in pursuit of peace, on behalf of the state. The chaplain, in discussing such questions, treads a careful line between acting as a pressure valve for inevitable questions arising out of the experience of combat, and opening up discussion that might undermine discipline. This prompts one to reiterate the question about how, given their ambivalent status, chaplains understand the relationship between their 'mission' and that of the armed services, to which the chapter will turn in due course. An answer to this question is further required in the light of the discussion about the chaplain having a 'subversive' role, however carefully interpretation of the word is nuanced.

The Genius of the Chaplain's Moral Engagement

Before turning to further consideration of the critical role of chaplaincy, it is worth asking, what is the particular contribution that chaplains make as they seek to underpin the 'moral component of fighting power'; in their role as 'moral compass'? It might be suggested that chaplains exercise a constraining role. This would be in keeping with the fact that chaplains are internal to the military, but introduce non-military perspectives, as part of their work with the military ethos. It would reflect the evidence of chaplains seeking to mitigate the effects of the military ethos, offered above. It would also be in keeping with the way chaplains have worked with, and advocated, the concept of 'restraint' in

---

[14]   On the principles of just war, both *jus ad bellum* and *jus in bello*, see, for example (Reed 2004; Reed and Ryall 2007); as well as Chapter 8 of this volume, by Coleman.

relation to military operations (see Todd 2008). But this may be something of an underestimate of the role.

In particular, it might underplay the importance of chaplains *connecting* moral domains. Their willingness to work with different moral contexts and discourses (military, faith-based, or drawn from contemporary society), and to bring those settings and diverse moral norms into dialogue with each other, may be one of the most significant aspects of chaplains' role and self-understanding. This approach, in all its richness, illustrates the way chaplains do act as both part of the state military operation *and* bring to bear a non-state moral perspective.[15] It might even suggest that military chaplains act as 'moral entrepreneurs' within the military setting, taking opportunities presented to them to reshape the military ethos and morality and consistently locating them within a wider frame (cf. Colonomos 2001).

This chapter has suggested that this ability to make connections is enabled by the ambiguous status of chaplaincy. That the chaplain is both part of the system and a symbol of that which is external to the military community appears to provide a space for military personnel to bring questions and concerns about the tension between being part of the military and also a member of wider society. It further enables chaplains to work with different moral systems, principles and contexts, as they respond to questions asked of them. This dynamic role is further facilitated by the chaplain's ambiguous role *within* the system – under the dual command of the RAChD and the commanding officer of the unit in which he or she serves; and outside the usual line of command. Exploiting this status in order to work with multiple moral perspectives is perhaps an aspect of the genius of military chaplaincy.

If Butler (2008) is right it may also be a necessary, or at least useful, part of the construction of a wider military identity, at least in the case of the army. He argues that the British Army is a 'clan' organisation (Ouchi 1980), with a high degree of socialisation of its members rooted in common values and particular traditions; and authority structures (particularly commissioned officers), which ensure the continued strength of army culture. Both values and authority structures are legitimated by external traditions, including Christianity which has a persistent role in army identity, to a different extent than in society at large. Chaplaincy thus contributes significantly to providing the 'sacred canopy' (Berger 1969) under which army culture is established and maintained. Butler too regards this role as not only significant, but also 'symbolic' (2008: 41).

---

[15]   Cf. the role of NGOs as private actors in public policy settings, discussed in Reinalda (2001).

The Chaplain as Interpreter

As we seek to locate the moral role of the military chaplain in wider frames of reference, hermeneutics provides an apposite lens. It should be already apparent that the chaplain has a significant responsibility as an interpreter of traditions. What is perhaps not yet obvious is the complexity of the chaplain's hermeneutical task. Gadamer (1979) suggests that we can only interpret a cultural tradition, as participants in that tradition. In other words, he is clear that all interpretation is historically situated. We interpret by becoming part of the 'effective history' (*Wirkungsgeschichte*), the continuing history of interpretation, of the texts in which the tradition is rooted. Such participation involves developing, or deepening, our effective historical consciousness (*wirkungsgeschichtliches Bewußtsein*). This consciousness grows through our awareness of our own 'horizon' and of others, especially the 'horizon' of a particular text which is significant within a tradition. Here 'horizon' connotes that collection of assumptions and understandings that maps our current perspective, or the perspective of the text. Interpretation, and more particularly 'understanding' (*Verstehen*), happens as we explore the difference of perspective between us and the other (the text); and as we come to points of common understanding, which represent what Gadamer calls a 'fusion of horizons'; at which point our perspective changes.

In the case of military chaplaincy, as in other aspects of life in contemporary society, interpretation is a plural affair. Chaplains are participants in plural traditions. For example, in relation to the discussion above of their moral role, they locate themselves within a faith tradition, a military tradition and traditions which shape contemporary society. The traditions become apparent as chaplains draw on aspects of those traditions and on particular texts. The latter include sacred texts, ethical texts (such as those which make up the just war tradition), military texts (such as the army's core values and the wider text of MoD 2000a), and texts relating to a tradition of human rights and individual freedom (such as those that are part of the history which leads up to the United Kingdom Equality Act 2010). Consciously, or unconsciously, chaplains work with plural 'horizons', both contemporary 'horizons' and historical ones. In their dialogue with military personnel about moral issues, as indicated above, a range of contemporary perspectives are apparent and are brought together in those conversations, as are the different cultural traditions which have given rise to those perspectives. The 'fusion of horizons', arriving at common understandings between chaplains and others, and between participants in such ethical conversations now and the traditions which feed discussion, is thus a complex interweaving of contemporary perspectives and strands of tradition.

To cast further light on the critical role of the chaplain in this, it is necessary to delve a little further into the world of hermeneutics, and in particular into the disagreement between Gadamer and Habermas that followed publication of the former's *Truth and Method* (1979).[16] As Mendelson (1979) makes clear, a primary focus of their disagreement lies in the place of critical reflection within interpretation of historical traditions. Looking at the debate in retrospect, it is clear that both thinkers agree that critical reflection is an essential part of interpretation of historical traditions, especially in understanding issues of reason, authority and prejudice – for example the way in which traditions may be distorted. Where they disagree, is in how that critical reflection takes place. For Gadamer, it is integral to hermeneutics; it arises from the interpreter's understanding of the historical distance between their 'horizon' and that of the text. For Habermas, however, critical reflection requires explicit use of critical theory to elucidate and critique the hermeneutical process.

Without evaluating the merits of the two positions, I want to suggest that together Gadamer and Habermas offer a way of elucidating the genius of military chaplaincy referred to above – the connecting of different perspectives apparent in their handling of moral questions. The question which arises from the Gadamer–Habermas debate is: how does critical reflection happen in chaplains' interpretative work? The proposal is that critical reflection, and therefore the richest hermeneutical understanding, arises when chaplains inhabit more than one historical tradition of understanding, in such a way that they bring traditions together as a critique of each other. This is, of course, to extrapolate the thinking of Gadamer and Habermas into our own context (but then that is what hermeneutics is about!). However, I would suggest that participation in different streams of tradition provides opportunity for effective critical reflection on understanding of each stream. If you like, this follows Habermas in recognising that critical reflection may not best be enabled by participating in what is perceived as a single tradition, but requires dialogue. It takes from Gadamer an understanding that engagement with any tradition will be hermeneutical (in this view critical theory is another tradition to be interpreted). It extends beyond both in recognising a plurality of interpretative traditions. For chaplains this means living in the theological tradition of their faith community, the tradition(s) of the military community and secular traditions that shape the life of society; bringing those traditions together; and allowing them to question each other. The mutual critique that may arise is, I would suggest, an example of the kind of intersubjectivity that both Gadamer and Habermas saw as integral to hermeneutics.

Thus, for example, McCormack's work (2005) brings together his understandings of the military context, contemporary society and his Christian tradition in order to develop a critique of the presence of slot machines which encourage gambling within army initial training establishments. Further, chaplains' responses considered above, which embedded their ethical dialogue within their pastoral relationship with military personnel, underline the way in which interpretation of traditions involves the chaplain inhabiting not only their

---

[16]   For key texts relating to the debate, see Gadamer (1986, 1990) and Habermas (1990a, 1990b).

faith tradition, but the mix of traditions experienced by other members of the military community.

While subtle, even artful, the chaplain's hermeneutic remains (as Gadamer's work reminds us) a human activity, rather than a technical one. It is a particular example of the way in which interpretation happens in human communities who live with and in plural traditions. The genius of the chaplain's role lies perhaps in its being self-conscious. The chaplain's effective historical consciousness is developed through a conscious process of reflection on their situation (rooted in listening to the multiple voices of those around them). It is this which enables them to articulate the critical significance of different traditions, and their interweaving, on behalf of the military community – bringing to the surface that which is already implicit in the life of that community.

The Mission of Military Chaplaincy

The suggestion that chaplains as part of their interpretative work need to live within different traditions, and not only their faith tradition, implies a particular model of mission. That model needs to capture the sense of wisdom arising as the chaplain facilitates critical engagement between traditions, each of which may generate insight as part of the dialogue between them. A prime candidate is the 'ecumenical missionary paradigm', which Bosch (1991: ch. 12) argues represents the dominant contemporary missiology. Three aspects of that model correlate particularly strongly with the picture of the chaplain's interpretative role sketched above.

First, the model is rooted in the understanding that mission is primarily God's mission (the *missio Dei*) – it is an 'attribute of God' (1991: 390). This shifts understanding of mission away from a strongly ecclesiocentric understanding. Mission is first the work of God to and in the world, in which the church participates. 'To participate in mission is to participate in the movement of God's love toward people' (1991: 390). Crucially for our argument, the *missio Dei* is larger than the mission of the church, because it 'embraces' the whole world (1991: 391). This mission is the work of the Holy Spirit in human history (1991: 391f.). That allows for people meeting God at work in traditions other than their faith tradition. Indeed it implies an imperative to be open to the work of God in different traditions as part of the church's participation in the *missio Dei*. The military chaplain needs therefore to be open to the work of God both within the military tradition and within the traditions which shape secular society. This is not about embracing those traditions uncritically, but rather about engaging with them in a spirit of critical reflection; seeking to discern the presence and activity of God. This opens up the critical question as to whether God's presence can be discerned in the midst of military operations.

Bosch identifies two further consequences for an understanding of mission that flow from the belief that mission is first an 'attribute' of God, which are important for this discussion. The first of these is that mission involves contextualisation, and must necessarily give rise to contextual theologies (1991: 420–32). The 'local' theologies that result ask the question, how is God's presence and activity to be discerned in this place? At the same time, in the spirit of discernment identified above, they do not simply construct an identity between God and the events of history. Such theologies represent a turn away from the illusion of a universal theology which may be applied straightforwardly in any socio-cultural setting. That turn involves identifying the 'universal' as a local (for example eurocentric) theology imposed on those of other cultures, which is in danger of silencing them rather than liberating them, because it has become closed to the question of how the gospel works in different locations.

It is important to note that, as Bosch makes clear (1991: 427–8), contextual theology must avoid both relativism and the new 'absolutism' of the local. Local theologies are not self-sufficient, but are rather interdependent with other such theologies. This is entirely in keeping with the hermeneutical picture derived from Gadamer (1979) of developing traditions whose interpretation is always historically situated. There are continuities and connections between different manifestations of the 'effective history' of a text, but also a contextual specificity to its interpretation. In their moral role, military chaplains are engaged in this work of contextual theology, seeking to discern how the gospel may become fully incarnate (cf. Bosch 1991: 426) in the military context. This is not about avoiding proclaiming the gospel, but rather about being clear that proclamation is part of a dialogue between a tradition and a particular socio-cultural setting, through which the gospel takes root amongst the people who live in that setting.

Mission, therefore, inevitably involves 'inculturation' (Bosch 1991: 447–57). This process replaces, in missionary thinking, earlier approaches in which the reception of the gospel by a particular culture could be characterised as the 'adaptation' of the gospel, or as 'accommodation' (Bosch 1991: 453), in which the primary agent was the missionary to that setting, rather than the local faith community. The agency of the local community is a key aspect of the dialogical process that is 'inculturation'. This continuing process involves the reshaping of both local culture and the gospel – 'the inculturation of Christianity and the Christianization of culture' (Bosch 1991: 454). Further, it embraces the whole of culture, rather than being selective about which aspects of culture are susceptible to Christianisation, as Bosch suggests earlier models of mission were.

The image of inculturation deepens understanding of the chaplain's moral role. It interprets their engagement with different traditions as precisely this kind of process. It elucidates the dynamic of chaplains' engagement by registering their primary concern with their faith tradition; but also underlines the importance of their inhabiting other traditions in order to promote an all-embracing inter-cultural dialogue.[17] The model further indicates the importance of a cooperative

---

[17]   Cf. 'The chaplain may militarise Christian virtues in the service of civil society – but the military and civil virtues are churched, if not baptised, in return' (Totten 2006: 55).

relationship between chaplains and military personnel, in which responsibility for the interpretation of traditions, including the faith tradition, is shared. This correlates with chaplains' facilitative approach to discussion of moral issues and questions. Their acting as a catalyst for shared ethical reflection is in keeping with an approach which looks for interpretation of the faith tradition by the military community that grows out of their culture.

If chaplains, as part of their mission and interpretative role, are committed to a thoroughgoing engagement with military culture and a dialogue between their faith tradition and the other traditions which are interwoven within that culture, then that returns us to the question about the dialogical encounter between the mission of the chaplain and the military mission. If the chaplain is engaged in contextualization and, more specifically inculturation, then he, or she, cannot be selective about engaging with military culture. In particular, if the chaplain is committed to inhabiting the military tradition, then that must involve a direct engagement with the central purpose of the military – to exercise lethal force, when authorised and required to do so, on behalf of the state, in the interests of re-establishing peace and justice. Chaplains cannot interpret the military tradition, while ignoring the central purpose around which that tradition is formed – this is part of their own inculturation.

More than this, as Butler has argued in the discussions that lie behind this chapter and elsewhere (Butler 2008), the chaplain must be committed to that purpose, recognising that they are indeed a 'force multiplier'. You cannot be a pacifist and a military chaplain, and you must believe that it is possible to be both a Christian and a member of the military. Of course this position needs to be critically examined, employing all the resources of military ethics and the just war tradition. In particular, the chaplain's participation in military operations must be rooted in their critical judgement that the operations are justified in the terms of the just war tradition, that armed conflict is necessary in this situation. If they cannot arrive at that judgement then they must resign their post, because they will then have become an alien within the military community, disabled from dialogue with its members and at risk of undermining their military identity.

It is the argument of this chapter that this embracing of the purpose of military engagement enables the chaplain to engage in mission which is thoroughly contextual, concerned with the inculturation of the gospel and open to discerning the presence of God in the midst of armed conflict, however strange that may sound to the ears of those who are theologically suspicious of the military. Only by being committed to the mission of the army can a chaplain act as an effective interpreter in the way that this chapter has proposed is vital to their moral role. It is this commitment that enables the chaplain to ensure that their faith tradition is included within a wider dialogue of traditions within the ethical reflection that they facilitate, as a contribution to keeping peace as the end in view. Paradoxically, it is this approach that then enables the critical role of the chaplain *within* the military community: providing space for military personnel to air their doubts, or raise questions about the rules that govern military life; acting as a critical friend to the commanding officer; questioning, when necessary, the way in which military strategy is carried out. The role of allowing different traditions to act as a critique of each other, including the faith tradition acting as a critique of the military one, is made possible by the chaplain's full membership of the military community and their being subject to the same discipline that enables others to be effective in executing the military mission. This is integral to chaplains' acting as a 'moral compass' and ensuring the 'moral component of fighting power'.

Coda: The Implications for 'Sending Churches'

Chaplains are only accepted for military service on the basis that they have the authorisation and support of their faith community – the 'sending churches'. And if those supporting faith communities are to be properly supportive of their chaplains, then there has to be congruence between the missiology of the chaplain and that of their church. One of the implications of this chapter, therefore, is that, if chaplains need to be committed to the military mission, as a corollary of their Christian mission, then the same must be true of the churches. That means that in the interests of supporting the moral role of chaplains discussed here, the 'sending churches' must also be supportive of the use of lethal force by an appropriately authorised military in support of peace and justice and must believe that serving in the military can be a Christian vocation. Otherwise the chaplain is at risk of discovering that in seeking to live out the gospel within the military community they have become isolated from their faith community.

Bibliography

Abercrombie, C.L. 1977. *The Military Chaplain*. Beverley Hills: Sage.

Achtar, A. 2010. Challenging Al' Qu'aeda's Justification of Terror, in *Just War on Terror? A Christian and Muslim Response*, edited by D. Fisher and B. Wicker. Aldershot: Ashgate, 25–36.

Adjutant General. 2004. D/AG Sec 108/1, Letter to Revd Peter Howson dated 6 August 2004.

Aldred, T. 2004. Stabilization – for Real People, in *War and Morality: Proceedings of a RUSI Conference – 'Morality in Asymmetric War and Intervention Operations' held on 19–20 September 2002*, edited by P. Mileham. London: Royal United Services Institute (Whitehall Paper 61), 147–50.

An-Na'im, A.A. 2002. Upholding International Legality Against Islamic and American *Jihad*, in *Worlds in Collision: Terror and the Future of Global Order*, edited by K. Booth and T. Dunne. Basingstoke: Palgrave, 162–71.

Army Doctrine Publication (ADP). 2010. *Operations*. Shrivenham: Development, Concepts and Doctrine Centre.

Arreguín-Toft, I. 2005. *How the Weak Win Wars: A Theory of Asymmetric Conflict*. Cambridge: Cambridge University Press.

Augustine, St. 2003. *City Of God*. London: Penguin Classics.

Avis, P. (ed.) 2003. *Public Faith? The State of Religious Belief and Practice in Britain*. London: SPCK.

Baarda, Th.A. van and Verweij, D.E.M. (eds) 2009. *The Moral Dimension of Assymetrical Warfare: Counter-terrorism, Democratic Values and Military Ethics*. Leiden: Martinus Nijhoff.

Bachrach, B.S. 2001. *Early Carolingian Warfare: Prelude to Empire*. Philadelphia: University of Pennsylvania Press.

Bachrach, D.S. 2003. *Religion and the Conduct of War c.300–1215*. Woodbridge: The Boydell Press.

Bachrach, D.S. 2004. The Medieval Military Chaplain and His Duties, in *The Sword of the Lord: Military Chaplains from the First to the Twenty-First Century*, edited by D.L. Bergen. Notre Dame: University of Notre Dame Press, 69–88.

Ball, J. 2006. *God still with us? How Far does the Retention of Uniformed Chaplaincy in the British Army Constitute an Unjustifiable Alliance of Faith with Nation?* Unpublished MTh dissertation, Cardiff University.

Beattie, D. 2009. *Task Force Helmand: A Soldier's Story of Life, Death and Combat on the Afghan Front Line*. London: Simon & Schuster.

Beck, U. 1992. *Risk Society: Towards a New Modernity*. London: Sage.

Bell, C. 1992. *Ritual Theory, Ritual Practice*. Oxford: Oxford University Press.

Bergen, D.L. (ed.) 2004. *The Sword of the Lord: Military Chaplains from the First to the Twenty-First Century*. Notre Dame: University of Notre Dame Press.

Berger, P. 1969. *The Sacred Canopy: Elements of a Sociological Theory of Religion*. New York: Anchor Books.

Best, G. 1994. *War and Law since 1945*. Oxford: Clarendon.

Bieler, L. (ed.) 1975. *The Irish Penitentials*. The Dublin Institute for Advanced Studies.

Blair, T. 2010. *Evidence to the Iraq Inquiry (Chilcot Inquiry) 29 January 2010*. Available at: http://www.iraqinquiry.org.uk/media/45139/20100129-blair-final.pdf [accessed: 9 August 2011].

Blair, T. 2011a. *Evidence to the Iraq Inquiry (Chilcot Inquiry) 21 January 2011*. Available at: http://www.iraqinquiry.org.uk/media/50865/20110121-Blair.pdf [accessed: 9 August 2011].

Blair, T. 2011b. *Statement to the Iraq Inquiry 14 January 2011*. Available at: http://www.iraqinquiry.org.uk/media/50743/Blair-statement.pdf [accessed: 8 August 2011].

Blewett, T., Hyde-Price, A. and Rees, W. 2008. *British Foreign Policy and the Anglican Church: Christian Engagement in the Contemporary World*. Aldershot: Ashgate.

Bobbitt, P. 2008. *Terror and Consent*. New York: Alfred A. Knopf.

Bolt, N., Betz, D. and Azari, J. 2008. *Propaganda of the Deed 2008: Understanding the Phenomenon*. The Royal Services Institute.

Bonhoeffer, D. 1964. *Letters and Papers from Prison*. London: SCM Press.

Booth, K. and Dunne, T. (eds) 2002. *Worlds in Collision: Terror and the Future of Global Order*. Basingstoke: Palgrave.

Bosch, D. 1991. *Transforming Mission: Paradigm Shifts in Theology of Mission*. Maryknoll: Orbis Books.

Bowyer, D. 2009. The Moral Dimension of Assymetrical Warfare: Accountability, Culpability and Military Effectiveness, in *The Moral Dimension of Assymetrical Warfare: Counter-terrorism, Democratic Values and Military Ethics*, edited by Th.A. van Baarda and D.E.M. Verweij. Leiden: Martinus, 137–67.

Bradshaw, P. and Melloh, J. (eds) 2007. *Foundations in Ritual Studies: A Reader for Students of Christian Worship*. London: SPCK.

Brinsfield, J.W. 1997. *Encouraging Faith, Supporting Soldiers: A History of the United States Army Chaplain Corps, 1975–1995*. Washington, DC: Office of the Chief of Chaplains.

British Army. 2011. Army website: Home/Joining the Army/Army Life/Values and Standards. Available at: http://www.army.mod.uk/join/20217.aspx [accessed: 16 August 2011].

Brown, C. 1997. *Understanding International Relations*. London: Macmillan.

Brown, C. and Snape, M. (eds) 2010. *Secularisation in the Christian World: Essays in Honour of Hugh McLeod*. Aldershot: Ashgate.

Brown, C.G. 2001. *The Death of Christian Britain*. London: Routledge.

Bugnion, F. 2004. Terrorism and International Humanitarian Law, in *War and Morality: Proceedings of a RUSI Conference – 'Morality in Asymmetric War and Intervention Operations' held on 19–20 September 2002*, edited by P. Mileham. London: Royal United Services Institute (Whitehall Paper 61), 47–55.

Burchard, W.W. 1953. *The Role of the Military Chaplain*. Unpublished PhD thesis, University of Berkeley.

Burleigh, M. 2010a. *Moral Combat: A History of World War II*. London: Harper Press.

Burleigh, M. 2010b. Is God on our side? Morality in World War Two (an edited version of the Annual Basil Liddell Hart Lecture). *Standpoint*, November 2010.

Butler, C. 2008. *Does a Chaplain on an Operational Tour have a Responsibility to Promote or Support the Aim of the Deployment?* Unpublished MTh dissertation, Cardiff University.

Byers, M. 2002. Terror and the Future of International Law, in *Worlds in Collision: Terror and the Future of Global Order*, edited by K. Booth and T. Dunne. Basingstoke: Palgrave, 118–27.

Carrette, J. and King, R. 2005. *Selling Spirituality: The Silent Takeover of Religion*. Abingdon: Routledge.

Challans, T.L. 2007. *Awakening Warrior: Revolution in the Ethics of Warfare*. Albany: State University of New York Press.

Chomsky, N. 2002. Who Are the Global Terrorists? in *Worlds in Collision: Terror and the Future of Global Order*, edited by K. Booth and T. Dunne. Basingstoke: Palgrave, 128–39.

Church of Scotland. 1991. *Agenda of the General Assembly*. Edinburgh.

Church of Scotland. 2000. *Agenda of the General Assembly*. Edinburgh.

Church of Scotland. 2001. *Agenda of the General Assembly*. Edinburgh.

Church of Scotland. 2002. *Agenda of the Church of Scotland*. Available at: http://www.churchofscotland.or.uk/downloads/forbesreport02.rtf [accessed: 4 January 2004].

Clausewitz, C. von 1993. *On War*. Edited and translated by M. Howard and P. Paret. New York and London: Knopf.

Coker, C. 2002. *Waging War Without Warriors*. London: Rienner.

Coleman, J. 1994. *Models of Ministry in the RAF Chaplaincy*. Unpublished PhD thesis, University of Nottingham.

Colonomos, A. 2001. Non-State Actors as Moral Entrepreneurs: A Transnational Perspective on Ethics Networks, in *Non-State Actors in World Politics*, edited by D. Josselin and W. Wallace. Houndmills: Palgrave, ch. 5.

Cox, H. (ed.) 1971. *Military Chaplains: From a Religious Military to a Military Religion*. New York: American Report Press.

Creveld, M. van 1991. *Transformation of War*. New York: The Free Press.

Cutler, D. 1968. *The Religious Situation*. Boston: Beacon Press.

Davie, G. 1994. *Religion in Britain since 1945: Believing without Belonging*. Oxford: Blackwell.

Davies, J.G. 1978. *New Perspectives on Worship Today*. London: SCM.

Deakin, S. 2008. Education in an Ethos at the Royal Military Academy Sandhurst, in *Ethics Education in the Military*, edited by P. Robinson, N. de Lee and D. Carrick. Aldershot: Ashgate, 15–29.

Dixon, P. 2009. *Peacemakers: Building Stability in a Complex World*. Nottingham, Inter-Varsity Press.

Elliott, B. 2006. *They Shall Grow Not Old: Resources for Remembrance, Memorial and Commemorative Services*. Norwich: Canterbury Press.

Elshtain, J. 2003. *Just War against Terror: The Burden of American Power in a Violent World*. New York: Basic Books.

Elshtain, J.B. 2010. Political Order, Political Violence, and Ethical Limits, in *Bonhoeffer and King: Their Legacies and Import for Christian Social Thought*, edited by W. Jenkins and J.M. McBride. Minneapolis: Fortress Press, 43–52.

Entous, A. 2010. 'How the White House Learnt to Love the Drone', 19 May. Available at: http://uk.reuters.com/article/2010/05/19/uk-pakistan-drones-idU KTRE64H5U720100519?pageNumber=3 [accessed: 21 May 2010].

Falk, R. 2005. Amid Normative and Conceptual Crisis, in *The Law of Armed Conflict: Constraints on the Contemporary Use of Force*, edited by H.M. Hensel. Aldershot: Ashgate, 241–6.

Fergusson, D. 2004. *Church, State and Civil Society*. Cambridge: Cambridge University Press.

Fisher, D. 2011. *Morality and War: Can War be Just in the Twenty-first Century?* Oxford and New York: Oxford University Press.

Fisher, D. and Wicker, B. 2010. *Just War on Terror? A Christian and Muslim Response*. Aldershot: Ashgate.

Flanagan, K. 1991. *Sociology and Liturgy: Re-presentations of the Holy*. London: Macmillan.

Freedman, L. 2002. A New Type of War, in *Worlds in Collision: Terror and the Future of Global Order*, edited by K. Booth and T. Dunne. Basingstoke: Palgrave, 37–47.

French, P.A. 2011. *War and Moral Dissonance*. Cambridge: Cambridge University Press.

Gadamer, H.-G. 1979. *Truth and Method*. 2nd Edition. London: Sheed and Ward.

Gadamer, H.-G. 1986. Rhetoric, Hermeneutics and the Critique of Ideology: Metacritical Comments on *Truth and Method*, in *The Hermeneutics Reader: Texts of the German Tradition from the Enlightenment to the Present*, edited by K. Mueller-Vollmer. Oxford: Blackwell, 274–92.

Gadamer, H.-G. 1990. Reply to My Critics, in *The Hermeneutic Tradition: From Ast to Ricoeur*, edited by G.L. Ormiston and A.D. Schrift. Albany: State University of New York Press, 273–97.

Gage, W. (Chairman). 2011. *The Report of the Baha Mousa Inquiry*. London: The Stationery Office.

Geach, P. 1977. *The Virtues*. Cambridge: Cambridge University Press.

Gennep, A. van 1960. *The Rites of Passage*. London: RKP.

Gilbert, P. 2003. *New Terror New Wars*. Edinburgh: Edinburgh University Press.

Grant-Jones, M. 2010. *What are the Implications for Military Chaplaincy of a Dialogue Considering the Relationship between Islamic Terrorism and the Just War Tradition?* Unpublished MTh Dissertation, Cardiff University.

Gray, C. 2002. World Politics as Usual after September 11: Realism Vindicated, in *Worlds in Collision: Terror and the Future of Global Order*, edited by K. Booth and T. Dunne. Basingstoke: Palgrave, 226–34.

Gray, C.S. 2005. *Another Bloody Century*. London: Weidenfeld & Nicolson.

Green, C.J. 2005. Pacifism and Tyrannicide: Bonhoeffer's Christian Peace Ethic. *Studies in Christian Ethics*, 18(3), 31–47.

Grimes, R. 1982. *Beginnings in Ritual Studies*. Lanham: University Press of America.

Gross, M.L. 2010. *Moral Dilemmas: Torture, Assassination and Blackmail in an Age of Asymmetric Conflict*. Cambridge: Cambridge University Press.

Habeck, M. 2004. *Knowing the Enemy*. Yale: Yale University Press.

Habermas, J. 1990a. A Review of Gadamer's *Truth and Method*, in *The Hermeneutic Tradition: From Ast to Ricoeur*, edited by G.L. Ormiston and A.D. Schrift. Albany: State University of New York Press, 213–44.

Habermas, J. 1990b. The Hermeneutic Claim to Universality, in *The Hermeneutic Tradition: From Ast to Ricoeur*, edited by G.L. Ormiston and A.D. Schrift. Albany: State University of New York Press, 245–72.

Hanson, V. 2005a. *A War Like No Other*. London: Methuen.

Hanson, V. 2005b. The Roman Way of War, in *The Cambridge History of Warfare*, edited by G. Parker. Cambridge: Cambridge University Press, 46–58.

Harding, T. 2010a. Paras Ready to 'Dance with the Devil' for Third Time in Helmand. *Daily Telegraph*, 17 May, 8.

Harding, T. 2010b. A 'Breeze of Change' Blows in Helmand. *Daily Telegraph*, 27 December, 23.

Harting-Correa, A.L. (trans.) 1996. *Walahfrid Strabo's* Libellus De Exordiis Et Incrementis Quarundam In Observationibus Ecclesiasticus Rerum: *A Translation and Liturgical Commentary*. Leiden: E.J. Brill.

Hauerwas, S. 1981. *A Community of Character: Toward a Constructive Christian Social Ethic*. Notre Dame: University of Notre Dame Press.

Hay, D. with Nye, R. 1998. *The Spirit of the Child*. New York: HarperCollins.

Hornsby Smith, M. 1987. *Roman Catholics in England*. Cambridge: Cambridge University Press.

Hornsby Smith, M. 1991. *Roman Catholic Beliefs in England: Customary Catholicism and Transformations of Religious Authority*. Cambridge: Cambridge University Press.

Howard, M. 1983. *The Causes of War*. London: Temple Smith.

Howard, M. 2002. *Clausewitz: A Very Short Introduction*. Oxford: Oxford University Press.

Howson, P.J. 2006. *The Nature and Shape of British Army Chaplaincy, 1960 – 2000*. Unpublished PhD thesis, University of Aberdeen.

Hutcheson, R.G. 1975. *The Churches and the Chaplaincy*. Atlanta: John Knox Press.

Ignatieff, M. 1998. *The Warrior's Honor: Ethic War and the Modern Conscience*. New York: Holt.

Iqbal, A. 2010. One Out of Three Killed by Drones is a Civilian, Says Study. *Dawncom*, 2 March. Available at: http://archives.dawn.com/archives/37108 [accessed: 15 May 2011].

Jenkins, W. 2010. Christian Social Ethics after Bonhoeffer and King, in *Bonhoeffer and King: Their Legacies and Import for Christian Social Thought*, edited by W. Jenkins and J.M. McBride. Minneapolis: Fortress Press, 243–57.

Jenkyns, R. 1980. *The Victorians and Ancient Greece*. Oxford: Blackwell.

Johnson, J.T. 1999. *Morality and Contemporary Warfare*. New Haven: Yale University Press.

Jones, C. 2006 *Who gets Hurt? Theological Reflections on Risk, Protection and Justice*. Unpublished article delivered to a college seminar at Ripon College, Cuddesdon, 17 January 2006.

Kaldor, M. 1999. *New and Old Wars: Organised Violence in a Global Era*. Cambridge: Polity.

Keegan, J. 1991. *The Face of Battle*. London: Pimlico.

Keegan, J. 1993. *A History of Warfare*. London: Hutchinson.

Keegan, J. 1999. *War and Our World: The Reith Lectures 1998*. London: Pimlico.

Keegan, J. 2004. *A History of Warfare*. London: Pimlico.

Kelly, G.B. 2010. Spiritualities of Justice, Peace and Freedom for the Oppressed, in *Bonhoeffer and King: Their Legacies and Import for Christian Social Thought*, edited by W. Jenkins and J.M. McBride. Minneapolis: Fortress Press, 207–18.

King, P. 2011. *Could the Use of Improvised Explosive Devices by Insurgents in Afghanistan be Considered an Act of Just War?* Unpublished MTh essay, Cardiff University.

Kramer, M.H. 2004. *Where Law and Morality Meet*. Oxford: Oxford University Press.

Krulak, C.C. 1999. The Strategic Corporal: Leadership in the Three Block War. *Marines Magazine*, January 1999. Available at: http://www.au.af.mil/au/awc/awcgate/usmc/strategic_corporal.htm [accessed: 12 August 2011].

Lattimore, R. 1961. *The 'Iliad' of Homer*. Chicago: Chicago University Press.

Lebor, A. 2006. *'Complicity with Evil': The United Nations in the Age of Modern Genocide*. New Haven and London: Yale University Press.

Leonard, R.A. 1967. *A Short Guide to Clausewitz On War*. London: Weidenfeld & Nicolson.

Lewis, B. 2003. *The Crisis of Islam: Holy War and Unholy Terror*. London: Random House.

Longley, C. 1985a. *The Times*, 4 September.

Longley, C. 1985b. Status of Armed Forces Chaplains may be Reviewed by Roman Catholic Bishops. *The Times*, 9 September.

Louden, S.H. 1996. *Chaplains in Conflict: The Role of Army Chaplains since 1914*. London: Avon Books.

McCormack, P.J. 2005. *The External Voice: A Model of Chaplaincy*. Unpublished MTh dissertation, Cardiff University.

McCormick, M. 2004. The Liturgy of War from Antiquity to the Crusades, in *The Sword of the Lord: Military Chaplains from the First to the Twenty-First Century*, edited by D.L. Bergen. Notre Dame: University of Notre Dame Press, 45–67.

McCready, D. 2009. Ending the War Right: *Jus Post Bellum* and the Just War Tradition. *Journal of Military Ethics*, 8(1), 66–78.

MacCulloch, D. 2009. *A History of Christianity: The First Three Thousand Years*. London: Allen Lane.

McGill, I. 1999. *Spiritual Needs Study: An Investigation into the Need for Spiritual Values in the Army*. Unpublished Ministry of Defence report.

MacIntyre, A. 1985. *After Virtue*. London: Duckworth.

MacIntyre, A. 1988. *Whose Justice? Which Rationality?* London: Duckworth.

MacKenzie, J.M. 1992. Heroic Myths of Empire, in *Popular Imperialism and the Military 1850–1950*, edited by J.M. MacKenzie. Manchester and New York: St Martin's, 109–38.

McLuskey, F. 1997. *Parachute Padre: Behind German Lines with the SAS France 1944*. Stevenage: Strong Oak Press.

Madigan, E. 2011. *Faith under Fire: Anglican Army Chaplains and the Great War*. Basingstoke: Palgrave Macmillan.

Main, A. 1992. Exploring a Tension for the Faithful. *Journal of the Royal Army Chaplains' Department*, 31(2), 24–7.

Mallinson, A. 2011. Army Chaplains 'Need to Show their Steel under Pressure'. *The Times*, 1 October, 111.

Mayer, J. 2008. *The Dark Side: The Inside Story of How The War on Terror Turned into a War on American Ideals*. New York: Doubleday.

Mendelson, J. 1979. The Habermas-Gadamer Debate. *New German Critique*, 18, 44–73.

Methodist Church. 1974. *Agenda of the Methodist Conference*. London: Methodist Publishing House.

Mileham, P. 2008. Teaching Military Ethics in the British Armed Forces, in *Ethics Education in the Military*, edited by P. Robinson, N. de Lee and D. Carrick. Aldershot: Ashgate, 43–56.

Mileham, P. and Willett, L. (eds) 2001. *Military Ethics for the Expeditionary Era*. London: Royal Institute of International Affairs.

Ministry of Defence (MoD). 2000a. *The Values and Standards of the British Army*. Army Code 63813 and 63812.

Ministry of Defence (MoD). 2000b. *Soldiering: The Military Covenant*. Army Doctrine Publication No.5 (ADP5), Army Code 71130.

Ministry of Defence (MoD). 2005. *The Manual of the Law of Armed Conflict*. Oxford: Oxford University Press.

Ministry of Defence (MoD). 2008. *The Aitken Report: An Investigation into Cases of Deliberate Abuse and Unlawful killing in Iraq in 2003 and 2004.*

Ministry of Defence (MoD). 2011. *The UK Approach to Unmanned Aircraft Systems, 30 March 2011: Joint Doctrine Note 2/11.* Available at: http://www.mod.uk/NR/rdonlyres/DDE54504-AF8E-4A4C-8710-514C6FB66D67/0/201 10401JDN211UASv1WebU.pdf [accessed: 15 April 2011].

Münkler, H. 2005. *The New Wars.* Cambridge: Polity.

Nabulsi, K. 2006. Conceptions of Justice in War: From Grotius to Modern Times, in *The Ethics of War*, edited by R. Sorabji and D. Rodin. Aldershot: Ashgate, 44–60.

Niekerk, S.G. van 2002. *The History, Role and Influence of the South African Military Chaplaincy, 1914–2002.* Unpublished DTh thesis, University of South Africa.

Nietzsche, F. 2000. *The Antichrist.* New York: Prometheus Books.

Norwegian Nobel Committee. 2009. The Nobel Peace Prize 2009 citation. Press release of 9 October 2009. Available at: http://nobelprize.org/nobel_prizes/peace/laureates/2009/press.html [accessed: 15 January 2010].

Obama, B.H. 2009. Full text of President Obama's Nobel Peace Prize speech. Available at: http://nobelprize.org/nobel_prizes/peace/laureates/2009/obama-lecture_en.html [accessed: 9 August 2011].

O'Donovan, O. 1999. *The Desire of the Nations: Rediscovering the Roots of Political Theology.* Cambridge: Cambridge University Press.

O'Donovan, O. 2003. *The Just War Revisited.* Cambridge: Cambridge University Press.

Oliver-Dee, S. 2009. *Religion and Identity: Divided Loyalties?* London: Theos.

Olsthoorn, P. 2007. Courage in the Military: Physical and Moral. *Journal of Military Ethics*, 6(4), 270–79.

Ouchi, W.G. 1980. Markets, Bureaucracies and Clans. *Administrative Science Quarterly*, 25(1), 129–41.

Paret, P. and Moran, D. (ed. and trans.) 1992. *Historical and Political Writings.* Princeton: Princeton University Press.

Paris, M. 2000. *Images of War in British Popular Culture, 1850–2000.* London: Reaktion.

Parker, G. (ed.) 2005. *The Cambridge History of Warfare.* Cambridge: Cambridge University Press.

Peacemaking: A Christian Vocation. 2006. London: Trustees for Methodist Church Purposes and the United Reformed Church.

Phillips, M. 2006. *Londonistan: How Britain is Creating a Terror State within.* London: Encounter Books.

Pugh, M. 1999. *Britain since 1789: A Concise History.* Basingstoke: Macmillan.

Ramadan, T. 2004. *Western Muslims and the Future of Islam.* Oxford: Oxford University Press.

Raymond, G.A. 2005. Military Necessity and the War Against Terror, in *The Law of Armed Conflict: Constraints on the Contemporary Use of Force*, edited by H.M. Hensel. Aldershot: Ashgate, 4–10.

Reed, C. 2004. *Just War?* London: SPCK.

Reed, C. and Ryall, D. (eds) 2007. *The Price of Peace: Just War in the Twenty-First Century*. Cambridge: Cambridge University Press.

Reinalda, B. 2001. Private in Form, Public in Purpose: NGOs in International Relations Theory, in *Non-State Actors in International Relations*, edited by B. Arts, M. Noortmann and B. Reinalda. Aldershot: Ashgate, 11–40.

Robbins, S. 2010. Loose Minute to DPS(A) on Pastoral Issues, dated 12 May.

Roberts, A. and Guelff, R. 2000. *Documents on the Laws of War*. Oxford: Oxford University Press.

Robinson, A. 2008. *Chaplains at War: The Role of Clergymen During World War II*. International Library of War Studies 11. London: Tauris.

Robinson, P., De Lee, N. and Carrick, D. (eds) 2008. *Ethics Education in the Military*. Aldershot: Ashgate.

Rodhe, D. 2012. The Obama Doctrine – How the President's Drone War is Backfiring. *Foreign Policy*, March/April. Available at: www.foreignpolicy. com/articles/2012/02/27/the_obama_doctrine [accessed: 27 February 2012].

Rodin, D. 2006. The Ethics of Asymmetric War, in *The Ethics of War: Shared Problems in Different Traditions*, edited by R. Sorabji and D. Rodin. Aldershot: Ashgate, 153–68.

Rogers, A.P.V. 2004. *Law on the Battlefield*. Manchester: Manchester University Press.

Rogers, P. 2008. *Global Security and the War on Terror: Elite Power and the Illusion of Control*. Abingdon: Routledge.

Ryall, D. 2001. The Catholic Church as a Transnational Actor, in *Non-state Actors in World Politics*, edited by D. Josselin and W. Wallace. Houndmills: Palgrave, ch. 3.

Sacks, J. 2005. *The Persistence of Faith: Religion, Morality and Society in a Secular Age*. London: Continuum.

Savage, S., Collins-Mayo, S. and Mayo, B., with Cray, G. 2006. *Making Sense of Generation Y: The World View of 15–25 Year Olds*. London: Church House Publishing.

Sedgwick, P. 2000. Liberation Theology and Political Theory, in *The Blackwell Reader in Pastoral and Practical Theology*, edited by J. Woodward and S. Pattison. Oxford: Blackwell, 164–71.

Shanahan, T. 2008. *The Provisional Irish Republican Army and the Morality of Terrorism*. Edinburgh: Edinburgh University Press.

Sherman, N. 2004. Educating the Stoic Warrior, in *War and Morality: Proceedings of a RUSI Conference – 'Morality in Asymmetric War and Intervention Operations' held on 19–20 September 2002*, edited by P. Mileham. London: Royal United Services Institute (Whitehall Paper 61), 105–26.

Silverman, A. 2004. Just War, Jihad, and Terrorism: A Comparison of Western and Islamic Norms for the Use of Political Violence, in *The New Era of Terrorism: Selected Readings*, edited by G. Martin. Thousand Oaks: Sage Publications, 149–60.

Sledge, M. 2005. *Soldier Dead: How We Recover, Identify, Bury and Honor Our Military Fallen*. New York: Columbia University Press.

Smith, R. 2001. Building Force and Unit Morale and Motivation (1), in *Military Ethics for the Expeditionary Era*, edited by P. Mileham and L. Willett. London: Royal Institute of International Affairs, 43–7.

Smith, R. 2005. *The Utility of Force: The Art of War in the Modern World*. London and New York: Allen Lane.

Snape, M. 2005a. *God and the British Soldier: Religion and the British Army in the First and Second World Wars*. London: Taylor & Francis.

Snape, M. 2005b. *The Redcoat and Religion: The Forgotten History of the British Soldier from the Age of Marlborough to the Eve of the First World War*. London: Routledge.

Snape, M. 2008. *The Royal Army Chaplains' Department: Clergy Under Fire*. Woodbridge: The Boydell Press.

Snape, M. 2010. War, Religion and Revival: The United States, British and Canadian Armies during the Second World War, in *Secularisation in the Christian World: Essays in Honour of Hugh McLeod*, edited by C. Brown and M. Snape. Aldershot: Ashgate, 135–58.

Stassen, G.H. 2010a. Peacemaking, in *Bonhoeffer and King: Their Legacies and Import for Christian Social Thought*, edited by W. Jenkins and J.M. McBride. Minneapolis: Fortress Press, 191–205.

Stassen, G.H. 2010b. *Just Peacemaking: Transforming Initiatives for Justice and Peace*. Kentucky: Westminster/John Knox Press.

Strachan, H. (ed.) 2000. *The British Army: Manpower and Society into the Twenty-First Century*. London: Frank Cass.

Strachan, H. 2006. Training, Morale and Modern War. *Journal of Contemporary History*, 41(2), 211–27.

Stringer, M. 1999. *On the Perception of Worship*. Birmingham: Birmingham University Press.

Stumpf, C.A. 2006. *The Gortian Theology of International Law: Hugo Grotius and the Moral Foundation of International Relations*. Berlin and New York: Walter de Gruyter.

The Tablet. 2010. On the Front Line, 22 May.

Thompson Brake, G. 1984. *Policy and Politics in British Methodism 1932–2002*. London: Edsal.

Thornton, R. 2004. The British Army and the Origins of its Minimum Force Philosophy. *Small Wars and Insurgencies*, 15(1), 83–106.

Thornton, R. 2007. *Assymetric Warfare: Threat and Response in the Twenty-First Century*. Cambridge: Polity Press.

Todd, A.J. 2008. Guest Editorial, Military Chaplaincy Today. *Crucible: The Christian Journal of Social Ethics*, Jan–March, 3–5.

Todd, A.J. and Tipton, L. 2011. *The Role and Contribution of a Multi-Faith Prison Chaplaincy to the Contemporary Prison Service*. Research Report to the National Offender Management Service. Available at: http://www.stmichaels. ac.uk/chaplaincy-studies-research-activity.php [accessed: 17 April 2012].

Torrance, I. 2000. The Moral Component, in *The British Army: Manpower and Society into the Twenty-First Century*, edited by H. Strachan. London: Frank Cass, 202–12.

Totten, A. 2006. *Military Chaplaincy under and after Christendom: Civilizing the Soldier?* Unpublished MTh Dissertation, Cardiff University.

Totten, A.J. 2010. SOI 4012: Chaplaincy, dated 9 July.

United Nations (UN). 1945. *Charter of the United Nations*. Available at: http://www.un.org/en/documents/charter/index.shtml [accessed: 8 August 2011].

United Nations (UN). 2002. *Resolution 1441 adopted 08 November 2002*. Available at: http://daccess-dds-ny.un.org/doc/UNDOC/GEN/N02/682/26/PD F/N0268226.pdf?OpenElement [accessed: 8 August 2011].

US Army and Marine Corps. 2007. *US Army and Marine Corps Counterinsurgency Field Manual*. Chicago: Chicago University Press (first published 2006).

Volf, M. 1996. *Exclusion and Embrace: A Theological Exploration of Identity, Otherness, and Reconciliation*. Nashville: Abingdon Press.

War Office. 1920. *Précis for the Army Council, Number 1026: Future Administration of the Royal Army Chaplains' Department*. London: War Office. [Copy in possession of P. Howson.]

War Office. 1923. *Report of the Committee on the Establishment of Royal Army Chaplains' Department*. A 02511. London: War Office [Copy in possession of P. Howson.]

War Office. 1956. Minutes of the Inter-denominational Committee on Army Chaplaincy Services P/(56)1, dated 17 April 1956, located in The National Archives WO 32/14820.

War Office. 1968. Inter-denominational Advisory Committee on Army Chaplaincy Services, Minutes of Meetings, located in The National Archives WO 32/14820.

Ward, G. 2000. *Cities of God*. London: Routledge.

Watkins, O.S. 1981. *Soldiers and Preachers Too*. London: privately published.

Weber, M. 1978. *Economy and Society: An Outline of Interpretative Sociology*. Berkeley: University of California Press.

White, N. 2009. *Democracy goes to War: British Military Deployments under International Law*. Oxford: Oxford University Press.

Wilkinson, A. 1981. The Paradox of the Military Chaplain. *Theology*, LXXXIV(700), 249–57.

Williams, B. 1985. *Ethics and the Limits of Philosophy*. London: Collins.

Winter, T. 2010. Terrorism and Islamic Theologies of Religiously-Sanctioned War, in *Just War on Terror? A Christian and Muslim Response*, edited by D. Fisher and B. Wicker. Farnham: Ashgate, 9–24.

Woodward, J. and Pattison, S. (eds) 2000. *The Blackwell Reader in Pastoral and Practical Theology*. Oxford: Blackwell.

Yates, R. 2004. Relief – a Human Right, in *War and Morality: Proceedings of a RUSI Conference – 'Morality in Asymmetric War and Intervention Operations' held on 19–20 September 2002*, edited by P. Mileham. London: Royal United Services Institute (Whitehall Paper 61), 139–41.

Zahn, G.C. 1969 *Chaplaincy in the RAF: A Study in Role Tension*. Manchester: Manchester University Press.

Zahn, G.C. 1991. *An Infamous Victory: The Burden of Proof Lies with the Warriors. Commonweal*, 118(11), 366–8.

Zimbardo, P. 2007. *The Lucifer Effect*. London: Rider.

Index